Austria Between East and West, 1945–1955

Austria Between East and West 1945-1955

William B. Bader

1966
Stanford University Press
Stanford, California

Stanford University Press
Stanford, California
© 1966 by the Board of Trustees of the
Leland Stanford Junior University
Printed in the United States of America
L.C. 66-17559

To John Howes Gleason

Preface

The city of Vienna as seen from the summit of the Kahlenberg flows across a juncture of the eastern Alps, the Sudetic Mountains, and the Carpathians. Literally a crossroads of east and west, Vienna serves as a gateway to both Germany and the Hungarian plains via the Danube, to Czechoslovakia up the Morava, and to the northern Balkans over the Karst plateau. It was from this same summit that King John Sobieski of Poland, in the summer of 1683, deployed his troops and drove the Turkish armies of Kara Mustafa from a siege of the city. Two and a half centuries later elements of another army from Eastern Europe would descend from the Kahlenberg heights to liberate Vienna—but the Soviet armies were not as anxious as their Christian predecessors to retire to the east once the city was free.

In the spring of 1945 the Austrian front formed part of a rough line of demarcation drawn from the Baltic to the Adriatic, defining the limits of the Soviet military advance into Eastern Europe. When the Soviet Union some ten years later withdrew its military forces from Austria, this action marked the first and thus far the only time this line of advance was adjusted. The stage for this unique event in postwar European history was set by the Four Power occupation, which began in the summer of 1945. The advertised design of the wartime Allies was to assist Austria, both economically and politically, to rejoin the democratic nations. But this objective was soon lost sight of when, during the long years of occupation, Austria became first a prize and then a pawn in a quiet, but often bruising, dispute between East and West.

The opponents in the struggle were, on the one side, the Austrian Communist Party supported by the prestige and resources of the Red Army, and on the other a Socialist-Conservative coalition backed by the Western powers. The pieces in play were the internal security forces, the loyalties of the economically and politically deprived, the trade unions, and the so-called "German assets" in Eastern Austria. The competition began in April 1945, when the Red Army took Vienna, and only subsided in the fall of 1950 with the abortive Communist effort to stage a general strike. After this last and most conclusive political failure of the Austrian Communists in 1950, the future of the Soviet zone of Austria, always dependent on external events, now rested entirely on the course of shifting East-West power relations, thereby providing a revealing chapter on the objectives and attitudes of the Cold War competitors.

What follows is not a chronological history of the Austrian occupation. It does not, for example, explore in any depth the pre-occupation policies of the wartime Allies, discuss and compare the occupation techniques of the Four Powers, catalogue the manner and effects of military censorship, or describe the revival of cultural life in Austria. Others have covered these questions thoughtfully and thoroughly. What I have done instead is to concentrate on certain aspects of the Austrian episode which I believe are specifically relevant to an analysis of the fate of the Communist challenge in Austria and to the evolution and interaction of Soviet and Western attitudes toward their role and stake in Austria. The text, therefore, concentrates on the revival of political life in Austria, the successes and failures of Communism, the East-West contest for control of the internal security forces and the trade unions, the development of the Soviet economic enclave in Eastern Austria, and finally an analysis of what has recently been described as the "lingering enigma" of the Soviet withdrawal from Austria in 1955.

The Austrian episode of the Cold War, particularly the period from 1945 to 1950, is richly documented not only in material on the development of Soviet policy, but on the maneuverings of the United States and the Socialist-Conservative coalition government backed by the United States. Although a mimeograph copy of the proceedings of the Allied Commission for Austria has long been in the public domain, the original U.S. set of Allied Commission records was first made available to the nonofficial scholar when the U.S. Department of State permitted me to use the records in 1962. This collection, used here for the first time, includes not only the corrected minutes of the executive sessions, with supporting U.S. position papers and reports, but also letters of the Austrian Federal Chancellory to the Allied Commission and correspondence between the Austrian Chancellor and various ministries with the U.S. element. This material was particularly useful as an account of Soviet attitudes and actions in Austria. Moreover, in addition to the normal Soviet sources, the Soviets had their own newspaper in Austria—the *Oesterreichische Zeitung*—which faithfully recorded Moscow's official pronouncements on the Austrian question. On the course of the Austrian State Treaty negotiations, the Dulles Papers, located at the John Foster Dulles Library, Princeton University, were most useful.

This study, which took me to Vienna for a year to gather the essential source materials, was made possible in large measure through a grant from the Center of International Studies, Princeton University, and the University of Pennsylvania. I am also grateful for the generous amount of time granted me for interviews by the late Leopold Figl, former Chancellor of Austria, and the late Oskar Helmer, Austrian Minister of the Interior during most of the occupation period. I wish particularly to thank Dr. Kurt Wessely of the Oesterreichisches Institut fuer Wirtschaftsforschung for putting at my disposal his collection of materials on the Soviet industries in Eastern Austria.

In my efforts to uncover the materials on the occupation, I received valuable assistance from the staffs of the Wiener Stadtbibliothek, the Sozialwissenschaftliche Studienbibliothek der Kammer fuer Arbeiter und Angestellte fuer Wien, the Historisches Institut der Universitaet Wien, the Bibliothek des Parlaments, the Nationalbibliothek, and Amtsbibliothek der Bundes-Polizeidirektion, Vienna, and the John Foster Dulles Library.

In the writing of this book I have benefited from the advice and encouragement of Cyril E. Black, Gordon A. Craig, and Gerald Stourzh. I would also like to extend thanks to Miss Dolores Unick for her kind help in the preparation of the manuscript. And finally, to Gretta, who shared it all—and much more.

W.B.B.

May 1966

Contents

Austria Between East and West, 1945–1955

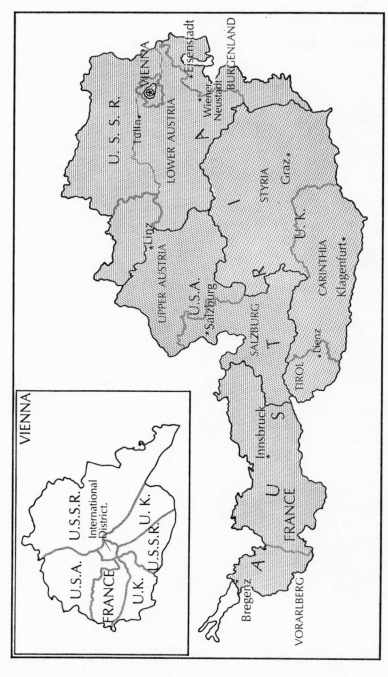

The 1945 Final Boundaries of Austria and (inset) Final Sector Boundaries of Vienna

Introduction

Throughout the winter of 1944–45 the Russian armies rolled relent-
lessly toward Vienna. It was only a question of time before the German forces, exhausted from the unsuccessful defense of Budapest,
would be driven from Austria. Doubtlessly all those immediately concerned with the future of the country—the Soviet military authorities, the Austrian Communists in their wake, those Socialists and
members of the Catholic party due to return from retirement or concentration camps—had good reason to wonder what sort of Austria
would emerge after the 11 years of dictatorship, Nazism, and war
which had begun in 1934 with the collapse of the First Austrian Republic.

The tragic blowup of 1934 which closed the tumultuous history of
the First Austrian Republic was the result of many interacting forces
—the unhappy circumstances that surrounded the breech birth of
that truncated and disorganized republic, the staggering economic
problems that came as a legacy of the shattered monarchy, the doc-
trinal intransigence of the left wing of the Social Democratic Party,
the fear and envy of the Catholic peasantry who saw in a Socialist
Vienna a threat to its very existence. While it is obviously not the
intention here to give a capsule history of the Socialist-Conservative
conflict which finally ended at the barricades in February of 1934, it
is nevertheless important to highlight certain features of that struggle
which helped to mold the political conditions of 1945.

I

The two dominant political parties of the First Republic—the
Social Democratic and Christian Social—have been characterized

most aptly as resembling *Lager,* or armed camps, rather than political parties.[1] The bitter antagonism between the two major parties stemmed from socioeconomic differences as well as political. From 1920, when the postwar coalition government of Socialists and Catholics collapsed, the Social Democrats remained in total opposition to a succession of Christian Social governments. When Otto Bauer, the unchallenged leader of the Social Democrats during the interwar period, led his party into political exile, he vowed that the party would not soil its ideological skirts with any coalition compromise until conditions were favorable—favorable in the sense that the Socialists must be the dominant partner in any such coalition. In the meantime the party would wage an unrelenting parliamentary struggle against the Christian Social leadership while simultaneously holding up for all to see a working model of what Socialist control could mean.

In keeping with Bauer's approach, the Socialists from 1920 to 1934 compiled an impressive record of accomplishments outside the national parliament. In Vienna, the Social Democrats made effective use of their undisputed political control of the city. Initiating a program of lavish public expenditures, Vienna soon became a European Socialist showpiece. Tax reforms, municipal recreation facilities, municipal housing, rigid rent control, public health programs—these are just a sample of the extensive social welfare schemes undertaken with great success by the Socialist city government.[2] Not the least of their accomplishments was the construction of 25,000 apartments during 1924–28. The Karl Marx Hof, the most impressive of the early municipal housing projects, alone contained 1,400 apartments and some 5,000 residents.* These buildings, erected by a Socialist government, gave safe and sanitary housing to thousands of workers, thus contributing heavily to what became a remarkably durable bond between the workers and their party. In 1945, the Russian troops would not believe that workers could live in such comparative luxury and the inhabitants would not be spared the looting and assault.

Complementing and supporting the Social Democratic successes in Vienna and in other municipal areas such as Graz was the elaborate and powerful party organization. Membership in the Social Demo-

1 Numbered notes (primarily source citations) will be found at the back of the book, on pp. 211–37.
* The very names of these municipal housing projects say a great deal about the ideological potpourri of Austro-Marxism: Karl Marx, Giacomo Matteotti, Ferdinand Lassalle, Robert Blum, Goethe, George Washington; and in 1961, George Marshall was added to the list.

cratic Party meant payment of regular dues collected by party volun-
teers. Such direct, active participation of the entire working class in
support of the party was valued above all else. As a result, the Social
Democratic Party in 1929—the year of peak membership—could
boast of 708,839 dues-paying members. Thus, more than 10 per cent
of the entire population of Austria was directly involved in the party
activity. Significantly, and in contrast to the greater diversity of the
Second Republic, 58 per cent of this total was concentrated in
Vienna.[3] The very size of the organized party ensured that there
would be no lack of funds for campaigns. It also meant that the party
could be confident of a strong election turnout.

Backing the political organization of the party was an elaborate
network of extra-party activities: newspapers, cooperatives, party li-
braries, affiliated trade unions, and the like. The possibilities for
affiliation with Socialist nonpolitical activities were virtually un-
limited. This remarkable pervasiveness of the party could theoretically circumscribe almost the entire life of a dedicated party member
—from nurseries to burial societies.

In sharp contrast to the Socialists' successes, the Austrian Communists, plagued by party factionalism and the Social Democrats' ability
to produce real and immediate social reforms, were badly outdis-
tanced in the race for popular support and remained until 1934 a
powerless splinter group. In the 1927 national elections, for example,
the party won but 16,119 votes, or 0.5 per cent of those cast throughout all of Austria. In Vienna, an industrial city, and a potential source
of great Communist strength, the total was 0.7 per cent of the votes
cast in 1927, 0.9 per cent in 1930. In 1932, during the depths of the
depression in Austria, the Communists could command but 21,813,
or 1.9 per cent of all the votes cast in Austria. There is perhaps no
better evidence that the Social Democrats' program was a resounding
success.

While the Communists floundered pathetically in their opposition
to the Socialists, the Christian Social Party leaders soon made it clear
that they had both the will and the capacity to stem the tide. It was
the Socialists' social welfare programs, particularly in Vienna, which
aggravated and disturbed the Christian Social Party. The very success
of these extensive social welfare programs which had so undercut
Communist popular support provoked a conservative reaction which
almost succeeded in destroying both the Social Democratic Party and
its works. What had begun, at least on the surface, as political rivalry
between the major parliamentary parties had become by 1934 a

heated and bruising struggle of world ideologies, with the contrasts and conflicts extending into every aspect of Austrian life.

Socialist control of Vienna proved to be the sharpest wedge driving the two parties apart. Derisively known as "Rotes Wien" to the peasantry, Vienna with its sophisticated municipal socialism based on a highly industrialized economy contrasted harshly with the agrarian, conservative, and strongly Catholic nature of the provinces. This contrast was highlighted by the industrial concentration of the interwar period. Vienna contained not only a disproportionately large percentage of the population—some 30 per cent—but the bulk of the industrial capacity.

The response of the conservative and agrarian sectors of the population to all of this was a deepening mood of fear generously mixed with envy. Time and the continuing Socialist successes only added to the explosive situation. It was apparent to all that the national parliament had become a hollow, powerless, caricature of a deliberative body. To the Christian Social Party it was clear that the opposition party represented not an alternative government but an alternate regime. The Social Democrats, therefore, had to be kept out of power at all costs. From 1920 until 1933, when Chancellor Engelbert Dollfuss finally "dispensed" with the parliament, the Christian Social Party could only maintain its slender majority by going progressively further to the right to form a coalition. A particularly explosive characteristic of this tense political situation was the existence of paramilitary formations on the right (Heimwehr) and left (Schutzbund). The Heimwehr grew out of the home guards, which defended Austria's borders in the early days of the Republic, but by 1930 the original purpose had been perverted and the Heimwehr became the military arm of the right. The Socialist counterpart was the Republikanischer Schutzbund, which had hidden arms caches throughout Austria.

In 1934 the collision long predicted by right and left came when a series of police raids of Social Democratic offices in search of arms and ammunition ended with barricades and bloodshed. When the shooting was over, Chancellor Dollfuss had won. Scores were dead; the Social Democratic Party had been eliminated from the political scene. But the First Austrian Republic was also finished, and the way was opened for Hitler.

The clumsy dictatorship begun by Chancellor Dollfuss survived his assassination by the Nazis in July 1934, only to be brought down by Hitler in 1938. In the meantime, the Dollfuss regime, despite its best intentions, was both inefficient and permissive in dealing with the now illegal Social Democratic Party. One result of this bungling was that Socialist Party cadres, despite the handicaps imposed by the new restrictions, continued to function. Consequently, the deep schism within the Socialist ranks which had arisen after the February debacle was soon clear for all to see.

The full story of the Socialist underground movement and the role of Revolutionary Socialists cannot be told here, but it should be noted that this was a time of hard reassessment of the basic tenets upon which the party had been based. To its members Social Democracy was much more than a means of fulfilling political aspirations; it was an entire way of life, and its followers drew their confidence and strength ultimately from the assurance that the party leadership was prepared to lead them to the barricades if the social revolution was seriously threatened. This had been the promise of the party's leader, Otto Bauer. In February Bauer and other leaders of the Socialist left were required to redeem this pledge. The response was one of indecision, confusion, and virtual paralysis of the party's leadership. Reluctant to gamble with the fruits of years of gradual progress, the Social Democratic leadership pleaded caution when the party's rank and file looked for a call to action. They hesitated just long enough for the workers to go into the streets without them. The result was more than a single military defeat; to many Socialists the pain and humiliation of the debacle was of small account when compared with the festering bitterness born of a sense of betrayal. The militant wing of the party—whose ideological radicalism had so successfully outflanked the Communists—had been bound to Bauer in the confidence that he would protect the social movement with force if necessary. Now the illusion was shattered, and the way was opened for a fragmentation of the party that only benefited the Communists.

To the rank and file the collapse of the party organization was primarily a loss of identity with a community that had filled their entire lives. For others, the defeat demanded a complete rejection of the party's commitment to achieving Socialist goals through democratic means. The new situation of illegality obviously required a shift in party organization from concentrating on the problems of mass membership to the direction of small militant groups operating under cover. More important than the organizational change, however, was the new spirit of militancy and activism. Most of the leaders of the party's left wing, including Otto Bauer, Friedrich Adler, and Julius Deutsch, had fled abroad; those who remained built highly disci-

plined military cadres prepared to use whatever means necessary to
bring about the violent overthrow of the Dollfuss dictatorship.[4] Symbolic of the new militancy was the dissatisfaction with the old party
labels. The underground newspapers were named *Die Wahrheit*
(truth or *Pravda*) and *Der Funke* (the spark or *Iskra*). Significantly,
the new political group that came to dominate the underground
movement called itself the Revolutionary Socialists.

At first the old leadership of the Social Democratic Party was subjected to scathing abuse from the underground party. Joseph Buttinger, Chairman of the Revolutionary Socialists from 1935 to 1938,
recounts that disillusioned young party members poured some of
their bitterness into an often quoted rhetorical question: Where were
the Jewish intellectuals when the workers manned the barricades?
In the train to Prague, where they are going to write new pamphlets
on the revolutionary struggle.*

In such circumstances of ideological ferment, where the "true"
Socialist was now also a practicing revolutionary, it was only natural
that strong interest would develop in the party with the most experience in such matters—the Communists. Of the remarkable resurgence of the Communist Party after 1934, Buttinger has written:

> The Communist Party of Austria, vegetating hopelessly in dark corners until
> 1934, got its only real boost from the February upheaval. The collapse of
> Social Democracy aroused curiosity about the Communists' message. The
> doubts that suddenly seized the workers, their need of comfort, and their
> outrage at the disappointments, combined to turn a mentally and politically
> insignificant handful of Communists overnight into a political movement.[5]

The compulsion became very strong for unity of the entire working class in the face of a common danger; the belief in such unity
soon "came to be the test of the revolutionary line, the mark of a
true leftist, the measure of an honest revolutionary and the only guarantee of victory."[6] This sense of common purpose soon broadened
into contact groups between the underground trade unions, intensive discussions between the party leaders, cautious joint proclama-

---

* Buttinger, p. 75. He notes that the number of Jews in the hierarchy of the interwar Social Democratic Party (including Bauer, Adler, and Robert Danneberg) was
so high that the party executive had established a secret ratio that would always
give the "Aryans" a majority of one. Buttinger also says (pp. 80–81) that at the
time 90 per cent of the editors of the official party paper, *Arbeiter-Zeitung*, were
Jewish. Whether the Jewish dominance of the party leadership was as pronounced
as Buttinger says is debatable. Nevertheless, it is clearly one of the major socio-
logical characteristics of the post-1945 Socialist Party that the Jewish element in
the party is virtually gone.

tions, and finally in May of 1936 an agreement on joint action. Another common bond was struck in 1936 when two Communists—Franz Honner, who became Minister of the Interior in 1945, and Friedl Fuernberg—were put on trial, together with a large group of well-known Socialists, including Austria's Foreign Minister from 1959 to 1966, Bruno Kreisky. Simultaneously, many Socialists including Ernst Fischer, Communist Minister of Education in 1945, and Heinrich Duermayer, the Communist Chief of the State Police in 1945, left the Social Democratic Party and joined the Communists.[7]

The extent of the Communist success in capturing popular support from the Socialists during the period of illegality cannot be determined with any real accuracy; the limitations of rank-and-file participation inherent in an underground operation, as well as the absence of free elections from 1934 to 1945, cloud any estimate. Nevertheless, the impact of the Communist surge after 1934 on the non-Communist left had been considerable, and there was no doubt that the Communists had gained significant support at the expense of the Social Democrats. Moreover, the Communists' reputation was also considerably enhanced by their creditable performance during the Spanish Civil War. The third boost to the Communist stock came after the Anschluss of 1938, when they earned the reputation as the most implacable foe of Nazism.

II

The initial reaction of the Austrian populace to Hitler's seizure of the country is difficult to gauge. But whatever enthusiasm for Anschluss existed was sorely put to the test by the Germans' behavior. Many of those who voted for Anschluss in a plebiscite stage-managed by the Germans after the occupation soon discovered to their chagrin and horror that the Germans' conception of what "union" implied was radically at odds with their own. To its Austrian supporters "Anschluss" meant entry into the Reich as a fully equal Federal State; some even nursed the dream of a Germany with two capitals—Vienna and Berlin. The Germans were not nearly so romantic. Austria was immediately subjected to a vigorous policy of economic and political integration aimed at destroying everything that was "Austrian." The very name of Austria was eliminated; it was rechristened by Hitler as the East March (Ostmark), later as the Donau und Alpen Gaue. The original nine provinces were transformed into seven *Reichsgaue*. The boundaries of Vienna were extended. The provincial diets, which enjoyed immense powers during the First Republic, ceased to exist. Finally, all vestiges of an Austrian central government were dissolved, and the Donau und Alpen Gaue were administered by the Germans taking their orders from Berlin.

Judged in the context of the immediate postwar period, when a record of stubborn resistance to Nazi fascism became an important political asset, the reputation of the Austrian Socialists suffered during the Nazi occupation. Karl Renner, leader of the right wing of the Social Democratic Party, was induced, in the hope of winning from the Nazis the release of his party colleague, Robert Danneberg, to support publicly the union with Hitler's Germany.[8] It might be noted that Danneberg was arrested and, tragically enough, despite Renner's efforts, executed because he was a Jew. Socialist Jews, whether they were of the right or left wing (and almost invariably they stood on the left) of the party, were either hounded out of the country or murdered. At the same time the right-wing Socialists such as Adolf Schaerf, Karl Renner, and Oskar Helmer—men who came to dominate the party after 1945—survived the war with little difficulty. Thus the Nazis helped shape the political complexion of Austria's postwar Socialist Party.

For their part, the Christian Social leaders incurred the wrath of Hitler, both for the humiliation they had caused him in calling on Mussolini for help in 1934 and for their resistance to the German takeover. Kurt Schuschnigg, Dollfuss' successor, refused to resign or flee Austria, and was imprisoned, and many party leaders, including the postwar People's Party leader, Leopold Figl, were packed off to Dachau.

But it was the Communist Party that had the unmatched record of resistance, and the party has never let Austrians forget it.[9] While the Socialists in March of 1938 were singularly cautious in their reaction to the Nazis' takeover, the Communists immediately issued a defiant proclamation of total resistance. The Communists who subsequently fought in the underground were almost indifferent to the toll in human life. The Communists have claimed that during the Nazi period almost 1,400 Communists were executed, including 13 members of the Central Committee.[10] Let it be said, however, that these figures do not tell the full story. This fearless and ultimately futile resistance of the Communists took its toll not from the hierarchy of the party but primarily from the young activists. The loss of such men cost the party dearly in terms of young leadership—a commodity that the Communists sadly lacked in the postwar period. The party leaders themselves—Johann Koplenig, Franz Honner, Ernst

Fischer, Friedl Fuernberg—spent most of the war comfortably living
in Russian hotels as guests of the Soviet Union while busily preparing
for that day when they would return to Austria.* In June 1944, however, Franz Honner and a small party of Austrian Communists were
flown into Yugoslavia, where Honner organized the first of what became two Austrian "Freedom Battalions." These units fought beside
Tito's partisans, and many were to become after 1945 members of a
Communist paramilitary group.

The Communists were able to bring to the postwar scene an impressive resistance record in spite of the fact that by 1943 Nazi countermeasures had all but snuffed out Communist resistance. This
record, commendable enough in view of the size of the party, was
considerably enhanced by the belated entrance of other parties into
open resistance. The non-Communist resistance movement, despite
the considerable attention it has been given in Austria, cannot be
compared with the highly effective units active in France and Italy
—a fact that caused considerable concern among the Allies.[11] It was
only in December 1944, some five months before the end of the war
in Austria, with the organization of the Provisorisches Oesterreichisches National Komitee and its military unit, known as the 05, that
active and effective resistance began.†

Against this background, the future must have seemed particularly
uncertain to the Austrian Socialists in the Spring of 1945, for the
constant turmoil of the past 11 years had had its impact. This once
powerful party had been torn apart, shorn of its mass organization,
its leaders hounded out of the country. Otto Bauer had died in exile;
Adler had grown old. Even the right wing of the party had faded out
of sight. Renner lived in retirement; Helmer was in the insurance
business; Adolf Schaerf practiced law. Eleven years was a long time
for the political machinery to stand idle.

For the Christian Social Party the excesses of 1934 had also left

---

* See Leonhard, pp. 183–277. Leonhard, who defected from the German Communist Party after the war, was a member of the Ulbricht group, which returned to
Germany from the Soviet Union in April 1945 to reorganize the party. While the
Comintern school, first in Moscow and later in Ufa, was still operating, Honner
was the leader of the Austrian group. In May 1943, when the school was closed,
Honner and the rest of the Austrian contingent moved to the Hotel Lux in Moscow. Ernst Fischer spent his time as the "voice" of Freies Oesterreich, broadcasting
propaganda to the Austrian troops in the German army and to Austria.
† The "05" was taken from the "Oe" in Oesterreich with "5" as the fifth letter
of the alphabet in place of the "e."

their mark. Kurt Schuschnigg, Dollfuss' successor as Chancellor, could never have formed a new Austrian government with Socialist participation. Even if a coalition of left and right could be arranged, could the result be any different than in 1934?

To the Austrian Communist leaders preparing to leave Moscow, however, the future must have seemed promising indeed. Admittedly, the apparent upsurge of the party's popular support, demonstrated during the period of illegality, had never been tested at the polls. But it was generally conceded that a strong base of support was there and that the party's record as the most uncompromising foe of fascism would be a great political asset after the war. Moreover, Otto Bauer's control over the entire Socialist party had been dramatically lifted as a result of the 1934 debacle, offering the distinct possibility that the Socialists would enter the postwar political arena a divided, querulous party. Finally, if the Soviet armies gained control of most of Austria, particularly Vienna, the entire weight of the Soviet Union could be brought into play behind the party's efforts.

But for the moment the most immediate concern was the liberation of Austria and the evolution of Allied policy for the country's future. As the Red Army swept across the Danubian plains, American and British troops were pressing in from the south and west. In April 1945 it became only a matter of days.

The Rebirth of Austria

In March 1945 the Germans launched a powerful counteroffensive in Hungary in hopes of breaking the Russian hold on Budapest. But the thrust was crushed at Lake Balaton, and the Soviet armies once again took up their drive on Vienna, this time encountering only token resistance. The first penetration of the Austrian border was made before the end of the month, and by April 7 Russian forces had moved into the southern suburbs of Vienna.

In Vienna itself the walls of the city were plastered with Gauleiter von Schirach's proclamation of a state of siege and notice of German determination to fight to the last round of ammunition. Nevertheless, the outcome of the battle for Vienna was never in doubt. The most the few SS divisions around Vienna could hope for was to force the Red Army to pay the highest possible price for the city. The one unanswered question—at least in the Allies' minds—was the extent to which the heretofore embarrassingly dormant Austrian resistance forces would participate in the liberation of the city.

I

On April 8 Radio Moscow broadcast a declaration on Austria, which proclaimed that the Austrian people had welcomed ". . . the Red Army cordially as the liberator of Austria" and that "the Soviet Union does not aim at appropriating any part of the Austrian territory or changing the social order."[1] The text also lauded the Austrian resistance forces for their part in disrupting the efforts of the German army to defend Vienna. This sudden burst of resistance activity that the Russians referred to included widespread acts of sabotage and some street fighting with SS troops. This action was spearheaded, at least in the popular imagination, by the 05 group. These Austrian resistance activities were finally and most dramatically capped by a contact made between the advancing Soviet forces and members of the resistance by the then Sergeant Ferdinand Kaes, an Austrian in the German army. Kaes presented to field officers of Marshal F. Tolbukhin's Third Ukrainian Front a plan of the Austrian resistance forces whereby the Soviet troops would strike Vienna from the ill-defended west, outflanking the Germans' main line of defense.[2] Whether there was in fact a direct cause-and-effect relationship between this suggestion of the resistance group and the subsequent Soviet decision to press their major attack from the west is open to question. Nevertheless, Kaes certainly provided the Soviets with valuable information and concrete evidence that a resistance group was operating in Vienna.

Although Vienna was effectively cut off by April 8, it still required five days of severe artillery exchanges and violent street fighting before the city was finally cleared on the 13th. Consequently, Vienna suffered considerable damage, particularly to the center of the city, where many priceless buildings including the Cathedral of St. Stephen were badly hit. But for the first time in seven years the Red-White-Red colors of Austria were raised in Vienna. The Anschluss nightmare was over.

The Russians had said they would come as a liberating army and that the lives and property of the Austrians would be safeguarded. There is little doubt that most Austrians, wearied of the war and bitter over Hitler's distortion of the dream of Anschluss, were prepared in April 1945 to welcome the Russians as "liberators." This predisposition disappeared with the arrival of the Russian troops. With brutal suddenness the Russian troops, many of them the most primitive of Mongolians, unleashed a holocaust of rape and looting that terrified and alienated the population. In their defense it must be said that the Russians had reached Austria after an immense and costly campaign. The subtleties of distinguishing between "Germans" were beyond most of them. They knew only that their homeland was an open wound as the result of a German invasion that had few historical peers in brutality and wantonness. Moreover, some 35 German divisions composed mainly of Austrians and officered partly by Austrians had been formed on Austrian territory. Most of these divisions had fought in the Soviet Union. The Russians could ask with justice whether the French, who were also "liberated," had a field marshal in the German army and a number of major generals. No collective hand-washing can remove the stains on the hands of many Austrians—the stains of complicity in or indifference to Hitler's brutalities. The Russians who in those first days got drunk, raped, and plundered rarely denied or apologized for it.* Whatever the provocation may have been, however, the results shocked and embittered the population. The effects of this experience on the outcome of the first postwar election have perhaps been exaggerated, but there is little doubt that the Austrian workers whose apartments were plundered and whose families were abused by marauding troops from the "Motherland of Socialism" took some painful memories to the polling places.

But for the moment Vienna was totally under Soviet control. By the end of the month the provinces of Lower Austria, Burgenland, and most of Styria were in Russian hands. Yet in Vienna, literally before the sound of battle had died away, the Russians turned their attention to the creation of a provisional government for Austria, although the country was still physically divided. With this decision political life began anew in Austria.

In contrast to the Austrian experience, by the time the war ended in Italy and France the resistance forces had become so well organized and powerful that they were able to play a major role in the postwar political settlement. No such parallel development went on in Austria, where, for a variety of reasons, the resistance activities only became really organized during the last few weeks of the war. As a result the o5 organization, which in any case lacked strong leadership, was soon swallowed up by the emerging political parties. Even the Communists, who had the best claim to a commendable role in partisan warfare, were left in April 1945 with the best of reputations but no on-the-scene organization, owing to the efficiency of the German countermeasures. Consequently, the postwar Austrian Communist Party, although it drew considerable prestige from its resistance ac-

* One important exception was an incident involving Oskar Helmer's brother and sister-in-law. Helmer, who became Minister of the Interior after the November elections, discovered soon after the fighting was over that his brother had been killed by the Russian troops when he attempted to defend his wife from repeated assault by Russian soldiers. To compound the tragedy, Helmer's sister-in-law immediately afterwards took just enough poison to die a slow and painful death. After Helmer's selection as Minister of the Interior, the Soviet High Command sent an officer to apologize for the incident. The apologies were not accepted. Helmer, pp. 204–5.

tivities, was forced to draw the bulk of its leadership from an exile group that had spent the war in the Soviet Union. The one important exception to this general rule was the Communist Franz Honner, who became Austria's first postwar Minister of the Interior. Honner led an Austrian brigade which fought in Tito's army. In general, however, the lack of a strong personality or personalities who could embody the Communist resistance movement hurt the party badly in the postwar years.

The provisional administrations set up under Russian direction in April 1945 were therefore put together primarily by men who, although they valued the sense of mutual purpose born of common suffering, were first and foremost party representatives. Long years of political inactivity had apparently not shaken the old political ties and party loyalties. The Austrian leaders who emerged in the earliest months of the liberation, whether from retirement (Schaerf, Helmer, Renner—Socialists), from a concentration camp (Figl—Conservative), or from the Soviet Union (Koplenig and Fischer—Communist), thought almost entirely in party terms. The negotiations of April 13 and 14 over the selection of a provisional mayor and city council for Vienna brought together for the first time the three major political factions of the postwar period. The selection of Theodor Koerner, a Socialist, was the result of hard bargaining between groups acting precisely like political parties, although the Socialist and Conservative parties had not as yet been formally reorganized. Because the postwar provisional administrations were formed by and simultaneously with the formation of the political parties, a brief survey of the immediate postwar grouping may be useful here.[3]

II

In a period of just four years (1934–38) the Austrian Social Democratic Party had been suppressed twice, first inefficiently by Dollfuss and then effectively by Hitler. As a consequence, two waves of political refugees poured over Europe, the Soviet Union, and the United States. The first group, driven out by the Dollfuss regime, consisted in the main of the left-wing faction—Bauer, Adler, Deutsch—which had controlled the party since 1920. The second group, fleeing before the Gestapo, were not political refugees in the proper sense, but Socialists of Jewish descent. As has been mentioned, those members of the former party directorate who remained in Austria during the war were primarily of the right wing of the party. This group included such men as Karl Renner and Oskar Helmer. The fact that there was no Austrian government in exile is probably due to a number of factors: Kurt Schuschnigg, the last Chancellor of the First Republic, had refused to go into exile and remained a German prisoner along with many of his cabinet; the Austrians, at least in London, were split into bickering factions and were unable, despite the encouragement of the British government, to present a united organization; finally, until roughly 1943 neither the Allies nor the refugee Austrians were agreed on the question of Austria's future.[4] As a result of this external disunity the Austrians who returned in 1945, whether from Great Britain, or from the United States, or the major Communist group from the Soviet Union, came as individuals with no other credentials than their former party membership and personal record. One result of the wartime exile of many of Austria's Socialists was the moderating effect on the political philosophy of many left-wing Socialists that prolonged residence in Great Britain and the United States seems to have had. For example, such men as Oskar Pollak, the long-time editor of the Socialist daily, *Arbeiter-Zeitung,* and Karl Czernetz, who is now perhaps the leading Socialist parliamentary spokesman on foreign policy, returned to Austria with their ideological outlook softened to a point where, for the first time, political cooperation with former philosophical antagonists such as Karl Renner was readily managed. The same may be said of the fiery former Social Revolutionary Bruno Kreisky, foreign minister of Austria for many years, who spent the war years in Sweden.

When we combine this change in the political philosophy of many of the prewar left-wing Socialists with the fact that Otto Bauer was dead and that Friedrich Adler chose to remain abroad, it is little wonder that the leadership of the reestablished party after 1945 fell to the right-wing Socialists, who had the added advantage of being on the spot when political life began anew.

Perhaps the best representative of the type of Austrian Socialist leader who came to dominate the party after 1945 was Dr. Adolf Schaerf. During the First Republic, when the Social Democratic Party followed the lead of Otto Bauer, Schaerf had served the party faithfully but without distinction, first as secretary of the Socialist faction in the parliament and then for a brief time before the 1934 uprising as a member of the upper house (Bundesrat) from Vienna. In 1934 he was arrested and briefly imprisoned, as was the case again in 1938 and 1944. In April 1945 Schaerf was one of the first Socialists on the scene and, with remarkable skill and energy, directed the reorganization of the party. For his efforts he was elected Party Chairman of the Socialist Party in 1945. Simultaneously he became a State Secretary and member of the inner political cabinet of the Renner provisional government. Later he became Vice-Chancellor in the first elected Austrian government of Leopold Figl, and in 1957 he was elected President of Austria, a position he retained until his death in 1965.[5]

Dr. Schaerf was a pragmatic, hardheaded politician, essentially disinterested in ideological argument. As a skilled political tactician he defended the interests of his party with vigor and intelligence. The involved strictures of Marxism obviously held no interest for Schaerf with his bread-and-butter concept of socialism. Schaerf, perhaps more than any other single Austrian, personifies the remarkable postwar transformation of Austrian socialism—a transformation so decisive that it has been noted that "no other Socialist party has travelled a longer road faster from Left to Right."[6]

This is not to suggest that the left wing of the party lacked representation when the party organization was re-established. And here the word "re-established" rather precisely describes what went on in April 1945. Former party functionaries very naturally drifted back to their old haunts, discovered old colleagues, and proceeded to reorganize the party in the same pattern as before 1934—i.e., a mass party structure with direct membership led by a party chairman and his secretariat in concert with the party's executive committee (*Parteivorstand*).

Less than 24 hours after the last German troops were driven from Vienna, a small group of Socialists, representing both wings of the party, met to discuss ways and means of revitalizing the party. The Revolutionary-Socialist faction of the party was represented most notably by Joseph Afritsch and Hilde Krones, and the Social Democrats by Oskar Helmer, Adolf Schaerf, and Theodor Koerner. After a good deal of give-and-take, they reached a compromise, expressed symbolically by renaming the Social Democratic Party "The Socialist Party of Austria (Social Democrats and Revolutionary Socialists)," and organizationally by the creation of a provisional executive committee of five members from each faction, with the position of party chairman held open for Karl Seitz, the former Social Democratic mayor of Vienna.[7] Indicative of the depletion of the former party leadership was the fact that only one member of the provisional executive committee, Oskar Helmer, had held a parallel position in the pre-1934 party. Nevertheless, the reorganization of the SPO (Sozialistische Partei Oesterreichs) moved swiftly, with the party secretariat functioning by April 19. By April 20 it was apparent that Karl Seitz, the party's first choice for party secretary, would be delayed in returning to Austria, so the position of temporary party secretary went to Dr. Schaerf.[8] Under Schaerf's steady hand the party broadened its scope of operation throughout the Russian-controlled area of Austria. (Once the French and the Americans had taken up their occupation positions, they refused to permit any sort of political activity until September 1945; this was not entirely true of the British.) Finally, in the last days of April Schaerf received formal permission from the Soviet military to organize the Socialist Party.*

Despite the fact that the Revolutionary or left-wing Socialists were amply represented in the executive committee, the influence of the more radical political philosophy which they theoretically represented had virtually no effect on the ideology and policies of the new party. This was due to a number of reasons: many of the Revolutionary Socialists, such as Josef Afritsch and Otto Probst, were by 1945 Revolutionary Socialists in name only and quickly fell in behind the leadership of the right wing; most of the pre-1934 left-wing Socialists had not returned to Austria or had almost unconsciously shed their radicalism during their prolonged exile; and finally, radical socialism came to be identified with the efforts of Erwin Scharf (not to be confused with Adolf Schaerf) to build a common front or unity party with the Communists.

Erwin Scharf, who was for many years the editor of the Vienna Communist daily *Volksstimme,* is one of the most controversial figures in postwar Austrian politics. To the Socialists, he was a party traitor, a Communist infiltrator, a man who caused the Socialist Party some of its most unhappy and painful moments. In his own estimation, Scharf is a man who attempted in vain to rescue the party from the taint of partnership with the bourgeoisie and place it in harness with the other party of the working class, the Communists, in order to strive for true Socialist goals.[9] Scharf, in some ways, is a typical example of the Socialist young left—he had reached manhood during the Dollfuss period, was an active member of the Social Revolutionary Movement, was imprisoned by the Nazis, and after his release escaped to Yugoslavia. While in Yugoslavia he fought alongside Tito's par-

* Schaerf, *Oesterreichs Wiederaufrichtung im Jahre 1945,* p. 65. Helmer (p. 212) contends that the Soviet delays were inspired by the fact that the Communist leaders—Koplenig, Fischer, and Honner—did not arrive in Vienna until the reorganization of the Socialist Party was already under way. Thus any obstacles the Russians put in the Socialists' way would help to offset this initial advantage.

tisans and finally joined with the Austrian partisan group led by the Communist Franz Honner. Upon his return to Vienna in April, he took up his old Socialist contacts, and whether because he was a talented representative of the young R-S faction or because of former contacts with the Austrian Communists and Russian military, or a combination of both, he was appointed one of the two central party secretaries. From this position, Scharf used all his influence and talent to persuade the party executive committee to work closely with the Communists, even to form an *Einheitspartei*. As early as May 1945, Scharf successfully promoted the idea of "contact committees" (*Kontaktkomitees*) with the Communists. At one point he convinced the Socialist executive committee to adopt a resolution calling for the Socialists to take common action with the Communists in such matters as nationalization, the Nazi problem, and restitution of damages from 1934.[10]

Scharf's hopes of binding the two parties together were soon hopelessly dashed by the stubborn resistance of such men as Schaerf and Helmer, and second, most decisively, by the crushing defeat the Communists received at the polls in November 1945. After the 1945 elections Schaerf, Renner, and Helmer had the Socialist Party well in hand, and Communist prospects for the creation of the type of Socialist unity party that had served Communist interests in other parts of Central Europe seemed very dim indeed.

One dramatic consequence of Erwin Scharf's final removal from the party in 1948 might be mentioned. Shortly after Scharf's dismissal, Hilde Krones, a personal friend of Scharf, who also stood on the far left of the party, took an overdose of sleeping pills and died. Whether the party would have dealt with her in the same ruthless manner as it did with Scharf is an open question. What can be said, however, is that the removal of Scharf and the death of Krones not only removed two Communist sympathizers from the hierarchy of the party but put a taint on left-wing socialism itself. As a result, the process of moving to the right was accelerated, with all things "left" falling into disrepute.

The rebirth of the Christian Social Party could have been a most awkward affair had it been handled badly; for this was the party of Dollfuss and Schuschnigg, and the 11 years since 1934 had been too few for many Socialists to forget. It is conceivable that the party could have been re-established under its old name, with the surviving members of the 1934–38 Dollfuss regime again directing the party. But the chances of cooperation between the two major parties would have been seriously prejudiced, and the creation of the Socialist–People's Party coalition which has ruled Austria since 1945 might never have taken place. Fortunately, the postwar leaders of Austria's conservative party chose to sidestep their unfortunate political legacy, devise a new name (Oesterreichische Volkspartei or OVP), and select new leaders such as Leopold Figl, who was relatively unmarked by the Dollfuss interlude and had spent time in Nazi prison camps, and Leopold Kunschak, a Catholic labor leader, who was known to have spoken out against the excesses of the Dollfuss regime. In April 1945 Kunschak became the leader (*Parteiobmann*) of the OVP. For his part, Leopold Figl won an excellent reputation for his work in rebuilding the party in Lower Austria, where he worked closely with Oskar Helmer, his Socialist counterpart. Partly as a result of this activity, Figl in September 1945 succeeded Kunschak as leader of the OVP throughout all Austria, while Kunschak, who was an elderly man, became the honorary President of the party. Incidentally, as a sop to the resistance movement, Raoul Bumballa, formerly prominent in the resistance movement, was given the position of second Vice-Chairman—a position he promptly lost after the election.[11]

The rebirth of the Christian Social Party may have produced a wave of new ideas, men, and symbols, but the organizational fabric of the party remained that of the pre-Anschluss period. The rechristened Austrian People's Party is essentially the political expression of three important interest groups—the Wirtschaftsbund (League of Businessmen), the Bauernbund (League of Farmers), and the Arbeiter- und Angestelltenbund (League of Workers and Employees). In other words, the OVP is supported by the same people—peasants, businessmen, some white-collar workers and laborers—who had followed the party's predecessor before 1938. But if the similarities between the prewar and postwar parties are important to note, particularly because they facilitated a rapid reorganization of the party, the differences are striking and most significant.

From the very first, the new leaders of Austria's conservative party were not so doctrinally intransigent as their predecessors. This is not to say that the postwar period saw a complete metamorphosis of the Austrian right, but the failure of the First Republic had indeed been a bitter lesson in the realities of Austrian political life. The Socialists made too large a lump under the carpet to be ignored; a means of mutual accommodation had to be found if an independent Austria was to survive. Persecution by the Nazis had built a common bridge between many Socialists, Conservatives, and Communists, and many members of the Austrian People's Party, notably Leopold Figl and Lois Weinberger, were determined to rebuilt the new Austria by emphasizing the feeling of comradeship born of shared wartime experience and a sense of common purpose in its reconstruction.

The Austrian Communists, for their part, were convinced in April 1945 that their moment had come. A few days after Vienna was taken by the Red Army, a dozen or so Austrian Communist functionaries, led by Party Secretary Koplenig and Ernst Fischer, landed at Voeslau airfield after being flown from Moscow via Budapest. They were taken immediately to Marshal Tolbukhin's headquarters.[12]

Koplenig knew that despite the lack of an on-the-spot Communist resistance organization, which could have taken considerable advantage of the party's excellent resistance record, the Austrian Communist Party would begin the postwar period with considerable assets: a party hierarchy that had remained intact from an early stage in the war and was fully prepared to begin reorganizing the party in Austria, an assured measure of support from those dissident left-wing Socialists who had been disillusioned in 1934 by the performance of the Social Democratic Party's leaders, the prestige of the Communists' role during the resistance, and, perhaps most significantly, the power and resources of the Red Army.

The Communist Party cadre that Johann Koplenig brought into the political arena in April 1945 was a self-confident and aggressive group, quick to take advantage of the new circumstances. Despite their dismal political record during the First Republic, the Austrian Communists immediately demanded, and received without much protest, a position of political parity with the other two parties. This admission of the Communists as political equals by the other two parties was prompted not only by the presence of the Red Army but by the assumption that the Communists had gained considerable strength and influence since 1934—how much strength no one really knew. Moreover, the Communists encouraged cooperation on the part of the other parties by behaving in such an accommodating fashion as to call into question whether this was really the party that had first attempted to overthrow the state in 1919 and had then withdrawn, at least until 1934, into snarling, almost nihilistic opposition.

In keeping with the "national front" approach that was serving Communist purposes throughout Eastern Europe, the Austrian Communists pressed hard for the establishment of such front organizations as unified youth movements, children's organizations, an organization for the victims of Nazi persecution, and of course a political *Freiheitsfront* in which all three political factions would merge as an "antifascist" front. Partially in response to Communist exhortations on the virtues of interparty cooperation, a whole rash of triparty organizations quickly sprang up. They included the Freie Oesterreichische Jugend, a "nonpolitical" organization for young men; a society for "democratic" teachers and educators; an organization primarily for former concentration camp inmates; and a newspaper edited jointly by the three parties, the *Neues Oesterreich,* which was the first Austrian newspaper to appear (April 23). Although Communist control of and plans for these organizations became increasingly apparent, at least after the first few months, the Communists had reason in the fall of 1945 to be satisfied with their efforts to build extrapolitical organizations that would complement the drive for the political unification of the three parties.[13]

At the same time as they were diligently constructing what they hoped would soon become effective front organizations, the Austrian Communists did not neglect the reorganization of their own party structure. Nevertheless, their patriotic appeals to all Austrians to put aside party differences in the reconstruction of the country soon reached such a crescendo that Leopold Kunschak, after listening to the Communists' brilliant orator Ernst Fischer on the subject of patriotism and national unity, was moved to remark to a friend that he expected Fischer at any moment to start singing "Gott erhalte Franz den Kaiser"—the national anthem of the old empire.[14]

Once the reorganization of Austria's political parties had begun, the Russians needed only the right man to head the government they hoped to control. When news arrived of the reappearance of Karl Renner, the Russians were sure they had found their man.

III

Karl Renner, the first Chancellor of the First Austrian Republic, was discovered by the Russians in April 1945 living in retirement in the small town of Gloggnitz located south of Vienna at the foot of the Semmering Pass. The story of how Renner was first brought before General Zheltov, Marshal Konev's political adviser, thoroughly interrogated, and finally, on April 20, brought to Vienna to assume again the role of Chancellor as he had after World War I, has become a near legend in Austrian political folklore.[15] At first thought it seems incredible that the Russians would pick Renner, an acknowledged and outspoken right-wing Socialist, to head the provisional government. However, Renner conformed to the type of political figurehead that the Soviets had pushed to the forefront of provisional governments throughout Eastern Europe: a non-Communist held in high regard by the population, preferably well along in years, where sheer physical exhaustion would foster a sense of compromise, and hopefully vulnerable to mild forms of political blackmail born of certain indiscretions committed during the Nazi period. Renner had most of these "qualifications," including a record of grudging endorsement of Hitler's Anschluss. Renner, then, must have seemed ideal for the role the Soviets hoped he would play. According to Anastas Mikoyan, Stalin is supposed to have exclaimed, when word was brought to him that Renner had been found, "What, the old traitor is still alive? He is exactly the man we need."[16] Apocryphal story or not—Renner was an old man and to the Austrian Communists he must have seemed an excellent choice for a figurehead.

When Renner was brought to Vienna on April 20, he and his family were quartered in a house in the fashionable section of Hietzing. Symbolic of his position was the billeting of a Russian detachment in the basement of the building, the assignment of a Soviet interpreter and aide, and a Soviet escort to accompany him around the city—this last service was also provided all cabinet members once the provisional government was formed.* Renner's original plan, formulated before he arrived in Vienna, was to recall the national parliament which Dollfuss had suspended in 1933. Renner theoretically had the power to do this, since he was one of the presidents of the Nationalrat in 1933. However, when he actually returned to Vienna and saw not only the practical difficulties involved in such a step (including the fact that the Communists were not represented in the 1933 Nationalrat) but the remarkable revitalization of the political parties, he decided that the parties were capable of representing the people.[17]

Thus, on April 22, representatives of the three political parties assembled at Renner's residence under the watchful eye of the Russians to bargain for cabinet positions—the Socialists led by Renner, Schaerf, and Koerner; the People's Party by Kunschak; and the Communists by Party Secretary Koplenig, Ernest Fischer, and Franz Honner.[18] Honner had been flown to Vienna ahead of his partisan troops, who would not arrive from Yugoslavia until early May.

* Renner, *Denkschrift,* pp. 106–7. Schaerf writes that most people, upon seeing him on the street followed by two Russian soldiers carrying automatic weapons, thought that he was a Russian prisoner—an impression that the Western Allies initially extended to the whole Renner government.

The bargaining took two full days, primarily because the Communists insisted on getting two of the most important positions in the cabinet—Minister of the Interior, with all its control of the internal security forces, and Minister of Education. Despite the greatest misgivings, Renner was realistic enough to appreciate that without Communist participation there would be no provisional government and that the Communists demanded these two positions as the price of joining the Renner government. Therefore, the Communists got what they wanted. Franz Honner became Minister of the Interior; Ernst Fischer became Minister of Education and Public Information; and Johann Koplenig became one of three secretaries without portfolio—Schaerf and Kunschak (later Figl) were the other two—who served as members of Renner's inner cabinet. As the full cabinet was finally composed on April 23, there were 13 main posts, with four going to the Socialists, four to the People's Party, and three to the Communists, with two nonparty men rounding it out.[19]

Despite the fact that the Communist position in the new cabinet was extremely strong (particularly since every decision of the provisional government had to be approved by the Soviets), it is at this early stage that we see for the first time the remarkable political acumen of the man the Communists thought would be so pliable. To counter Communist influence in these critical posts, Renner proposed an ingenious idea of the appointment of two undersecretaries for each cabinet position except finance and justice (which had nonpolitical men); these undersecretaries were to be drawn from the two parties that did not have the top spot. For example, in the Ministry of the Interior Honner had Socialist Oskar Helmer and Dr. Bumballa of the People's Party to look out for the interests of their respective parties. One result of this decision, which the Communists agreed to, apparently figuring that they would have a man in every ministry, was considerable inefficiency. At cabinet meetings there were often 33 or 34 members present, and although the undersecretaries could veto a decision of the minister, the normal process was to refer disagreements to the cabinet.[20] One technique used by Karl Renner to get the required cabinet unanimity of the three parties was to hold the cabinet sessions in the evening and then keep the most controversial issues to the very last. In a city where in 1945 between 400 and 800 calories of nourishment per day was the normal fare, the knowledge that the wine and food would not be served until the cabinet business was concluded served to dampen argument.

Thus, under Renner's capable guidance, the provisional government operating as both a legislative and executive body somehow did

manage to govern the Soviet-occupied area of Austria, and later all
of Austria. And in the process, owing in large measure to the "watchdog" undersecretaries, the Communists were hampered in the full
exploitation of their powerful offices.

Once the cabinet was installed, the formal process of establishing
the government went swiftly. On April 27 the provisional government issued a five-point proclamation to the Austrian people declaring the Anschluss null and void and officially declaring the establishment of a democratic Austrian republic "to be organized in the
spirit of the constitution of 1920." The proclamation was signed by
Karl Renner as provisional Chancellor and the three members of
the political or inner cabinet, Schaerf, Kunschak, and the Communist Koplenig.[21]

This declaration and two transitional constitutional laws subsequently approved on May 13 served as the legal underpinning of the
provisional government, thereby sparing Austria some of the political confusion that often plagued other Eastern European countries in 1945. The first of these laws provided that the provisional
government would be guided in its temporary role of performing
both executive and legislative functions by the 1920 constitution of
the First Republic as amended in 1929. Once a freely elected parliament convened, this body would assume the legislative role and be
empowered to modify the constitution as required. The second major decision of the provisional government was to declare that all
legislative and executive decrees promulgated by March 5, 1933, were
valid, while those after March 5, the date Dollfuss suspended the last
freely elected Austrian parliament, were held to be invalid. Adolf
Schaerf considered these constitutional steps among the most important decisions for the future of Austria made in the postwar period.[22]
This is a fair appraisal; for these decisions not only gave legal authority to the provisional government in the most expeditious manner
but served to sidestep a source of possible conflict between the Socialists and Conservatives over the Dollfuss interlude.*

* The contrast between the Russians' view of these laws before and after the November 1945 national elections is interesting and bears out Schaerf's point on the
importance of these constitutional steps. In May 1945 the Russians were obviously
in favor of Renner's constitutional solution, since the Soviets had unchallenged
control over the actions of the provisional government. In December 1945, when an
Austrian parliament virtually free of Communist influence because of the elections
submitted to the Allied Commission for approval the very constitution the Russians had backed in May, the Soviet representative vetoed the measure. Moreover,
at the insistence of the Soviets the Austrian Parliament was ordered to prepare a
new constitution, to be submitted by July of 1946. That the Austrians chose to

On Austria's "day of independence," April 27, the entire cabinet was feted by Marshal Tolbukhin, who, amid the general festivities, informed the Austrians that the Soviet Union had recognized the Renner government. But before the Austrians could toast this event, Tolbukhin added that Russia's allies had refused to follow the Soviet Union's example. Schaerf has written of the deep concern and disquietude this obviously unexpected news caused the Socialists and the People's Party.[23] For the moment, however, whatever misgivings many Austrians might have had about this turn of events were muted by the ceremonies of April 29, when the Second Austrian Republic was born, with the formal installation of Renner as its first Chancellor.[24] However natural and appropriate it might have seemed at the time, the presence of a Russian military band, the large number of ranking Soviet officers attending and participating in the ceremonies, and the patronizing tone of their speeches, all caused a disturbing impression abroad. Although the Austrians were virtually unaware of it, the Soviet Union's allies were becoming increasingly suspicious that the Renner government was nothing more than a Russian pawn.

---

disregard this order and got away with it is best explained in terms of the new occupation control agreement described in Chapter 4. See the *Proceedings of the Allied Commission*, Minutes of the Allied Council Meeting of March 25, 1946, ALCO(46)19, and Minutes of the Executive Commission, Meeting of March 30, 1946, EXCO(46)30. In 1950 the Soviets would charge that Austria did not have a constitution (Allied Council Meeting of January 27, 1950, ALCO(50)115). Given the fact that the Allied Commission had supreme authority in Austria and no constitution was ever formally approved by the Council, the Russians were technically correct.

Austria and the Western Allies

The question of recognition of the Renner government by the Western Allies, which was debated at the Potsdam Conference in 1945, is best seen against the background of the Allied political planning for the postwar period.[1]

The first declaration on Austria's postwar future came as a result of a conference between the foreign ministers of the United States, the United Kingdom, and the Soviet Union held in Moscow at the end of October, 1943.[2] Here it was agreed in the Moscow Declaration of November 1, 1943, that "Austria, the first free country to fall victim to Hitlerite aggression, shall be liberated from German domination."[3] The German annexation of Austria was condemned as the Allies declared their intention "to see reestablished a free and independent Austria." With this declaration as a guide, the European Advisory Commission, established at the Moscow Conference to study the postwar political problems and to draw up the occupation control agreements, began to negotiate the occupation settlement for Austria.

In its discussions on Austria the European Advisory Commission (EAC) was soon hopelessly deadlocked on arrangements over zones and occupation machinery. This situation resulted in large measure from Soviet insistence on zoning Vienna for occupation by the Four Powers along city limits delineated before 1938. The Western Allies contended that such an arrangement would deprive them of the necessary area to support their forces in the city and would leave no airfields within the Vienna zones. This deadlock and other points of disagreement continued for months, with the result that the zoning agreement was not signed until July 9, 1945, and the Western Allies were unable to move their headquarters into Vienna until August 23.

This was four full months after the Soviet army had full control of the city.[4]

Considering the vexing Soviet delays in the zonal arrangements, the announcement by the Soviet Union that on April 24 it had permitted the Socialist Karl Renner to form a provisional government came as an unwelcome surprise. The American and British representatives in Moscow first heard of it from Andrei Vyshinsky, who contended that Renner, by virtue of his former position as one of the presidents of the Austrian parliament when it was dissolved, had every legal right to take this initiative.[5] The Western Allies were obviously disturbed by this news, which came less than two weeks after the Russian army took Vienna. When further word came via Radio Moscow that on April 29 the Soviet Union had recognized the Renner government, a government in which the Communists had one-third of the cabinet positions, Churchill was outraged. He immediately wired President Truman requesting coordination on a strongly worded protest to Stalin.[6] The President agreed to protest the unilateral action but not to comment on the composition of the Renner government.

Western indignation was further aroused by the obvious effort of the Soviets to delay the entrance of Allied troops into Vienna until they had a better settlement on the remaining zonal conflicts before the EAC. On July 2, 1945, the American Ambassador in the Soviet Union, Averell Harriman, wired Washington that the Soviet Commander in Austria had refused to allow American troops to take up their positions. On June 16, in reply to Truman's protest, Stalin had promised to set July 1 as the date of occupation of these positions. According to Stalin this delay was to give the EAC time to complete its work.[7] This sort of pressure was successful in reducing Western demands and prolonging the period of unchallenged Soviet control of Vienna and the Renner government.* But such blackmail was certainly not endearing, nor did it help bring the Western Allies closer to acceptance of the Renner government.

Once the initial reaction to the Soviet Union's unilateral action on the Renner government was spent, policy discussion on the issue between the United States and Great Britain soon followed. On the

* On July 4, the American representative on the EAC, John G. Winant, was finally instructed by Washington to accept the Soviet counterproposal on the airfield issue—i.e., to accept Tulln and Schwechat rather than the three fields heretofore insisted upon. *Potsdam Conference*, I, Doc. 281, pp.350–51. The final agreement was signed on July 9.

morning of May 31, the American Acting Secretary of State, Joseph
C. Grew, handed President Truman the British proposals for a Potsdam agenda. Under the heading of Austria, the British suggested discussion of an Austrian government that would be "satisfactory to all
three Allied governments."[8] Following Truman's request for a study
of various points, on June 14 Grew submitted to the President point-
by-point comments on the British proposals. Grew's memorandum
begins with the observation that Churchill's list "is so drawn as to
give the appearance largely of a bill of complaints against the Soviet
government, which seems hardly the proper approach to the forthcoming meeting."[9] The comments on the Austrian government situation are significant in pointing up the developing difference in policy
toward the Renner government between the United States and Great
Britain. Grew recommended that the United States agree to "give
prompt consideration" to the question of recognizing the Renner
government after the questions still before the EAC were resolved and
the Allied troops had taken up their positions. He suggests, "We
should also stipulate that the Renner government should be prepared
to hold elections as soon as possible, under the supervision of the Occupying Powers, for a constituent assembly."[10]

The inclination of the United States government to accept the
Renner government without a major cabinet revision is most clearly
defined in the briefing paper prepared on the subject for use of the
American delegation at Potsdam.

Whatever might be the regrettable nature of the Soviet action [in unilaterally recognizing the Renner government], it appears beyond serious doubt
that, in terms of the men themselves and in terms of representation of political forces, the Renner government is as good a coalition as could be devised
at the present time. It equally appears that the distribution of offices among
the three Austrian parties is not a serious misrepresentation of current political forces although the allocation of the Interior portfolio to a Communist
suggests a special advantage for the Communist group by virtue of the importance of that office. The portfolio of Public Instruction and Worship in
the hands of a Communist may appear dubious from our point of view, but
Ernst Fischer, the incumbent, is a post-1934 convert to communism and a
cultured man highly esteemed by persons of contrary political outlooks. . . .
Generally Austrians at home and abroad, except Fascist and Monarchist
elements, have approved the Renner government. . . . The British take
a less favorable view of the Renner cabinet than we do, and may insist that
it is too far to the left to recognize without some changes.[11]

The "Monarchist elements" referred to in the briefing paper sought
to stay U.S. recognition of the Renner government by stressing the

Communist influence in it. In a letter to President Truman dated July 2, 1945, Archduke Otto of Austria minced few words about the character of the Renner government. Contending that he was "in daily contact not only with the former Austrian resistance movement, but also with the majority political parties and local administration," Otto charged that:

The Russians have been sponsoring a Communist-dominated regime of their own in Vienna. There have been rumours that the Allies will eventually recognize this Communist regime, the so-called "Provisional Government." I can assure you that the overwhelming majority of the Austrians would refuse to accept such a Government, because they do not want the elections controlled by the Austrian Communists, who avowedly strive for dictatorship and would do anything to impair the honesty of the elections.[12]

In contrast with the American position, the British were very wary and suspicious of the Austrian Provisional Government. This position is best illustrated by an extract from the political directive sent in July by the British government to Lieutenant General McCreery, Commander of the British Forces of Occupation in Austria. McCreery's instructions were:

One of your first tasks will be to secure, in agreement with your Soviet, United States, and French colleagues, an early transition from the Renner Government to a fully representative Austrian Government which it will be possible for the four controlling powers to recognize.

With a view to bringing this about, you should take the following line in discussion with your colleagues. While admitting at a time when only a limited part of Austria had been liberated, you should assume that there can be no question of that Government, recruited on so narrow a territorial basis, continuing to survive once Austria is placed as a whole under Allied control.[13]

The directive goes on to instruct McCreery to press for a general Austrian conference representing the various provincial administrations to meet in Vienna under Allied supervision. This conference would then nominate a "representative Austrian Government" which would hold office until free elections could be held. In other words, this was not a question of broadening the Renner government but of beginning again.*

* General McCreery very carefully pursued this policy at the Allied Council meetings beginning in September. He adamantly refused to consider any declaration by the Council that referred to a "provisional Austrian government" until after the late September conference of provincial representatives. McCreery also refused to discuss extension of the administrative authority of the Renner government until this time. By early September, however, the British had gained enough con-

These differences among the Allies about the future of the Renner government were finally persistent enough to require the attention of the Big Three at the Potsdam Conference.

I

The "Tripartite Conference of Berlin," most commonly referred to as the Berlin or Potsdam Conference, took place from July 17 to August 2, 1945. During this period the heads of government of the United States, the United Kingdom, and the Soviet Union met in 13 formal or plenary meetings in Schloss Cecilienhof, the former palace of Crown Prince Wilhelm of Prussia, in Potsdam. Here the victorious wartime Allies made many major decisions affecting the postwar future of Europe. Two questions of great importance to Austria's future were discussed at Potsdam. The first was of course the recognition of the Renner government by the Western Allies. The second issue was the question of reparations from Austria.

Considering the intense and often bitter nature of the disagreement over the Renner government and occupation arrangements, the actual negotiations at Potsdam on these issues were something of an anticlimax.

On July 20 during the Fourth Plenary Session of the Big Three— President Truman, Prime Minister Churchill, and Generalissimo Stalin—Churchill accused the Soviet Union of obstructing Western occupation of the agreed zones and delaying entrance of Allied officers into Vienna. Stalin suggested that Churchill seemed unnecessarily indignant considering that general agreement on the question of zones had just been reached.* Therefore, Stalin continued, movement of troops could begin in one or two days.[14]

At the Sixth Plenary Meeting on July 22, Stalin said that withdrawal of Soviet troops from the Western zones had begun. This announcement, coupled with a letter from Marshal Ivan S. Konev, the Soviet Commander in Chief in Austria, to his Western counterparts

---

fidence in Renner that they were content with the broadening of his government by the inclusion of Western Austrians rather than continuing to insist on an entirely new government. See Allied Commission for Austria, *Proceedings of the Allied Commission*, Minutes of the Allied Council Meeting of September 11, 1945, ALCO(45)1, pp. 4–7, and Minutes of the Meeting of September 20, ALCO(45)3, pp. 5–10.

* Stalin was referring to the Four-Power agreement on control machinery which was approved by the EAC on July 4, and a similar agreement on the zones of occupation in Austria and the city of Vienna signed in London on July 9, 1945. See also Chapter 5 below. Truman signed both of these agreements on the morning of July 20.

stating that he had been instructed to extend cooperation to the
Allied Forces, paved the way for a series of meetings of the four
Deputy Commanders, which began on July 24.[15]

Churchill and Truman seemed pleased by Stalin's immediate response to their protests of July 20, and it was in this moment of good
will that the question of the authority of the Renner government was
discussed. In addition, Stalin at the Big Three meeting of July 23
had presented the case for the Renner government very well indeed.
He suggested that the Western Allies consider not recognition of the
Renner government but extension of its authority to the Western
zones as one answer to the pressing question of collection of food in
Austria.[16] At the Eighth Plenary Meeting, on July 24, Churchill himself raised the question and stated that once the Western forces arrived in Vienna, they would take up the question of extension of the
administrative control of the Renner government. Churchill added
that he agreed with the extension in principle. Truman concurred.[17]

This compromise was consistent with British policy on the Renner
government as defined in the political directive to General McCreery.
Deferring any decision until Western forces were securely in Vienna
would avoid any danger of a rash commitment and provide time for
a closer assessment of the situation. American policy with respect
to the Renner government was certainly less cautious. There is no
evidence to indicate that the United States during the Potsdam Conference departed from its initial position that the Renner government was acceptable in its original form. It is conceivable, then, that
the United States would have been willing to extend the authority
of the Renner government in Austria until such time as elections
could have been held.

The result of Russian initiative on this question was the inclusion
in the Potsdam Protocol of the following paragraphs:

The Conference examined a proposal by the Soviet Government on the extension of the authority of the Austrian Provisional Government to all of
Austria.

The Three Governments agreed that they were prepared to examine this
question after the entry of the British and American forces into the City
of Vienna.[18]

Certainly the Soviet Union could claim that at Potsdam it was the
champion of Austrian interests. The use to which they put this image
would only emerge in the months to come.

The Austrian reparations question at Potsdam was an infinitely
more complex problem than that of recognition of the Renner gov-

ernment. To the Soviet Union reparations were not simply a matter of compensation for war damage, but an effective economic lever in the general process of sovietization of Eastern Europe.[19] To demand reparations of the Austrians, however, would make a mockery of the Moscow Declaration, which clearly specified that Austria would be considered a liberated country.

Nonetheless, during the Moscow Conference, the Soviets had made a determined effort to impose upon Austria the burden of reparations—the amount and duration not to be specified. Andrei Vyshinsky, the Soviet representative on the Drafting Committee, had insisted on including the phrase "Austria bears full political and material responsibility for the war." After much heated argument the Western Allies finally agreed to the inclusion of a compromise statement, which formed the third paragraph of the Moscow Declaration: "Austria is reminded, however, that she has a responsibility which she cannot evade for participating in the war on the side of Hitlerite Germany, and that in the final settlement account will inevitably be taken of her own contribution to her liberation."[20] This concession to the Soviet Union, made in the interest of Allied harmony, firmly rooted subsequent Soviet claims for reparations from Austria.

The U.S. position on Austrian reparations, unlike the one taken on Germany where the principle of substantial reparations was granted, was well defined months before the Potsdam Conference. In a position paper prepared for the use of the American delegation at the conference, the official policy of the United States is perhaps best summarized:

The United States government is opposed to the exaction of reparations from Austria despite her contribution to the German war effort. It feels that such an attempt would be economically unrealistic and would have dangerous political implications in Central Europe. . . . A program of reparations for Austria analogous to that projected for Germany would be inconsistent with the sense of the Moscow Declaration and would require a reversal of the policy on which the Declaration is based. This policy implied an undertaking on the part of the subscribers to the Moscow Declaration to create economic conditions favorable to the preservation of Austrian independence. . . . It is believed that an attempt to force reparations from Austria would turn the Austrians against us and tend ultimately to strengthen Germany in future years by forcing Austria back into her arms.[21]

The paper goes on to say that the United States would, however, approve a reparations program "limited to the transfer of existing capital equipment clearly in excess of the healthy peacetime requirements of the Austrian economy, such as machinery in armaments plants erected since 1938."[22]

However, on the very day that the position paper on reparations was drawn up, an important concession on the Austrian reparations issue was made in London. On July 4, John G. Winant, American Ambassador to the United Kingdom and United States representative on the European Advisory Council, wired the new Secretary of State, James F. Byrnes, that he had been forced to agree to the inclusion of a Reparation, Deliveries and Restitution Division in the occupation control agreement for Austria he had just signed.[23] Winant reported that at the signing of the agreement he had qualified the U.S. position on this point by stating that the EAC "was not empowered to consider and did not consider the substantive aspects of the question of Austrian reparation." He conceded that his government did recognize Austria's obligation in principle to pay reparations if the general economic condition of Austria warranted it. Despite Winant's qualifying remarks, the fact remained that the Austrian control agreement provided for a reparations division, and this concession plus the "responsibility" clause in the Moscow Declaration gave real weight to the subsequent Soviet demands at Potsdam.

Once at Potsdam, the Soviet delegation was not long in testing the strength of the Western Allies' position on Austrian reparations. The American Secretary of State, James F. Byrnes, first raised the question at the Third Meeting of the Foreign Ministers on July 20. The Foreign Ministers agreed from the outset that the Austrian issue should be taken up by the reparations subcommittee.[24] The first concrete proposal, however, was not made until the Seventh Meeting of the Foreign Ministers, on July 24, when Molotov circulated a paper dealing with Austrian reparations. The proposal was brief and explicit:

Regarding Reparation from Austria:

1. To establish the general sum of reparation from Austria of $250,000,000 to be liquidated in equal parts during six years commencing with July 1, 1945.

2. To exact reparations generally in the form of deliveries of products of Austrian industry.

3. Reparations to be exacted to compensate for losses caused by the war to the Soviet Union, Great Britain, the United States of America, Yugoslavia.[25]

The position of the Western Allies was equally simple and straightforward, as expressed by the British proposal: "Reparations will not be exacted from Austria. Removal of plant and equipment and other goods from Austria as war booty or otherwise will, in future, be a matter to be settled by the Control Council."[26]

At the Ninth Meeting of the Foreign Ministers, on July 27, Secretary of State Byrnes and Molotov met head on over the issue of reparations from Austria. Molotov heatedly rejected Byrnes's contention that it was impossible to hope for reparations from Austria or Italy. Italy, according to Byrnes, had already received some $500 million in aid and would probably require more. Austria was in a similar situation. Any reparations demands, then, would come out of aid from the Western Allies and would mean, in effect, that this would go to the Soviet Union as reparations. Molotov rejoined that the United States had not been occupied by Austrian troops, that these troops had wrought great damage in Russia, and that "they could not let the Austrians go unpunished."[27] The meeting ended with the dispute unresolved. Molotov's admission, however, that Austria must be punished, and his insistence on coupling Austria and Italy in the reparations question, are certainly evidence that, to the Soviet Union, Austria was considered a defeated enemy power and not a liberated country in the spirit of the Moscow Declaration.

On July 28 Marshal Stalin, perhaps impressed with the firmness of the Western position, abruptly signaled a change in Soviet attitude on Austrian reparations. At the Tenth Plenary Meeting of the Big Three, Stalin, when the question was again raised on the matter of reparation demands from Italy and Austria, allowed that it was conceivable that reparations could be lifted from Austria because Austria, unlike Italy, did not have her own army in the field during the war.* Nevertheless, apparently reluctant to lose a bargaining point without something in return, Molotov, on July 30, submitted another proposal on reparations. Italy was to pay a total sum of $300 million to the Soviet Union, Yugoslavia, Greece, and Albania; Austria was to pay an amount to be established by the Austrian Control Council to the Soviet Union and Yugoslavia.[28] When Byrnes mentioned Stalin's concession of July 28, Molotov replied that they might be prepared to drop all reparation claims against Austria if Yugoslavia, who was to share in the Austrian reparation payments, would receive compensation from another source.[29]

Understandably the Western Allies must have felt most satisfied at this stage in the negotiations over Austria: the decision to resist

---

* *Potsdam Conference*, II, Tenth Plenary Meeting, Llewellyn E. Thompson Minutes, p. 464. Between the Ninth and Tenth Plenary meetings (July 25 and July 28, 1945) Churchill was replaced at Potsdam by Clement Attlee, and Anthony Eden by Ernest Bevin. Attlee had been at Potsdam as an observer until both he and Churchill returned to England to await the results of the July 1945 election.

any effort to burden the country with reparations had been well defended and Austria seemed to be free of all damaging economic penalties. Unfortunately, a more serious threat to the economic viability of Austria was building up in another quarter—over the German reparations question.

In comparison to the prolonged and heated struggle over the issue of German reparations, the Austrian reparations question was of little moment. Definitions of "war booty" and the Russians' insistence on a fixed reparations sum had continually plagued the negotiations, and it was only on July 29 that the discussions reached the stage of hard cold percentages of industrial equipment in Western Germany. It was finally agreed that the Soviets, who had already gained the right to independent action with regard to reparations in the Soviet Eastern Zone of Germany, would be entitled to 25 per cent of such industrial equipment as was unnecessary to the peacetime economy in the Western zones.[30]

Despite this agreement, the report of the Drafting Committee on Reparations from Germany, submitted on the last day of the Potsdam Conference, August 1, stated that no final agreement on the matter of German reparations had been reached.[31] The point of disagreement was over a phrase that would be well known in Austria for years to come—the German external assets. The United States and the United Kingdom representatives on the committee had insisted that in return for the percentages of capital equipment in the Western zones previously awarded the Soviet Union, the Soviets must drop their claims to the "German Corporations in the Western Zones."[32] At this time the draft of the section in the Potsdam Protocol on German reparations consisted of seven paragraphs. Six of the seven embodied the already-agreed-upon percentages of industrial capital equipment awarded to the Soviet Union. The only point of discord was paragraph three, which read in the draft: "The reparations claims of the United States, the United Kingdom and other countries entitled to reparations shall be met from the Western Zones *and from German external assets.*"[33] The phrase "and from German external assets" was objected to by the Soviet representative, who argued that the Soviet Union also had rights to some of the German foreign assets.[34]

At Potsdam, the United States took the position that the German assets should be subject to the jurisdiction of the powers occupying Germany and the Allied Control Council in Germany. This was the essence of a U.S. proposal advanced on July 22.[35] It is at this point that the basic fallacy in the Western position on German assets becomes painfully clear. The objective of U.S. policy with regard to the German external assets was to win for the Allied Control Council in Germany the power of disposition over the German-owned assets. Well and good, as far as it went. But in the process of winning this point, the delegation neglected considering the most important point —just what is a German external asset. On August 1, the United States and Great Britain, following this line of reasoning, recommended that the following paragraph be included in the protocol: "Appropriate steps shall be taken by the Control Council to exercise control and the power of disposition over German-owned external assets not already under the control of the United Nations which have taken part in the war against Germany."*

At the Eleventh Meeting of Foreign Ministers, on the same morning, it was agreed to send the problem to the Big Three.[36] It is not difficult to imagine the tense, almost frantic atmosphere that must have reigned at the last two meetings of the Big Three on this same day. At this point most of the Western delegates were physically and mentally spent by the seemingly endless hours of what President Truman has called "prolonged and petty bickering." They were exhausted, annoyed with "all the repetition and beating around the bush," anxious to leave, and seemingly confident that time would smooth everything out; so there is little wonder that the issue of German assets was resolved in such a bizarre and, for Austria, unhappy fashion.†

Secretary Byrnes opened the Twelfth Plenary Meeting of the Big Three around 4:00 P.M. on August 1 by reading the report of the Drafting Committee on Reparations from Germany, which consisted of the seven-paragraph draft described above. Stalin then suggested as a solution to the problem of the German foreign assets that the Soviet Union would first drop its claim to German gold which the Western Allies had found in Germany. Then, with regard to German foreign investments, the demarcation between the Soviet and Western

---

* *Potsdam Conference*, II, Doc. 1002, August 1, pp. 963–64. At the time, the Soviet representatives stated that "they had very little interest in the matter" and reserved judgment. This paragraph did, in fact, go into the Potsdam Protocol unchanged (Doc. 1383, II, para. 18, p. 1485).

† Harry S. Truman, *Year of Decisions*, pp. 410–11. The President notes in his memoirs that it was three o'clock in the morning of August 2 before the Potsdam Conference formally adjourned. Nevertheless, after returning briefly to the Little White House in Babelsberg, Truman's party left immediately for the Gatow airfield to return home. Truman speaks of how anxious he was to leave Potsdam.

zones could also serve as a dividing line for the division of the German assets—everything to the West going to the Western Allies, the Soviet retaining all the assets to the East.[37] President Truman then asked if this division along the demarcation line meant from the Baltic to the Adriatic. Stalin replied in the affirmative and cited, as an example, that the German investments in Hungary and Rumania would go to the Soviet Union. Stalin then raised the question of Austria and Yugoslavia, Austria being divided into zones and Yugoslavia being partly on the Soviet side of the demarcation line. It is at this point that Benjamin Cohen, a special assistant to the Secretary of State, records the following exchange:

> *Stalin:* Austria is divided into two parts—how shall we deal with those?
> *Bevin:* You better give it to us.
> *Stalin:* You want all of Austria. You can have part of Austria and [all of] Yugoslavia.[38]

It was finally agreed, then, that the Soviet Union would renounce all claims to both German gold and foreign properties on the Western side of the demarcation line and that the "German assets" would be divided on a similar geographic basis. The German properties in Austria would, therefore, go to the occupation powers on a zonal basis.[39]

One of the great ironies of the Potsdam Conference is the fact that at this very meeting where the German assets question was settled in such a casual fashion, the Western policy of no reparations from Austria was finally agreed upon. The long hours of careful and determined negotiation had been successful—Austria was spared the $250 million in reparations, only to be exposed to a more costly form of exploitation.[40]

The really extraordinary element in the German assets issue as it affected Austria was not the seemingly cavalier manner in which the decision was made, for much more important decisions were made at the Big Three level with much less ceremony, but the wording of the paragraphs within the Potsdam Protocol embodying the decision. In those few hours between the adjournment of the 4:00 P.M. meeting and the beginning of the last meeting of the Big Three, scheduled for 9:00 P.M., the original seven paragraphs of the Potsdam Protocol relating to the assets problem were expanded to ten.[41] The section on German reparations now included the following three articles:

8. The Soviet Government renounces all claims to shares of German enterprises which are located in the Western Zones of Germany as well as

to German foreign assets in all countries except those specified in paragraph 9 below.

9. The Governments of the U.K. and U.S.A. renounce their claims to shares to German enterprises which are located in the Eastern Zone of occupation in Bulgaria, Finland, Hungary, Rumania, and Eastern Austria.

10. The Soviet Government makes no claim to gold captured by the Allied troops in Germany.[42]

So as a result of a decision that was made in an atmosphere of Western impatience and exhaustion and put on paper in terms that are a model of ambiguity and imprecision, the Soviet Union received full and unqualified title to all "German foreign assets in Bulgaria, Finland, Hungary, Rumania, and Eastern Austria." Small wonder that the author of a distinguished book on diplomacy has cited the "German assets" decision as a prime example of the dangers of impatience in diplomatic negotiation.*

There is a curious sequel to this part of the story, which indicates that the Soviet negotiators at Potsdam were pursuing a carefully conceived line of policy. During the last meeting of the Big Three, Molotov proposed that the decision not to demand reparations from Austria be included in the Protocol but not in the communiqué.† When Truman asked if the whole section on Austria should be taken out, Stalin quickly interjected that they wanted only the part concerned with reparations left out. When Truman said that he would take out the whole section or a part, Stalin repeated that it was only the paragraph on reparations he wanted deleted from the communiqué. The result of all this was that in the communiqué released on August 2, 1945, Section VIII on Austria states:

The Conference examined a proposal by the Soviet Government on the extension of the authority of the Austrian Provisional Government to all of Austria.

The three Governments agreed that they were prepared to examine this question after the entry of the British and American forces into the city of Vienna.[43]

The Protocol, on the other hand, released much later, has an additional paragraph: "It was agreed that reparations should not be ex-

* Charles Thayer, in *Diplomat* (p. 96), quotes the American Commissioner of the Reparations Committee, Edwin W. Pauley, as replying apologetically when asked about this blunder: "We seemed to have overlooked that point in our hurry to wind up and go home."
† The communiqué of the Potsdam Conference was released by the respective governments on August 2, 1945; the text of the Protocol was not released by the Department of State until March 24, 1947, and by the Soviet Union not until 1955. The Protocol could be called a corrected copy of the communiqué; the changes, with some exceptions, were editorial in nature.

acted from Austria."[44] The reasoning behind all this, Molotov added, was simply that it was better for the Austrians to hope for this decision than to know it had been made. He felt that "Its publication in the communiqué would tie our hands unnecessarily."[45]

Immediately after the conclusion of the conference, President Truman undoubtedly felt some official uneasiness about the "German assets" solution, for he sent a long and detailed memorandum to Lucius D. Clay, Deputy Military Governor, United States Zone in Germany, on the German external property question.[46] Truman cited Section II, Paragraph 18, of the Potsdam Protocol as his reference, which instructed the Control Council in Germany to assume control over the disposition of the German-owned external assets not already in Allied hands.[47] He then instructed Clay to urge the adoption of an enclosed draft decree on the subject. Ironically enough, the draft decree defined the term "German assets" with all the precision that was so lacking in the Potsdam Protocol. Truman told Clay that this matter was "most urgent."

Any hopes of handling the German assets problem at the Control Council level were soon shattered. Although the German External Property Commission called for in the draft decree was established, General Clay himself has admitted that "the necessity for diplomatic negotiations with the various governments made the work of the Commission impracticable."[48] The Soviet Union obviously had no interest in pursuing the issue any further; the definition of German assets, or lack of definition, agreed to at Potsdam was more than enough for their purposes.

II

The Potsdam Conference gave the Soviet Union the opportunity to assume two seemingly contradictory roles in Austria—champion of the Provisional Government and heir to the German external assets.

The Russians in Austria were eager from the very beginning to profit from their role of liberators. There is little doubt that the majority of Austrians in the spring of 1945, despite the brutality of the first wave of Russian troops, would have seconded Karl Renner's sincere expression of gratitude to the Russian army given on the occasion of the official celebration in Vienna, April 29, 1945, of the formation of the Provisional Government. Renner gratefully acknowledged that "only through the strength and through the victorious advance of the Red Army has Austria been able to regain its independence."[49]

What was known in Austria of the Potsdam Conference from the communiqué would certainly have strengthened the impression that the Soviet Union was Austria's strongest supporter. The communiqué was explicit in stating that the conference examined "a proposal by the Soviet government on the extension of the authority of the Austrian Provisional Government to all of Austria." Reluctance to recognize the Provisional Government obviously came from the Western side, and the Austrian leaders felt this mistrust most keenly.[50]

After the entrance of the Western Allies into Vienna, the Soviet element continued to press for extension of the Renner government's authority. From the first meeting of the four Commanders in Chief on August 23, 1945, the Soviet position on immediate extension of the authority of the Provisional Government was strongly argued.[51] At the meeting of the Allied Council on September 20, a memorandum from Dr. Renner was discussed. Here Renner suggested calling a conference in Vienna of representatives of the provinces to discuss the inclusion of representatives of Western Austria in the government. At the Allied Council meeting the Soviet element proposed that the Renner government be granted immediate permission to extend its authority. After 30 days, consultation with the provincial governments could be arranged to discuss changes in the government.[52] In other words, the Russians were not interested in any conference that would broaden the base of the Renner government; what they wanted was to maintain the Renner government in its original form for as long as possible. Any changes in the cabinet made to include Western Austrians would, by the very conservative nature of that part of Austria, weaken Communist strength in the government.

Nevertheless, the conference took place September 24–26 in Vienna, with the result that the Provisional Government was broadened to include Western Provincial representatives.[53] As a result of this conference, the Allied Council on October 1 recommended to their respective governments that the Provisional Government be recognized, with the provision that the elections be held no later than December 1945.[54] On October 20 formal notification of recognition of the Renner Provisional Government, subject to the conditions of a free election to be held before December 31, was handed to Dr. Renner.[55] An election date of November 25 was quickly agreed to by all parties concerned. Thus, before the streets had been cleared of rubble, Austrians began a frantic political campaign under the watchful eyes of the occupying powers for an election that was to prove one of the most critical moments in Austria's history.

The Elections of November 1945

It is not completely clear why the Austrian Communists and the Soviet military authorities supported with such enthusiasm the holding of a national election in November of 1945. But certain factors undoubtedly weighed heavily in their decision to support early elections. First, the Communists were clearly convinced that the Austrian Communist Party was finally a "third force" in Austrian politics and that any election would demonstrate this new political reality. Since they already controlled the Ministries of Interior and Education—albeit under the watchful eyes of the other parties—they were certainly optimistic enough to believe that their electoral mandate would be large enough to at least retain these two key posts. Second, the Communists respected the organizational skills of the Socialists, and now that the Socialists had successfully resisted Communist efforts to build a common front, the Communists may have thought it was tactically wiser to have an election before the Socialists could completely reorganize their party apparatus. Finally, and perhaps most important, in late September of 1945, when the decision was made to hold an election, the appeals of communism as expressed in free elections had not as yet been tested in those countries that Soviet armies had overrun. All that was known was that in Western Europe the current was very strong to the left.

I

The technical details of the impending elections were agreed upon at the Second Austrian Provisional Conference held in Vienna from October 9 to 11.

The decision that only three parties—Communist, People's, and

Socialist—would participate in the election campaign had been made
for all practical purposes by the Allied Council on September 11,
when the Council gave these three parties, and only these three, permission to organize. From the vantage point of almost two decades
of the Cold War, it seems ironic that all three parties were described
by the Allied Council's election proclamation as "anti-Nazi and
democratic."[1] The major decision that came out of the Second Provisional Council itself was a ban on Nazi participation in the election.
As drafted, the prohibition was virtually a blanket indictment, making no provision for less implicated Nazis who had joined, or who had
applied for membership in, the party primarily because they were
fearful of the consequences of refusing to do so. On this issue the
People's Party, as might be expected, wanted to make a distinction
between active and passive Nazis; conversely, the Communists championed the banning of all Nazis. The Socialists' position was one of
compromise.[2]

The Communists ultimately won their point—and in doing so revealed their basic strategy for the election campaign. They were going
to run against fascism rather than against the opposition parties.
Moreover, during the ensuing campaign the Communists never let
the public forget that the Kommunistische Partei Oesterreichs (KPO)
was the most relentless foe of fascism and had the best resistance record.[3] At first the Communists made no attempt to tar the other parties
with the taint of Nazism. But as the campaign progressed, this initial
discretion vanished. Representative of this change was the following
Communist jingle:

> Bis du ein Nazi, dann steht's dir frei
> beizutreten der Volkspartei.
> Wenn du ein Gegner der Nazi bist,
> hilft dir nur einer: der Kommunist![4]

There was also a positive side to the Communists' program, and
this aspect of the campaign provides particular insight into their
assessment of the political situation in postwar Austria. The Communist platform was outlined in the so-called *Sofort-programm* (urgent measures) and included the following:

1. A radical purge of all Nazis from all levels of government, suspension of their pensions, and confiscation of the property of Nazi
war criminals.

2. Confiscation of all German property.

3. Nationalization of basic industries, especially the heavy industries and the mines.

4. Establishment of an eight-hour day and social insurance for all.

5. Selection of a number of trade delegations to be sent into Eastern Europe in order to establish closer trade relations.[5]

What was particularly startling, however, to the average Austrian, who remembered the Communist Party of the interwar period and its doctrinaire bolshevism, was the effort of the KPO to broaden the scope of the party's appeal by catering to the interests of the small businessman and the peasant. In a most un-Communist gesture, the KPO solemnly upheld the principle of private property, demanding only "that the state confiscate that which was ... German and fascist.[6] For the Catholic vote, the Communists provided the tortuous gyrations of Dr. Viktor Matejka, a former Catholic who in 1945 was the director of education for the city of Vienna. In one remarkable piece of election literature, Matejka went to great pains to demonstrate that the "true" Christian who heeded the call of Leo XIII would vote Communist.[7]

The campaign to convince the Austrian peasantry to support the Communists was directed by Laurenz Genner, the Communist Undersecretary for Agriculture in the Provisional Government. Here the Communists hit a stone wall so thick that the futility of this particular operation must have been apparent to the most optimistic of party members. Although Genner stressed the common bond of suffering under the Nazis and the need for a "just division of the land," there was a hollow ring to the entire effort.[8] The reason for this is clear enough. The destruction of the old empire had left Austria with a peasant class that was ethnically homogeneous; furthermore, the peasants invariably owned their land in freehold. With the exception of a Slovenian minority—whose role during the election is described below—Austria had no ethnically discontented or land-hungry peasants. And this hurt the Communists badly.

In addition to the official platform and appeals directed at specific groups, the Communists had many other strings to their political bow: the police for the first time were under the control of members of the working class (i.e., the Communists) and had to remain so if the workers were to be assured that the police would never again fire on crowds; the Russians not only were the liberators of Austria but had championed Austria's interests at the Potsdam Conference; the Red Army led all the other occupying powers in its donation of food, building materials, and money (including an extremely politic and sizable donation to the rebuilding of the State Opera House).[9]

Despite all the indications of the Communist success at the polls—indications that stretch back to the shattering of the Social Democratic Party of 1934—it still seems that the KPO was being overly optimistic in its expectation that its strength could so multiply. From complete lack of representation in the Nationalrat throughout the interwar period to near parity with the Socialists and the People's Party was certainly a great leap forward. Nevertheless, the Communists and the Soviets were apparently confident of success and willing to take a gamble which might eventually bring all of Austria under Communist control. It is obvious enough that the Communists could have opted for a test of strength in the Eastern zone before undertaking a national election, but they chose to go all the way. It must be said again at this point that the results of the national elections throughout Western Europe—in Great Britain, France, Norway, and Denmark—showed very clearly that the trend was to the left. The Austrian Communists made a great point of playing up these victories and were apparently convinced that the situation would be no different in Austria come the November election.[10]

The other two parties conducted a campaign that emphasized the necessity for Austrian traditional parties to return to full strength. The Socialist platform was perhaps best summed up by their own slogan—Wir sind wieder da! (We have returned!). Arrogant as this might seem, the Socialists logically enough ran on their greatest asset—their social welfare record. The working class of the larger cities were of course surrounded by examples of what the Socialists could do if they had the power, and the Socialist campaign in the fall of 1945 consisted primarily of reminding them of this. Their appeal, then, was not only that of well-articulated promises but tangible evidence of what they could do—in this the Austrian Socialists were in 1945 perhaps unique in Europe. As for any latent conflict between the Social Democratic and Revolutionary Socialist wings of the party, the party emphasized that this was not the merger of two parties but the recombining of two organizational forms of the same movement.[11]

As has been noted, Austria's conservative party had successfully muted much of the resentment that might have been directed against the party because of its past by assuming a new name and new leaders. In addition, the party consciously underplayed its clerical heritage; and the Austrian Catholic hierarchy responded to this desire of the party to steer clear of close connections with the Church by forbidding for the first time active participation in political activities by all clerics.[12]

This new-found moderation on the part of the People's Party may not have had any particular bearing on the outcome of the election per se, but it did become extremely important after the election when the Socialists and the People's Party sought to build a viable coalition. Moreover, the fact that the Allied Council had dictated that there would be only three parties virtually assured the conservative forces in Austria of a united front.

II

As the elections drew near, the Communists suffered many a disquieting moment. Although the French and Danish elections had gone well for the respective Communist parties, things were not encouraging closer to home. In both the Budapest municipal election of late October and the more important national election of November 4, the Hungarian Communists had done poorly, with the Small Landowners Party winning the honors. The Austrian Communists ruefully explained away this unpleasant turn of events by complaining that the Nazis had been able to vote in both elections.[13] Nevertheless, if the Austrian Communists were able to conceal this anxiety over the impending elections, the Russians were not. A few days before the elections the Russians called leading members of both the Communist and Socialist parties to Soviet headquarters in Vienna. What the Soviets wanted of the Austrians was their last-minute estimate on the probable course of the elections. Schaerf says the Communists contended that they would get at least 25–30 per cent of the vote; he estimated that his Socialist Party would receive some 40–44 per cent of the vote, or some 73 seats in the new parliament.

The elections of November 25, 1945, were the first free national elections held in Austria since 1930. These elections from all appearances were conducted in a free and orderly manner without direct pressure from the occupying powers.[14]

The Austrian Communists, after viewing the course of events since 1934, saw in the 1945 elections an opportunity to establish themselves as a legitimate political power in Austria. The results speak for themselves:[15]

Austrian People's Party	1,602,227	49.80%
Socialist Party	1,434,898	44.60%
Communist Party	174,255	5.42%
Democratic Party of Austria	5,972	.18%

In terms of seats in the Nationalrat, the Communist showing of some 174,000 votes entitled them, after the tortuous process of proportional representation had run full course, to four seats, while the People's Party and the Socialists won 85 and 76, respectively.[16]

Interestingly enough, owing mainly to the war and the disen-
franchisement of the former Nazis, some 670,000, or 20 per cent, fewer
ballots were cast in 1945 than in 1930, and of the 3.5 million Austrians who finally voted in 1945, 64 per cent were women—a fact that
certainly magnified the electoral impact of Soviet misbehavior.[17]
Moreover, the Communists could draw no particular comfort from
the provincial breakdown of the elections. They drew their heaviest
vote (8 per cent) in both Vienna and Carinthia, their lightest in Tyrol
and Salzburg (2 per cent); so there were no areas of heavy Communist
concentration.[18] The defeat, then, was as devastating as it was unexpected.

The elections had clearly shown that the People's Party was the
strongest party in Austria. Therefore, on November 28, Dr. Renner
officially dissolved the Provisional Government, and Leopold Figl,
the acknowledged leader of the People's Party, set about constructing
a government that would both reflect the results of the election and
please the Allied Commission. The reaction of the Soviet element to
Figl's proposals signaled the beginning of a new phase in the struggle
for Austria.

Figl's letter of December 8, 1945, suggesting the composition of the
new Austrian government actually contained few surprises. The proposed cabinet, the result of hard bargaining between the parties, consisted of six ministers and one state secretary representing the Peoples'
Party; four ministers and one state secretary representing the Socialist
Party, in addition to a Vice-Chancellor (Schaerf); two nonparty members; and finally, as a tactical gesture to the Communists, a Ministry
of Power and Electrification was created for the Communist Karl
Altmann.[19]

Only a few of the nominees need be mentioned: Figl was slated for
Federal Chancellor, Adolf Schaerf for Vice-Chancellor; a Socialist,
Oskar Helmer, took the position of Minister of the Interior away
from the Communist Franz Honner, while a People's Party man, Dr.
Felix Hurdes, took the Ministry of Education and Religious Affairs
over from the Communist Ernst Fischer. The Communists, apparently in order to fend off Russian charges that the KPO was unrep-
resented in the cabinet, were "entrusted" with the makeshift Ministry
of Power and Electrification, a position that was done away with
when Altmann resigned from the cabinet in 1948. The principal
structural changes were the abolishment of the triparty political cabinet, the re-establishment of the vice-chancellorship, and the abolition of the system of state secretaries. The only exceptions to the latter

change were in the Ministry of the Interior, where a state secretary from the People's Party was placed in order to keep an eye on the Socialist Minister Helmer, and in the Ministry of Public Property, where the situation was reversed.

The U.S. reaction, which mirrored that of the British and French, was one of complete acceptance of the proposed cabinet.* The same could not be said of the Russians. There is no evidence that would indicate exactly why the Russians objected to certain members of the proposed cabinet or whether all four changes that occurred after Soviet objections were raised were the result of Soviet pressure. This much is clear, however; the original list included the following four nominees: Minister for Trade and Construction, Julius Raab (OVP); Minister of Food, Andreas Korp (SPO); Minister of Property Control and Economic Planning, Vinzenz Schumy (OVP); and Minister of Social Administration, Johann Boehm (SPO).[20]

The Russians apparently objected to Raab and Schumy because both had served in cabinet positions during the Dollfuss/Schuschnigg era.† The case of Boehm, a trade union leader of impeccable reputation and the force behind the organization of the postwar Austrian Trade Union Federation, is particularly difficult to understand.[21] Possibly Boehm's removal was the result of an intra-party decision once the other three men had to be replaced. There is every evidence, however, that the Russians demanded the removal of Andreas Korp primarily in order to humiliate Karl Renner. Korp had retained his position in the Austrian Consumers Cooperative movement during the Dollfuss and Hitler periods at the personal request of Renner, who until 1934 had been President of the Central Association of the Austrian Consumers Union. In other words, as Renner put it in a letter to the Allied Council when Korp was later turned down for another position, he had told Korp that "I will shield your behavior from the public." And now, Renner went on, "I must keep the prom-

---

* *Proceedings of the Allied Commission,* Special Report No. 4, p. 3. The United States apparently thought the Soviets might raise objections to the inclusion of Ferdinand Graf (OVP) as Minister of Foreign Affairs on the grounds of "pro-Fascist utterances in campaign speeches." Apparently the British and French were completely dumbfounded by Russian objections, and when a revised list was submitted to the Executive Committee on December 14, they wanted to know why Figl had suddenly "changed his mind." *Proceedings of the Executive Committee,* Meeting of December 14, 1945, EXCO/UM (45)21, p. 10.

† Shortly before the Anschluss, Raab was Minister of Commerce and Transportation in the Schuschnigg cabinet. Schumy had been Minister of the Interior under Dollfuss.

ise because I . . . regard it as a debt of honor."[22] Despite Renner's
pleas, the Russians continued to veto Korp's appointment to any position. This was a hard blow for Renner, but the Russians had some
small revenge for their disappointment in his performance.

What is particularly significant about the Soviet rejection of the
original cabinet nominees is the fact that *all four* were in the original
Provisional Government—a government organized under the direction of the Soviets and strongly supported by them. This complete
reversal in policy is perhaps the best illustration of why the 1945 elections were such a watershed in Austrian postwar history. The Communists from this point forward were decidedly on the defensive. Once
they were effectively shut out of the legitimate government, they
turned on it in the hope that in harassing the government's operations
and intimidating its members they could severely weaken it.

III

The elections of November 1945 left the Austrian Communist Party
in a state of almost complete disarray, only dimly aware at first of the
consequences of their defeat. In a few short hours the tide had been
reversed and the Communists were suddenly confronted with the
realization that little had changed since 1934. To be sure, they had
won the support of some 5 per cent of the voters and had four seats
in the Nationalrat, but what was this compared to the convincing
demonstration that the two traditional parties had held the loyalties
of their members throughout the long years of political hiatus?

The reasons for the Communists' defeat seem clear enough. First,
they had completely misjudged the political and psychological tem-
perament of the mass of the Austrian people. The image of the raping
and looting Russian was decidedly clearer than that of the Russian
"liberator." The Soviets had obviously read too much into the results
of the elections in Western Europe, overlooking the fact that there
communism was identified primarily with a political philosophy and
not, as in Austria, with the reputation of the Red Army. Second, the
Austrian Communists had completely misjudged the strength and
appeal of the Socialist Party. A former German Communist, who had
returned to Berlin with Ulbricht's original party, recounts that
shortly before the election the Austrian Communists had informed
their German counterparts that the KPO expected to win as many
votes as the Socialists. After the results of the Austrian elections
arrived in Berlin, the German Communists, deeply disturbed by the

Austrian debacle, turned their entire attention to building an *Einheitsfront* with the German Socialists rather than confronting the Socialists directly in an open election.[23]

Third, one tactical mistake the Communists made which probably contributed to their defeat was the decision to run as the unforgiving foe of all Nazis. Unsavory as it may seem, the unqualified condemnation of all Nazis—active or nominal—undoubtedly irritated the families of the disenfranchised, while simultaneously cutting the Communists off from the Nazi voter, who, out of sheer protest and lack of Fascist alternative, would have voted *against* the majority parties. The German Communists apparently learned from the Austrian experience and, shortly after the Austrian election, began stressing the difference between "kinds" of Nazis.[24] Nor were the Austrian Communists long in changing their position on the question of the Nazi vote, and by 1950 they were in open alliance with the Soviet-sponsored neo-Nazi National Liga.* Fourth, the Communists were unable to discover any widespread economic or ethnic discontent that could be turned into elective support. There were two exceptions to this generalization which suggest what might have happened. In the 1945 elections the Communists received a surprising amount of support from the Slovenian minority in the Austrian province of Carinthia—a minority that prior to 1945 had voted the conservative ticket. Yet in the 1949 election this support all but disappeared. The answer was of course the Communist break with Tito. The Austrian Slovenes apparently saw in communism a common bond with their Yugoslav fellow Slovenes and the possibility that under an Austrian Communist government their minority rights would be safeguarded.[25]

The other case of support for the Communists coming from an unlikely quarter involved a question of land reform. In 1946 the Soviet military forces confiscated thousands of acres of Austrian land, to be used primarily in support of Soviet troops. Among the properties confiscated was that of the Esterhazy family in Burgenland. Part of this land was divided up by the Russians and given to landless peasants. When this land was returned to the Austrian government in

---

* In 1949 the franchise was restored to former Nazis, and from that day to this, there has been occasionally an unseemly scramble on the part of *all* the parties in Austria to win their votes. In 1956, for example, the Socialists, in a crude attempt to win a few former Nazi votes, used an election placard that showed two Socialists side by side with two of the Nazis who had shot Dollfuss. The point was that all four had been executed by the Dollfuss dictatorship. See Simon, p. 132.

1955, the authorities had an extremely difficult time with the Soviet-installed owners, who were obviously sorry to see the Russians go and with them the right of possession.[26] Unfortunately for the Communist interests in Austria, such opportunities to win the loyalties of the peasants were definitely the exception. Moreover, there were no German minorities to drive out, as was the case in Czechoslovakia or Poland, where the new owners of the confiscated land had a strong personal interest in perserving the Communist *Einheitsfront* government which had given them the property.

The Austrian Communists have their own explanation for their dismal performance in 1945. In a speech to the Austrian Communist Party faithful in 1957, Friedl Fuernberg, the party's chief theorist, attributed the defeat in part to the premature ending of the Japanese war. The unexpected collapse of the Japanese allowed the United States and Britain to concentrate on Western Europe before the KPO expected it. More important, however, was the presence in Austria of the "armies of the imperialist countries," whose activities "suppressed the revolutionary energies of the people."[27]

As for the Russians, it is also apparent that they were misinformed on the political climate of Austria by the local party. Fundamentally, however, there were probably two factors that weighed heavily in the Soviet decision to allow the Austrian elections to take the form they did: as has been mentioned, an almost complete lack of experience with elections held in areas where the Russian army was in full or partial occupation, and, as an extension of this lack of experience, a willingness to take a chance in a country where vital Soviet interests were not as directly engaged as in Poland or Germany. The situation afforded some latitude, and the Russians, basing their actions on advice of the KPO, were willing to wager on winning the whole country before the other political factions or the Western Allies could make their influence felt.

There was another result of the election that was truly a surprising phenomenon, considering the prewar history of Austria. This was the formation after the elections of a remarkable coalition pact between the Socialists and the People's Party, which departed radically from the familiar pattern of European parliamentary democracies. Building on the experience of the Provisional Government, the two parties devised in 1945 a system of permanent coalition government that has been described as "government by party cartel," or less flatteringly as a "two-party dictatorship."[28] Popularly known as the "proporz," or proportional system, the political arrangement worked out by the two major parties devised a method of distributing cabinet and administrative posts in accordance with the strength each showed at the last national election.

The first such *Koalitionspakt* (coalition pact) was drawn up in great secrecy in 1945 between the top leadership of the two parties, and the very existence of such arrangements was denied. Nevertheless, by 1956 enough of the details had gotten to the press so that the two parties agreed to publish the 1956 pact.[29] Similar pacts were negotiated after every election until 1966, when the People's Party won a clear majority and decided to rule alone.

In essence, the *Koalitionspakt* is the political instrument of an Austrian "grand coalition," in which the two parties agreed to take joint responsibility for guiding government policy. Because it is government by an oligarchy of top party leaders, the national parliament is, for all practical purposes, bypassed in the formulation of major decisions. The pact also provides for a division of administrative posts. In order to ensure that the principle of double veto is applied, the man in the top position has a "watchdog" from the other party as his second in command. This intertwining of party representatives has led many Austrians to believe that there are three men for every government job—"a Red and a Black and the man who does the work." And, as many critics contend, these complicated pacts do tend to breed inefficiency and occasionally eruptions of scandal because of the absence of a genuine political opposition.[30]

For its many faults—and the stultification of parliamentary democracy is the most serious—the "proporz," or proportional system, served Austria well, particularly during the occupation. This device allowed the coalition partners to exclude the Communists from government by simply stating that their performance at the polls did not warrant inclusion (although there was one Communist in government until 1948 as a sop to the Russians). More important, the system allowed the two major parties, whose electoral support from the prewar to the postoccupation elections had remained remarkably stable and evenly divided, to function as a team. Had one or the other been in opposition, the government in power probably could not have functioned unless the Socialists were willing to cooperate with the Communists, or the People's Party with the German nationalist element, which was to emerge in 1949 as the Union of Independents (Verband der Unabhaengigen). Thus Communist hopes of exploiting the traditional differences between the major parties were dealt a serious blow by "government by party cartel."*

The existence of these pacts did not mean that there was always complete harmony between the two major parties. There were large areas of Austrian political and economic life where no attempt was made to agree; controversy over these areas, such as the particulars of nationalization and Austrian foreign policy, was often intense, even during the occupation. One long-time observer of this curious brand of political behavior has likened the coalition "to a clinch in which neither party ever ceases to hit, bite and gouge."[31]

In sum, this permanent coalition technique may have outlived its usefulness, now that the occupation is over, but from 1945 to 1955 it served a vital function of holding two very wary old enemies in common harness. As Austria's long-time Foreign Minister, Bruno Kreisky, put it in defending the coalition: "In the coalition stand on one

* Parliamentary elections, 1930–56, break down as follows:

Party	1930	1945	1949	1953	1956
Social Democrat	1,517,251 (72) 41%				
Socialist		1,434,898 (76) 45%	1,621,275 (67) 39%	1,818,517 (73) 42%	1,873,295 (74) 43%
Christian Social	1,315,328 (66) 36%				
People's Party		1,602,227 (85) 50%	1,844,850 (77) 44%	1,781,777 (74) 41%	1,999,986 (82) 46%
German Nationalist	428,265 (19) 12%				
Union of Independents			489,132 (16) 12%	472,866 (14) 11%	
Liberal					283,749 (6) 6%
Heimwehr Bloc	227,402 (8) 6%				
Communist	20,951 (0) 0.6%	174,255 (4) 5%	213,066 (5) 5%	228,159 (4) 5%	192,438 (3) 4%

Additional Election Results

	1962	1966
Socialist	(81) 45%	(85) 48 %
People's Party	(76) 44%	(74) 43 %
Liberal	(8) 7%	(6) 5 %
Communist	(0) 3%	(0) 0.4%

Numbers in parentheses are number of seats in parliament. Totals of some minor parties have been eliminated so that total is not always 100 per cent.
Source: *Oesterreichisches Jahrbuch* (Vienna: Austrian State Printing Office), appropriate years.

side people who were in jail between 1934 and 1938 [the Socialists] and on the other those who put them there. Yet they work well together. I don't deny that the old situation could be conjured up again if the coalition should break down."[32] In such a statement one has neatly most of the elements of a *Koalitionspakt*—a useful arrangement which does not prevent a bit of "biting and gouging"; an arrangement motivated in part by a vague uncertainty that perhaps 1934 could come again if the "clinch" were broken up.

The March 6, 1966, elections have now given Austria the chance to experiment with a "normal" parliamentary democracy. After winning just four additional seats in the Nationalrat, the People's Party took the first clear majority the Austrian electorate has given a political party since the war and decided to go it alone. Although a return to the old system is still possible, Austria may finally have begun a transition to a genuine parliamentary democracy. Only time will tell.

Kreisky's fears of another 1934 raise another important point about the post-1945 period—that is, the mood of Austrian postwar politics. The 1934 clash was in large part the result of the collision of irreconcilable ideologies. Time and the experience of both parties from 1933 to 1945 served to temper the political passions and to dilute the ideological wine of most Socialists and Christian Socialists to a point where chances of another 1934 became remote. In stark contrast to the prewar Austrian, the most notable characteristic of the postwar Austrian is his disdain for world ideologies and ideological commitment. Austria emerged in 1945 as perhaps the most politicized yet ideologically empty country in Europe. Apparently the average Austrian has seen too many political movements, banners, and demonstrations along the dismal road from Hapsburg to Hitler. In such an atmosphere of ideological exhaustion, a *Koalitionspakt* is almost gratefully accepted whatever its flaws, while the personal commitment, exertion, and personal sacrifice required for an aggressive Communist movement dedicated to changing things is generally lacking. To its many other woes, the Austrian Communist Party had to contend with the negative Austrian who had already reaped too many of history's whirlwinds.

In sum, these elections, held but a few months after the country was freed from German control, mark a true turning point. The staggering election defeat represented a jarring check of the Communist momentum in gaining control of the country. The loss of the Ministry of the Interior was particularly hard, curtailing the wholesale packing of the security system, which had been going on since April 1945.

However, in December 1945 the struggle for control of Austria was far from over. Arrayed against the coalition government's momentary control of the administrative apparatus were strong Communist forces in the trade unions and the security systems. Moreover, the Austrian Communist Party could count on the military and economic assistance of the Soviet forces in Austria, a factor that played a varying and often significant role in Communist takeovers throughout Eastern Europe. If Communist influence in the security forces and trade unions could be increased to the point where they became reliable and effective Communist power levers, the handicap imposed by the election disaster could be rapidly overcome. For their part, the Soviets could bring to bear the military and political pressure provided by their position as an occupying power as well as the economic levers so capably won at the Potsdam Conference.

Ranged against this Soviet Military–KPO combination was the Austrian coalition government of Conservatives and Socialists, backed—albeit hesitantly at first—by the Western Powers. No sooner had the coalition government of Chancellor Figl been installed than a new phase of Austria's postwar history began. The East-West conflict for control of Austria came out of the shadows of the Provisional Government period and became a quiet but open conflict. This was a battle fought on a strategic no man's land between East and West. In the ensuing competition neither side labored under the sort of impossible strategic disadvantages that confronted the Western Allies in Rumania, or, conversely, the Soviet Union in Italy. Once the lines were clearly drawn and a rough balance of power was struck, the critical issue centered on the question of just how much power and prestige the Soviet Union and the Western Allies were willing or able to commit in order to maintain or extend their influence in Austria.

The following chapters will attempt to portray the prolonged conflict that took place in Austria from 1946 to 1950 between the Austrian Communists and the Conservative-Socialist coalition for control of the security forces, the trade unions, and that important segment of Austria's industrial capacity awarded to the Soviets at Potsdam. Although the narrative will naturally center on the activity in the center of the ring, it should be borne in mind that it was the occupying powers who made the rules and covered the bets on the outcome. Since the Allied Commission for Austria formally represented the interests of the occupying powers in Austria, a description of its activity, or lack of it, is clearly the place to begin.

The Allied Control Commission

Future historians seeking to unravel the tangled web of Austrian affairs in the postwar period may be puzzled by the Four-Power occupation. Here were the four most powerful nations in the world, with combined populations of some half billion, administering a country of some 32,000 square miles and a population roughly equal to that of New York City. Small wonder, then, that Karl Renner in a bittersweet moment is said to have referred to the occupation as a case of "four elephants in a rowboat."* Nevertheless, as crowded as the "boat" may have seemed to Renner and his fellow Austrians, there is little doubt that the Allied Control Commission played an important if not decisive role in the sustained East-West conflict over Austria.

I

The Austrian Allied Control Commission was only one of a number of inter-Allied military groups set up during the last months of the war to perform such chores as supervising the execution of armistice terms, as in the case of Bulgaria and Hungary, or coordinating occupation policies, as in Germany or Austria. Despite some differences in function, organization, and staff, there was one practical

---

* According to American estimates, the Red Army in Austria numbered in December 1945 some 200,000 men in 17 divisions (from a report sent to Secretary of State James F. Byrnes by Secretary of War Robert P. Patterson, dated January 11, 1946). Found as appendix to *Proceedings of the Allied Commission,* ALCO/M (46)14. U.S. forces were given in the same report as 47,000 in two divisions, French forces as 40,000 in one division, and British forces as 65,000 in two divisions. Thus there was approximately one member of the occupation forces for every 20 Austrians.

common denominator to all the control councils regardless of where they were located: influence and authority within these councils was directly proportional to the military force the participating power had in the immediate area.

American and British representatives on the Allied Control Commissions in Bulgaria, Hungary, and Rumania soon discovered the liabilities of operating from an insufficient power base. Representative of what happened to Western influence on commissions where no Western military forces were readily available to back up Western arguments is the complaint contained in a U.S. Department of State paper on Bulgaria prepared for use at Potsdam. The paper reported: "The American and British members have not been permitted to take any part in the work of the Commission. Only two meetings of the Commission have been held despite formal representations by the American and British representatives. Decisions in the name of the Commission have been taken by the Soviet chairman without prior consultation or subsequent notification to his Allied colleagues."[1]

This particular knife, however, cut both ways, as the Russians soon learned to their dismay in Italy. Anxious for Soviet influence in the Italian settlement, Molotov, at the Moscow Conference in 1943, asked for and received from the Western Powers Russian representation on the Inter-Allied Advisory Council for Italy. Since the Russians were deprived of representation within the Allied Military Government and on the Allied Control Commission for Italy, the Advisory Council was obviously intended as a pacifier. The United States' position on the Advisory Council, outlined in the following background paper for use at the Potsdam Conference, shows the same attention to the hard facts of power politics that undoubtedly motivated the Soviet Union in its dealings with the Allied Commissions within the Soviet sphere of unchallenged influence.

Should it be decided that further efforts to use the existence of the Advisory Council for Italy as an argument in obtaining adequate representation for ourselves and the British in Soviet-controlled territory are futile, the only remaining reason to maintain this body in Italy would disappear.[2]

It was soon evident, then, to East and West that the legal right to participate in the postwar affairs of occupied territories was meaningless unless the territory to be "jointly" administered was "jointly" occupied by military contingents of approximate strength and strategic position. Only Austria and Germany fell into this category; elsewhere the Allied Commissions soon disappeared and with them all semblance of meaningful inter-Allied control.

In Germany and Austria, where inter-Allied control actually functioned, the Four-Power occupation machinery was almost identical. An inter-Allied Control Council met at frequent and fixed intervals. This Council was backed up by a support committee composed of the deputies of the Allied Commanders and known as the Executive Committee in Austria and the Coordinating Committee in Germany. This Committee was charged with preliminary discussions of issues submitted to it by internal security, traffic, legal, and other Allied directorates. The similarity went as far as calling the inter-Allied commands in Berlin and Vienna the inter-Allied *Kommandatura*.

But there were also important differences which far outweighed the procedural similarities. The most obvious difference was that of geography. All of Austria could have been placed within one of the occupation zones in Germany. Germany's population was ten times that of Austria. Moreover, prolonged separation of one zone from another in Austria would not only have been politically absurd but economically impossible, as the Allies were quick to learn during the first few months of the occupation, when the borders of the zones were all but closed.

More important, perhaps, was the general attitude of the occupying powers. The Moscow Declaration had effectively clouded the issue of Austrian war guilt by including, at Russian insistence, the charge that Austria "could not evade responsibility for participation in the war," while simultaneously agreeing in the same declaration "that Austria, the first free country to fall victim to Hitlerite aggression, shall be liberated from German domination."[3]

For its part, the United States emphasized the latter point. This is reflected in the directive given to the Commander in Chief of United States Forces in Austria regarding the military government of Austria. The directive stated that the basic American objective in Austria was the "elimination of German domination and Nazi influences." The directive went on to call for the administrative reconstitution of Austria, its economic development, and "the restoration of local self-government and the establishment of an Austrian central government freely elected by the Austrian people themselves."[4]

Contrast this directive with the one issued to the Commander in Chief of the U.S. Forces in Germany:

Germany will not be occupied for the purpose of liberation but as a defeated enemy power. . . . The principal Allied objective is to prevent Germany from ever again becoming a threat to the peace of the world. . . . The administration of affairs in Germany shall be directed towards the decentralization of the political and administrative structure and the development of local responsibility. To this end you will encourage autonomy in regional, local, and municipal agencies of German Administration.[5]

There was also the question of whether the Allies should create central governments for Austria and Germany. The demand for decentralization in Germany, supported in varying degrees by all the powers, was born partially of the hope that such a measure would militate against the return of a strong and potentially dangerous German government. This was obviously not the case in Austria. France had no objections to a central Austrian government, and the Americans and British, although initially suspicious of the Renner government, were after all confronted with a central government already in existence, which lacked only the approval of the Western Allies to extend its authority beyond Soviet-controlled territory.

Another significant difference was that Austria had a civilian government while Germany was without such an authority until the creation of the Federal Republic. Because the Austrians actually operated the machinery of government, "control" by the occupation authorities came in time to mean indirect control. In Germany, on the other hand, the military authorities had direct control over civilian activities; the occupation powers were the central government. This difference between Germany and Austria became increasingly important, as events—and the Austrians—gradually eroded the "supreme authority" of the occupation powers.

To these considerations must be added the element of timing. Vienna was in Russian hands and a provisional government was already constituted before Germany capitulated. In addition, communication and transportation facilities, although severely damaged in Austria, were in relatively good condition when compared with those in Germany. The very size of Austria facilitated the rapid reconstruction of the state machinery. Moreover, Germany was obviously the key issue in Soviet and Western plans for Europe. Caution in committing prestige and power was natural. Since the stakes were higher, the game was bound to be played more methodically. It would also be well to bear in mind that many of the most important events of Austria's postwar history, i.e., the establishment of the Provisional Government, the elections of November 1945, and the Second Control Agreement described below, took place before the late summer of 1946—that is to say, before the general deterioration of East-West relations.

There is one additional distinction between the Austrian and

German control organizations which after 1946 proved extremely significant. In Vienna the Soviet Union agreed to the establishment of an international zone to be occupied jointly by the Four Powers, with administrative control rotating each month. This zone, encompassing the Innere Stadt or First District of Vienna, contained the bulk of the Austrian administrative and legislative buildings. Four-Power control of the Innere Stadt was perhaps best symbolized by the "Four Men in a Jeep." These four military policemen, who represented the occupying powers, patrolled the international district together during the entire occupation. This symbol of Allied unity captured the imagination of many Westerners in the immediate postwar years, when hopes of East-West cooperation were still high. The symbol soon became tarnished, but the ritual continued right down to the end of the occupation in 1955.

But to the Socialist-Conservative coalition government which took over in December 1945 the international zone itself was much more than a symbol. The fact that the coalition government, its administrative offices, and the legislative bodies were physically located in an area where it was difficult for any one power to apply direct pressures gave the government great freedom of action. Berlin, although its central district approximated Vienna's Innere Stadt in size and function, was not so divided. How this international zone in Vienna was created is a curious episode in the negotiations that went on in 1944 and 1945 at the European Advisory Commission.

As has already been noted, the EAC, charged with negotiating certain postwar problems affecting the interests of the Big Three, had as one of its missions the establishment of zones of occupation in Austria. Despite the fact that the formal meetings of the Commission began in January 1944, no substantial progress on the question of how Austria was to be administered was made until the fall of that year. One reason for this delay was the determination of President Roosevelt not to accept a zone in Austria or even to participate in control at the national level. This barrier was only removed when the United States, under heavy pressure from Great Britain, dropped its claim for a zone in northwest Germany and accepted the southern area. Once this decision had been made, American participation in the occupation of neighboring Austria became a practical proposition and the United States shortly thereafter accepted a zone.

In the meantime the Soviet representative on the EAC presented a proposal for the tripartite zoning of Austria. The Soviet Union would control the eastern halves of the provinces of Lower Austria and Styria; Great Britain the western halves of those provinces and Carinthia; the United States the rest of Austria. (See the map facing page 1 for final zonal boundaries.) According to the Russian plan, Vienna was to have been divided into three zones, with the Russians occupying the Innere Stadt alone.[6]

The British counter to the Soviet proposal took the form of a new draft. This draft, submitted on January 29, 1945, also took into account the French desire to participate in the occupation. As an alternative to the Soviet plan, they suggested a quadripartite division that followed the Austrian provincial boundaries of 1937. Russia would control Lower Austria; Great Britian, Styria, East Tyrol, and Carinthia; the United States, Salzburg and Upper Austria; France, Tyrol and Vorarlberg. Vienna proper was to be partitioned between the Four Powers, its boundaries to be those of the German enlargement of the city limits. (See the map facing page 1 for final sector boundaries.) The central district of the city—the Innere Stadt—was to be jointly occupied under the immediate control of an Inter-Allied Governing Authority *(Kommandatura)*.[7]

In response to this draft the Soviet representative indicated agreement if certain amendments were approved by the Western Powers. Russia wanted that part of Upper Austria which lay north of the Danube and bordered on Czechoslovakia and the Styrian part of Burgenland which bordered on Hungary. If the Western Powers were prepared to agree to these changes, the Soviets would agree to the rest of the British proposals on zonal boundaries. The boundaries of Vienna, however, would be those of the pre-1938 period—i.e., a smaller Vienna which would have placed all the air facilities within the Soviet zone.

At this point the negotiations became rather muddled. The Americans on the EAC, after finally winning Washington's approval for U.S. participation in the occupation, pressed for Vienna's postwar city boundaries to be those of the swollen Gross-Wien established by the Nazis. Division of this larger area (see map of Vienna) would have provided the American occupation forces with not only a more manageable administrative area but control of at least one of the airfields located around the city. The American delegation also joined the British in demanding that the First District or Innere Stadt, containing the bulk of Austria's administrative and legislative facilities, be placed under Four-Power control. Both of these proposals were of course in direct conflict with the Soviet plans to divide the smaller pre-1938 Vienna into individual sectors on the Berlin model and to retain exclusive control of the critical First District.

The bargaining over occupation arrangements remained deadlocked right on into April 1945, despite the fact that Vienna was about to fall to the advancing Soviet armies. Finally, during the second week of April, a way out of the deadlock was found. First, the British agreed to give the Soviet Union the trans-Danubian part of Upper Austria which bordered on Czechoslovakia and that part of Styria which bordered on Hungary—thus sealing off Czechoslovakia from the American zone and Hungary from the British zone.[8] The Soviets agreed to move out of the eastern half of Styria, leaving the area to the British. The controversy over the administration of the First District and the boundaries of Vienna was resolved at the same time, with the Soviets getting the smaller Vienna as the basis of occupation and the Western powers gaining Four-Power occupation of the First District.

With these issues resolved, the agreement on control machinery and zones of occupation was finally signed in London on July 4, 1945, and an agreement on the administration of the city of Vienna was signed on July 9.[9]

Assessed purely in terms of an East-West power relationship in Austria, it appears on balance that although the Soviets gained control of all access roads to Vienna's airfields and reduced the territorial base of Western presence in the city as a result of the EAC negotiations, the Western Powers got the better of the deal. But this is only a judgment bolstered by the wisdom of hindsight; in April 1945 the Soviets enjoyed the advantage of having set up the very government that would now be partially free of direct pressure. Moreover, when the EAC decisions on Austria are taken out of their immediate context, the Soviet Union probably considered a further insulation of Czechoslovakia and Hungary worth a few more concessions.

II

Despite the advantages provided by the existence of the international zone, Chancellor Figl's government was initially tightly controlled by the Allied Council. According to the terms of the control machinery for Austria signed on July 4, all decisions concerning Austria and the actions of its government had to be unanimously approved by the Council.[10] Therefore, the fact that Figl's government was pro-Western meant very little if the Soviet representative on the

Allied Council could veto any Austrian legislative action. The consistent use of the veto prerogative could destroy the effectiveness of the Figl government and that of the Allied Council, as became the case in Germany. Such a situation could only have worked to the advantage of the Austrian Communists. Moreover, if the Allied Council in Austria had been completely paralyzed, unilateral action on the part of any of the powers could have been easily justified.

That the Soviet Union, with the signing of the Second Austrian Control Agreement in June 1946, voluntarily gave up this right of veto and thus presented the Figl government with a remarkable degree of political independence remains one of the most decisive moments in the history of the Cold War in Austria. To make some sense out of this apparent Soviet blunder, we must go back to the first days of the Four-Power occupation.

III

The first Western occupation troops moved into Vienna shortly after the Potsdam Conference had ended. Although there had been a number of Western missions to Vienna to discuss occupation particulars, it was only on August 23 that the headquarters of the three Western powers were moved to the city.[11] The first official meeting of the Allied Council was held in the Hotel Imperial on the afternoon of September 11, 1945.[12] The line-up of military personalities representing the occupation powers was impressive. The Soviet Union was represented by Marshal I. S. Konev, Commander of the Soviet occupation forces in Austria and Hungary, who after Zhukov was probably the most highly respected Soviet general of World War II. His deputy was Colonel General A. S. Zheltov, graduate of the Lenin Military Political Academy, assistant to Bulganin as representative of the Central Committee upon appointment of Zhukov as Commander of the Western Front, in 1942 a Deputy Commander in Chief for Political Work.[13]

The United States Commander in Chief, General Mark W. Clark, had commanded the American Fifth Army in Italy. He was initially seconded by Major General Alfred M. Gruenther. The British were represented by Lieutenant General Sir Richard L. McCreery, who had commanded the British Eighth Army in Italy; the French by Général d'Armée M. E. Béthouart.

The first meeting of the Council was devoted mainly to approving the organization of what was officially to be known as the Allied Commission for Austria. The highest deliberating body of the Allied Commission, the Allied Council, was to meet at least once every ten days, and in emergency session upon request of any one of the members. Below the Allied Council was the Executive Committee, headed by the Deputy Commanders, which was responsible for the various staffs and divisions. There were twelve divisions: Economic, Finance, Air, Naval, Military, Internal Affairs, Legal, Reparations (included at the insistence of the Russians, although the Potsdam Protocol specifically relieved Austria of any reparations burden), Labor, Prisoners of War and Displaced Persons, Transport, and Political.

At the September 11 meeting the Allied Council officially assumed supreme authority in Austria.[14] In the proclamation to the Austrian people, the occupying powers set the tone for their policy in Austria:

The Allied Council bases itself on the Moscow Declarations in which the Governments of the United Nations declare their intention to see restored a free, independent, and domocratic Austria.

. . .

The Allied Council considers the next task to be the creation of a firm political, economic, and cultural foundation for the reestablishment of a truly democratic, free and independent Austria for the safeguarding of a lasting peace.[15]

Although real differences of policy immediately arose at the Allied Council on such questions as the recognition of the Renner government, there is no doubt that the general atmosphere of the Allied Commission was, for at least the first few months, one of hesitant, if not occasionally friendly, cooperation.

At the lower levels the Soviet representatives invariably came to the negotiating table with firmly fixed positions on any given point. But, at least initially, there was more give-and-take at the Allied Council level, with the Russians willing to discuss issues and to seek new instructions. It was only with the worsening of East-West relations during the spring of 1947 that this more relaxed atmosphere was dispelled. As a result, the minutes of the meetings after 1947 became increasingly more the record of position papers read by the various elements, with little or no comment from the other side.

When the Allied Council on September 11 assumed "supreme authority" in occupied Austria, this meant that the Allied Commission formally assumed the right to censor all forms of communication, to supervise the reestablishment of the education system, to approve or disapprove all legislation or dictate that particular pieces of legislation be enacted, to approve the selection of cabinet ministers, and to approve all government ordinances and decrees, no matter how minor.

The effort involved in handling all these affairs, judging from the records of the Allied Commission, must have been immense. Despite the existence of a central Austrian government that was constantly pressing to extend its powers, the supervision of Austrian internal and external affairs would have been difficult enough for military men of just one foreign nation; that an increasing number of decisions, mostly of extremely minor importance, had to be formally discussed and approved by the representatives of four countries divided by language and political tradition must have seemed at times an overwhelming burden. On this basis alone there was soon general agreement among the Four Powers that the occupation machinery had to be simplified to meet the changing conditions. Fortunately, modification of the original Control Agreement of July 4, 1945, had been anticipated by Article 14: "The nature and extent of the Allied direction and guidance which shall be required after the establishment of a freely elected Austrian Government recognized by the Four Powers will form the subject of a separate agreement between those Powers."[16] Even before the election of November 25, the British representative won approval at the Allied Council meeting of November 16 for a study to be made by the Executive Committee on how Article 14 of the Control Agreement could be implemented.[17] The British followed up this proposal with a draft agreement which they presented in February 1946. General L. V. Kurasov, Konev's replacement as Commander in Chief of the Soviet Forces, indicated at the Allied Council meeting of March 25, 1946, that he had read the reorganization draft submitted by the British element and was ready to discuss the matter.[18]

Although the original British draft was modified through quadripartite negotiations, its basic structure remained.[19] In the final agreement signed on June 28 the main structure of the original Control Commission remained intact. The members of the Allied Council were now to be called High Commissioners; the departmental staffs were reorganized to better correspond to their opposite number in the Austrian government; and the Commission would now exercise its powers primarily through the Austrian ministry directly concerned. The Council reserved for itself the right to intervene directly in certain sensitive matters such as war criminals, matters directly affecting the occupying forces, the German assets question, and demilitarization. More important was the final removal of all zonal restrictions on commerce and trade. The economic integrity of the country was thus reestablished.[20]

As important as the above provisions were in extending the authority of the Austrian government and increasing its powers, the new Control Agreement contained an additional article of the greatest importance. Adolf Schaerf, writing in 1955, called the Control Agreement "after the unification of Austria under Renner probably the most important victory for Austria since 1945."[21] What Schaerf was specifically referring to was Article 6(a) of the new agreement, which read:

All legislative measures, as defined by the Allied Council, and *international agreements which the Austrian Government wishes to make, except agreements with one of the Four Powers,* shall, before they take effect or are published in the State Gazette, be submitted by the Austrian Government to the Allied Council. *In the case of constitutional laws, the written approval of the Allied Council is required, before any such law may be published and put into effect. In the case of all other legislative measures and international agreements it may be assumed that the Allied Council has given its approval if within thirty-one days of the time of receipt by the Allied Commission it has not informed the Austrian Government that it objects* to a legislative measure or international agreement. Such legislative measures or international agreement may then be published and put into effect. The Austrian Government will inform the Allied Council of all international agreements entered into with one or more of the Four Powers.[22]

In essence, Article 6(a) introduced the principle of "the reverse veto" into the control mechanism. In all legislative matters submitted by the Austrian government except those of a constitutional nature, it would henceforth take the unanimous disapproval of all the powers to kill the measure; otherwise it would become effective thirty-one days after receipt at the Allied Secretariat. In addition, the Austrian government was allowed to conclude bilateral agreements with any of the occupying powers, subject only to the notification of the other three.

To Westerners long familiar with the effective use the Soviet Union has made of its veto prerogatives—whether it be at the Security Council of the United Nations or on the German Control Commission— the very idea that the Russians would voluntarily give up such a powerful weapon is astounding. Various explanations have been offered why the Russians consented to this fundamental change in the control mechanism, ranging from the suggestion that the Soviet element was dozing the day it was approved to failure to send the agreement to Moscow for approval.[23]

What the documents show is that the real explanation for the Soviet concession is a great deal more complicated than that of a heavy lunch followed by a warm afternoon in the Control Council, and they also tell us a great deal more about Soviet policies and objectives in Austria.

IV

The original British draft was first submitted to the Quadripartite Political Division. Among the differences that immediately arose was the wording of Articles 6(a) and 1(c). (In the final draft these two sections were fused as Article 6(a).) In the original British text, Article 1(c) stated:

Agreements made by the Austrian Government with any international organization or with any Government other than the Government of one of the Four Powers, and laws and administrative action of the Austrian Government and subordinate Austrian Authorities shall be subject to the power of veto of the Allied Commission as further described in Article 6 below.[24]

During the ensuing discussion various proposals departing from the British draft were offered. The following text for Article 1(c) was finally acceptable to the British and Soviet representatives:

Agreements made by the Austrian Government with any international organization or with any Government *other than the Government of one of the Four Powers* and *legislative measures* and administrative actions of the Austrian Government shall be subject to the power of veto of the Allied *Council* as described in Article 6 below.[25]

The American and French members said that they could not accept the phrase "other than the Government of one of the Four Powers." The Soviet element, however, said that the Soviet Union would not accept this article without the inclusion of that particular phrase.[26]

At this early stage in the negotiations any final decision on this point was delayed because the entire article was ultimately dependent on the wording of Article 6(a). The British text read:

All laws and international agreements, other than agreements with one of the Four Powers, which the Austrian Government wishes to make, shall, before they take effect or are published in the State Gazette, be submitted to the Allied Commission by the Austrian Government. If within twenty-one days of the time of communication the Allied Commission has not informed the Austrian Government that they object to a law or international agreement, the Allied Commission shall be deemed to have no objection thereto and the law or international agreement may be published and put into effect.[27]

The United States proposal for Article 6(a) stayed close to the original British draft:

All legislative measures, as defined by the Allied Council, and international agreements which the Austrian Government wishes to make, shall, before they take effect or are published in the State Gazette, be submitted by the Austrian Government to the Allied *Council.* If within *thirty-one* days of the time of receipt by the Allied Commission it has not informed the Austrian Government that it objects to a *legislative* measure or international agreement, the Allied *Council* shall be deemed to have no objection thereto, and the *legislative measure* or international agreement may be published and put into effect.[28]

The proposal the Soviet representative offered for the wording of this article is particularly interesting as a reflection of the Soviet position on what subsequently became the "reverse veto" principle. The proposal ran:

All legislative measures, as defined by the Allied Council, and international agreements which the Austrian Government wishes to make, other than agreements with one of the Four Powers, shall, before they take effect or are published in the State Gazette, be submitted by the Austrian Government to the Allied *Council* for approval. *The Allied Council must consider legislative measures or international agreements submitted to it within twenty-one days.*[29]

These various proposals were first discussed at length at the Quadripartite Political Division level. The question then went to the Executive Committee, where, after failing to reach any agreement whatsoever on these two articles, the entire matter was finally submitted to the Allied Council for consideration at the meeting of May 24, 1946. The new Control Agreement by this date had been under consideration for some two months. The differences on the two critical articles were by this time well defined. The Soviet Union was insistent on the inclusion of a clause that would permit the Austrian government to conclude bilateral agreements with any one of the four occupying powers without first receiving permission of the other three. At the same time the Russians were not prepared to renounce their veto rights and were only willing to offer the Austrians a speed-up in the control machinery.

The Western position was less precise. The British were apparently willing to go along with the Soviet proposal on bilateral treaties, and the French seem to have been equivocal on the thirty-one-day clause. The Americans would not agree to a bilateral international agreement proposal. They were also insistent, along with the British, that the Austrian government be given the freedom implicit in the thirty-one-day clause.

At the Allied Council meeting of May 24 a compromise was hammered out. In order to gain the inclusion of the clause on bilateral agreements strongly opposed by the Americans and the French, the Soviet element agreed to the Western proposal that the legislation of the Austrian government would go into effect thirty-one days after its receipt at the Allied Secretariat if the government had not been informed by that time of an Allied veto—a vote, in this case, meaning the unanimous disapproval of all the powers. At the same time both proposals were slightly modified. With regard to bilateral treaties between Austria and any one of the powers, the other members of the Council had to be informed of the contents of any such agreement. With respect to legislative matters, unanimous approval of the Council was still required of all laws that were "constitutional" in nature.[30] As to the logical and important question of defining a "constitutional law," the Four Powers merely agreed at the May 24 meeting to submit the question to the Quadripartite Legal Division for a definition. With this action the Allied Council, perhaps inadvertently, set the stage for what can only be described as a colossal Soviet diplomatic blunder.

Acting on the instructions of the Allied Council, the Legal Division did, in fact, produce a definition of a constitutional law that was subsequently approved by the Executive Committee, on May 31. The text finally approved by the Four Powers is as follows:

An Austrian Constitutional Law is an act of the Austrian Parliament which: (1) creates or amends the Austrian Constitution or amends an existing constitutional law; (2) is entitled a constitutional law; (3) is required, under Austrian law, to be adopted at a session of Parliament at which not less than one-half of the members of that body are present; (4) is required, under Austrian law, to be adopted by a majority of at least two-thirds of the votes cast.[31]

Beyond specifying that an amendment to the constitution was a constitutional law, the definition approved by the Executive Committee was more concerned with procedure than substance.

Nevertheless, the committee agreed to place this definition in the hands of the Legal Division, pending action by the Allied Council on the draft of the new Control Agreement. They further agreed "that each deputy would report the matter to his Commander in Chief."[32] And there the matter of a definition of a constitutional law rested until the violent controversy over the nationalization bill, passed by the Austrian parliament in July 1946, brought home to the Russians just what they had agreed to a month earlier.

In the meantime, however, all Four Powers submitted the final draft of the new Control Agreement to their respective governments for approval. As early as June 14 the Soviet and British representatives reported to the Allied Council that they had been authorized by their governments to sign without amendment.[33] Thus the theory is not logical that the Soviet representatives in Vienna approved the measure in a moment of oversight without reference to Moscow. Delay in the signing actually came from the Americans and the French. The French wanted a minor amendment included, and the Americans were in hopes that the Foreign Ministers Conference, which reconvened in Paris on June 15, would take action on Austria which would make the new Control Agreement unnecessary.[34]

Since no agreement was reached in Paris, the Allied Council on June 28 formally signed the new Control Agreement, the text of which was officially released on July 14.[35]

With the signing of the new Control Agreement, the Austrian coalition government attained a degree of independence that would have been thought impossible in the dark days of September 1945. Considering that this government after December 1945 was almost totally free of Communist influence, with the one cabinet position held by a Communist of minor importance, the fact that the Soviet Union consented to giving Figl's government such latitude has long puzzled Western observers. The best explanation is to be found, I believe, if we relate what we know of Soviet objectives during the course of the Control Agreement negotiations to what was going on at the same time between the Soviets and the Austrian government.

Although Soviet efforts to integrate part of Austria's industrial resources into a satellite economy are discussed elseswhere, part of this story impinged on Control Agreement negotiations.

Immediately after the Soviet occupation began, the Russians sought an agreement with the Austrians by which they would gain control of the country's oil resources. The first major effort to gain such an agreement came in September 1945, before the Allied Council officially assumed supreme control. These negotiations were broken off by the Renner Provisional Government. The Russians continued to press for such an agreement until the late spring of 1946. Examination of these prolonged negotiations indicates that the Russians would have preferred to gain control of the oil fields through a bilateral agreement rather than using the German asset pretext. With this in mind, the reasoning behind the Soviet demand that the new Control Agreement include a provision permitting the Austrian government to conclude bilateral agreements with any of the Four Powers without approval of the others becomes perhaps more understandable.

There are, however, certain flaws in this argument. We know that the Russians were heavily engaged in negotiations with the Austrians at least until the first week in June, that is, during the entire time the Control Agreement was under discussion.[36] Nevertheless, by the time the Control Agreement was ready for signature on June 28, it was probably clear to Moscow that the Austrians were not going to accept the Soviet terms. Despite this, however, the Russians went ahead and signed. One reason for this may have been that Moscow's approval of the agreement, which was given on June 12 and relayed to the Western Allies on June 13, probably came at a time when the outcome of the Austrian negotiations was still in doubt.[37] On the premise that the bilateral clause was the key to Soviet support of the agreement, it is difficult to say why the Russians formally signed the Second Control Agreement on June 28. They probably reasoned that it would have been both difficult and extremely awkward to attempt to renege on an agreement to which they already had given formal diplomatic approval. Then, too, the Soviets may have entertained some hope that the Austrians would still come around. Soviet hopes to reach some agreement with the Austrians seem only to have been finally dashed during the first week of July, when a Soviet military order—backdated to June 27—formally confiscated the German assets.

Whether this analysis is the real explanation is not entirely clear. What is certain, however, is that the Soviet Union was willing to pay a considerable price to gain this right to negotiate bilateral agreements with the Austrian government. If the Soviet objective was to pave the way for a legal agreement with the Austrians on the oil fields and other "German assets" that would not be subject to approval by the other three powers, the effort was wasted.

Less than a month after the signing of the Second Control Agreement, the Russians discovered what a serious miscalculation they had made in approving it. First, the Austrians refused to sign over the German assets, forcing the Russians to expropriate them—thus the right to conclude bilateral agreements which the Austrian government so painstakingly won during the quadripartite negotiations suddenly became a pointless victory. Now the Austrian parliament had dared to pass a law nationalizing the bulk of the assets taken by the Russians. What's more, if the Russians were unable to prove that the nationalization act was contrary to the provisions of the new Control Agreement or that it was a constitutional law, it would go into effect in thirty-one days if but one of the other powers refused to disapprove it. Rarely has the Soviet Union been hoist so high with its own petard.

Justifiably outraged with the turn of events, the Soviet representative on the Allied Council, Colonel General Kurasov, called an extraordinary meeting of the Allied Council for August 2. Kurasov demanded at this meeting that the nationalization bill be declared illegal because it affected former German property located in eastern Austria which was now the property of the Soviet Union. Kurasov then cited Article 5 of the new agreement, which prohibited actions by the Austrian government concerning "the disposal of German property in accordance with existing agreements between the Allies."[38] The reaction of the American and British, who were suddenly cast in the role of champions of nationalization—a role in which at least the Americans, who discouraged the idea in Germany, must have felt slightly uneasy—was to plead ignorance of the issue and defer discussion. The British delegate did say, however, that there was so much uncertainty as to what properly constituted a German asset that this must certainly be discussed first before the merits of Soviet objection could be determined.[39]

Presumably because the Russians had consistently refused to discuss the German assets question at the Allied Council, contending it had already been decided at Potsdam, this particular tack was subsequently played down, although the Soviet element was on firm legal ground. Instead, they decided that, if it could be demonstrated that the nationalization law was constitutional in nature, unanimous approval of the occupation powers would be required, and thus the measure could be killed with a Soviet dissent. It was on this point that the Soviet representatives staked their case. At the Executive Committee meeting of August 20, the Soviet element with the support of the French presented a resolution which said in part: "The Draft Law on Nationalization changes the structure of the Austrian economy, and, being an act of the Austrian Parliament, is a constitutional law."[40]

When this resolution was brought before the Allied Council on August 23, the British hotly denied that the Nationalization Law was a constitutional law. When the definition of a constitutional law, approved at the Executive Committee meeting of May 31, was cited, the Soviet representative surprised the British and Americans by contending that this definition had not been approved by the Allied Council and the Soviet Union was not in agreement with it. Any definition would require more study.[41] Apparently by this time the

Soviet element had realized that the definition they had consented
to in June was now a threat to Soviet interests. As long as the Austrian
government did not directly amend the constitution, entitle a law
"constitutional," or specifically use the legislative procedure for constitutional measures, any law could be called nonconstitutional.

The British countered quickly by stating that at the time the
definition was approved by the Executive Committee it was agreed
by all four elements to refer the measure to the respective Commanders in Chief. According to the British representative this was done,
at least by the British element, and since no question was raised about
it even at the time the agreement was signed, the matter was therefore
settled. The malicious glee with which the British and American
representatives viewed their Soviet colleague's discomfiture is well
illustrated by the following exchange:

> *General Sir James Steele to General Kurasov:* Why did you allow two
> and a half months to elapse before you admitted this? I most certainly
> would not have signed the Control Agreement until I was satisfied as to
> what was the definition of a constitutional law.
>
> . . .
>
> *Kurasov:* I only knew that when I signed the new Control Agreement,
> neither you nor I had a definition of a constitutional law.
> *Steele:* Would General Kurasov mind my asking him a very direct ques-
> tion? Did he, as I did, submit the definition of a constitutional law to his
> Government?
> *Kurasov:* I had planned to submit to my Government a definition which
> would include our remarks.
> *Steele:* Might I suggest that that is not an answer to my question?[42]

One wonders whether Moscow, at this point, was asking Kurasov
the same question. Where the mistake was made we will probably
never know; but a serious mistake it was, for with this default in
definition, the rider the Soviets had attached to the thirty-one-day
clause was useless.

Finally, when all else had failed, the Soviet, stubbornly contending
that the nationalization bill had violated the Control Agreement,
refused to recognize the validity of the law in the Soviet zone. This
whole affair may seem unreal enough when one considers that the
United States emerged as the champion of nationalization while the
Soviet Union violently opposed the measure. But another and most
interesting aspect of the nationalization issue comes with the realization that, given a fair reading of Article 5 of the 1946 Control Agreement, the Soviets were probably right in denying the validity of the
nationalization law. In fact, when the United States element queried

its own legal division on the issue, it was advised that the nationalization bill was indeed invalid.* Needless to say, the Soviet element was never apprised of this considered opinion.

Once the seriousness of the situation had sunk in, the Soviet element attempted to recoup lost ground by introducing a series of resolutions which would have weakened the terms of the Control Agreement. One such device was a resolution to send a letter to the Federal Chancellor concerning the procedure for application of the Control Agreement. The proposed directive to the Austrian government included the following instructions: "The Allied Council informs the Austrian Government that the new Control Agreement will be put into effect by degrees and that the Allied Council will determine the extent, the method and the dates on which responsibilities will be transferred to the Ministries of the Austrian Government."[43] This resolution received no support from the Western side and was therefore dropped.

The sense of frustration the Soviet element must have felt in subsequent attempts to prevent particular pieces of legislation from becoming law is well illustrated by an exchange that took place at the Executive Committee meeting of October 18, 1946, between Major General C. D. Packard (U.K.) and the Russian representative, Major General G. K. Tsinev. The particular law in question is not important, but the dialogue shows the handicap under which the Russians were now operating.

Tsinev: I have a question to put to Mr. Chairman [Packard]. Is Law No. 13 a constitutional one or a nonconstitutional one?

Packard: This is not a law, it is an Ordinance. Yes, Law No. 13 is not a constitutional law.

. . .

Tsinev: I don't understand where we have the right to regard some constitutional laws as not being constitutional laws. Now as far as I understand, my colleagues are implying the following: that all modifications and all

---

* In a position paper prepared for General Clark's use at the August 9 meeting of the Allied Council, where the nationalization law was debated, the U.S. legal advisers after a thorough analysis of the law wrote: "In passing the Nationalization Law, the Austrian government had therefore violated the new Control Agreement. As the Allied Council had not given its prior written approval, this law cannot go through the regular channels provided by Article 6(a) of the new Control Agreement, but is, as far as the Allied Council goes, legally non-existent" (included in the Official Operations Branch File Copy of the Amended Minutes of the *Proceedings of the Allied Commission*, ALCO/M(46)29, p. 2, as a four-page position paper).

amendments made to constitutional laws may be considered as nonconstitutional ones. Am I correct in such an understanding?

Packard: No.

Tsinev: If we accept a separate Ordinance, we may change the political essence of the law itself. Therefore, I deem it more correct that in the future all amendments to constitutional laws be dealt with as constitutional measures.

Packard: But this is not an amendment. A constitutional law is an act of Parliament.

This law we are dealing with is an Ordinance made by the Ministry.

Tsinev: Yes, but it relates to the constitutional law.

Packard: The constitutional law gives the Minister the issuing power.

Tsinev (after a prolonged conversation in this vein): I beg to submit the question for discussion at the meeting of the Allied Council.

Packard: If you wish to put it on the agenda of the Allied Council then it must go on. I would not suggest it myself.[44]

What General Packard meant was that in view of the lack of agreement on the measure, plus the fact that the Soviets could not prove it was constitutional in nature, the ordinance in question would become effective upon expiration of the thirty-one-day period. This situation would be repeated innumerable times before the occupation was over. Sometimes it would work against the interests of one of the Western powers, but on the whole, as long as the pro-Western government was in power, the West was well satisfied with this limitation on the powers of the Allied Commission. President Schaerf's view that the signing of the Second Control Agreement was one of the decisive moments in Austrian postwar history is well taken. For this he can perhaps best be thankful for Soviet miscalculation rather than any masterful effort on the part of the Western negotiators.

The crowning irony of this entire episode came in 1947, when the Austrian government, over the violent protests of the Soviet element, signed a bilateral agreement with the United States and joined the Marshall Plan. The justification for the agreement given by both the United States and the Austrian government was simple enough: Article 1 of the new Control Agreement denied the Austrian government, with one exception, the right to conclude bilateral agreements with any international organization or foreign power. The exception was of course bilateral agreements with "the Government of one of the Four Powers" who were occupying Austria. Thus, the very provision for which the Soviet negotiators had sacrificed so much in order to get it into the Control Agreement was now the means by which Austria could defy the Soviet Union and take a very long step

Westward. Conversely, the United States, which had fought against
the inclusion of this phrase, now profited from it.

V

The Austrian people, now quite independent and prosperous, will
certainly never recall the memory of the Allied High Commission
with any pride. Too many indignities were suffered for that. Nevertheless, its very existence contributed substantially to Austria's independence. It is probably true that with the important exception
of the Second Control Agreement the direct actions of the Allied
Commission were not impressive. The general deterioration of East-
West relations worked against any cooperative action on the part of
the occupying powers.

What the Allied Commission did do was improve the tone of the
East-West conflict over Austria. The physical pressures of the four
occupying powers more or less established the rules of how the game
would be played. Allied control of communications and education
ensured that both sides would get a fair hearing.

It is true that behind the scenes the struggle was waged with the
velvet gloves off—kidnappings were a common means of retaliation
on the part of the Russians, particularly in 1948. But on balance,
the existence of the Allied Commission helped keep such direct forms
of pressure to a minimum.

Although many Western political analysts contend the Soviet
Union has little regard for legal procedure and no respect for signed
agreements, in Austria at least this was not the case.[45] The Russians
bargained hard and would exploit any ambiguity or loophole they
could find. But when they lost, as in the case of the Second Control
Agreement, after trying every possible means of covering their losses,
they accepted the consequences.* One outstanding exception was,
of course, the nationalization law, but here I have suggested that
the Russians had just cause in refusing to accept its validity in the

---

* After their experience with the Austrian control argument, the Soviets carefully sidestepped Western attempts to apply the Austrian "model" to Germany.
During the Council of Foreign Ministers meeting in Paris in 1949, U.S. Secretary
of State Dean Acheson pressed for a German control agreement on the Austrian
model. A. Y. Vyshinsky immediately rejected the idea, stressing that Article 6,
which included the unanimous disapproval principle, was particularly ill suited
for Germany. *Dulles Papers*, Category VIII, Council of Foreign Ministers Minutes,
Paris, May 23–June 16, 1949, Vol. 1, USDEL(49)(P), 2nd Restricted Meeting, June
4, 1949.

Soviet zone. Time and again in their dealing with the Austrians and the other occupying powers one notices a Soviet preoccupation with legal refinements; a compulsion to justify their actions in terms of Four-Power agreements such as Potsdam. This passion for legality, then, seems to have been one of the most characteristic attributes of Soviet policy in Austria.

Internal Security

When the internal security system of a country becomes an instrument of policy rather than law enforcement, the very fabric of a free society is threatened. Where the partisans of a particular political philosophy control the forces of law and order and use them for political purposes, no dissenter is safe. Opposition meetings may be disturbed or broken up by thugs while the police ignore this violation of the right to dissent; armed mobs may roam the streets abusing those who oppose them while the police are conveniently somewhere else. Deprived of the right of personal protection, suspicious of the "impartiality" of the law, the dissenters lose heart and opposition collapses.

All this the Communists clearly understood. In Eastern Europe the internal security forces—police and gendarmerie—are invariably highly centralized and under the control of the Ministry of the Interior. In Austria control of this ministry, therefore, became a prime Communist objective. In the formation of coalition governments after the war, the Communists in Eastern Europe deferred to other parties in the selection of a premier—but the Minister of the Interior was something else again. Once the Communists had this position, they used it with the greatest effect. Consequently, the democratic elements within the country were soon buffeted by a police force indifferent to the personal safety of the non-Communists and quick to use the power of arrest as a political weapon.

I

The Austrian Communists were as aware as their compatriots throughout Eastern Europe of the importance of seizing control of this most important lever of power. During the negotiations between the three parties in April 1945, the Communists had pressed for and eventually won the post of Minister of the Interior. Chancellor Renner was keenly aware that the Minister of the Interior directs a highly centralized police and gendarmerie system with authority throughout all Austria. But Renner, like his counterparts in Eastern Europe, also knew that he had no choice—without this post the Communists would not participate in the government and without them there would be no government. Thus, in April 1945, the Communist Franz Honner was given full control of the most potentially powerful civil force in Austria. But to be really useful to Honner and his party, the internal security system had first to be rebuilt to Communist specifications.

By April 1945 all semblance of law and order had vanished from Vienna and throughout most of Austria. This security vacuum was in part the consequence of German efforts after 1938 to integrate the Austrian police into the German security system. As a result, many of the pre-1938 Austrian police officials were imprisoned or purged as the police became progressively more military and German in character. Finally, the siege of Vienna brought orders from the Nazis to withdraw both the police and the fire-fighting units from Vienna. Therefore, when Soviet troops entered the city, they were able, in the complete absence of local police authority, to rebuild the internal security system from the ground up.[1]

Following standard Red Army procedure, Russian military authorities quickly established a series of command posts throughout Vienna for the purpose of administering the now liberated city. It should be remembered that during the first weeks in April much of the city had no water, heat, or communication facilities. Not only was it virtually impossible for Austrians to pass from one district to another, but in the absence of telephone communications, it was difficult for them to know what was happening in other parts of the city. Under these conditions it is not difficult to understand why the reorganization of civil authority was so patternless. In most cases it was a matter of initiative on the part of the Viennese. Once the fighting had died down, an aspiring Austrian would appear at the Russian command post. There he would state his qualifications and party affiliation and offer his services, whether for mayor or police commissioner of a particular district.

In all probability this was precisely the manner in which Rudolf Hautmann first came into contact with the Russians. A former mem-

ber of the Socialists' prewar paramilitary organization, the Schutzbund, and now a Communist, Hautmann was picked by the Russians
on April 21 to be police chief of all Vienna. Operating under Russian protection and support, Hautmann proceeded to fill the important police commissioner posts in the 26 districts of Vienna with
as many Communists as he could find.[2] As a consequence of Hautmann's appointments, the Communists controlled, even after the
arrival of the Western Allies, 17 of the 26 police commissioners.[3]

While Hautmann was industriously recruiting Communists for
the rebuilding of the police, former members of the pre-1938 Austrian
police force, unaware of Hautmann's activities, were also attempting
to reorganize the security system. Meeting for the first time on April
12 in the headquarters of the Austrian resistance movement, the
Palais Auersperg in Vienna, this group moved the next day to the
abandoned headquarters of the police commissioner for Vienna's
Seventh District. From here, Dr. Huettl, head of Vienna's riot police
in the prewar days, issued a proclamation to all former police officials,
ordering them to report to Huettl's headquarters for assignment.
This ambitious program soon ran afoul of Hautmann, and as a result
of Soviet orders the Huettl group soon found itself under Hautmann's command, charged with the registration of all possible candidates for police positions.[4]

Thus by the beginning of May, the great attention the Communists
had given to the reestablishment of the police was paying dividends—
a great majority of the police districts were in Communist hands;
the provisional Chief of Police of Vienna was a Communist, as was
the Minister of the Interior in the Provisional Government.

The Communist position was further improved with the return
of the Second Austrian Freedom Battalion—Zweites oesterreichisches
Freiheitsbataillon. Organized in Yugoslavia from German army
deserters, escapees from concentration camps, and scattered Austrian
resistance fighters, this battalion and its predecessor had fought under
the command of Marshal Tito. It will be recalled that Franz Honner
had been flown from Moscow to take command of the Austrian partisan forces. The majority of these men were probably Communists;
this was certainly true of the officers. Ludicrous as it may seem, the
marching music of the battalion ranged from the Radetzky March to
the Internationale, and their uniforms were Yugoslavian with the
Red Star sewn on over the Austrian eagle.

The Second Battalion returned in force to Vienna on May 14, and
the reception the battalion received the next day in the square before

Hofburg provided an indication of the great hopes the Communists had for this group of well-armed and trained men. Surrounded by a crowd of some 10,000 Austrians, the batallion was praised by all the Communist leaders including Honner, who had been flown to Vienna some weeks before to participate in the formation of the provisional Austrian government. Under the command of Peter Hofer, who as late as September 1950 was the Police Commissioner of Vienna's 25th District, the battalion raised the cry of "Hitler brought war, Stalin peace!" and "Long live Marshal Tito," while Honner, paraphrasing Austrian poet Grillparzer's paean to Field Marshal Radetzky, assured them that "Your camp alone preserves Austria, and in the spirit which moves you, a new Austria will be built."[5]

The extent to which Honner strove to make this prophecy come true was only revealed to the Allied Council in February 1946 and has never really been known to the Austrian people. In response to a Soviet charge that there were still fascist military and paramilitary groups in the Western zones, an inter-Allied military commission carried on an investigation over all Austria. Paradoxically, the one really startling bit of information this commission uncovered was that Honner had incorporated the two Communist "Freiheits Bataillone" directly into the Austrian security system. The commission's report related that the two battalions had retained their wartime uniforms and

. . . had been employed by the Minister of the Interior to assist the police in frontier and police duties in Vienna. The company in Vienna remained as an organized sub-unit under its own officers wearing its own uniforms and insignia of rank. While on duty they carry personal weapons. Their machine guns, mortars, and other weapons are now stored in a police magazine.[6]

Considering how poorly the majority of the police were armed—a subject that will be discussed at length below—the control of such a group was a great asset to the Communists.

In order to overcome the appalling lack of qualified police officers, the Austrian authorities, with the approval of the Russians, organized a large group of temporary policemen called the "Polizeilicher Hilfsdienst fuer die Kommandantur der Stadt Wien." These men assisted the Russians in maintaining order in the city. They wore their civilian clothing and arm bands of white (in some districts red) material. Later as material became easier to obtain, they wore red-white-red arm bands with "police" on them. With few exceptions, this was a rag-tag mob of undisciplined, unqualified men who very often had criminal records. Moreover, since these men were appointed with the advice and consent of the Russians by a Communist police chief or by police commissioners who were mainly Communists, the group soon became a refuge for many of the party faithful.[7]

During the first weeks of May the city of Vienna pulled itself together; communications were reestablished; a city government was organized and the authority of the central administration spread slowly over the city's districts. In time the necessity for centralizing and legalizing the police authority became apparent. With the decision of the Renner government to reorganize the police system along pre-1938 lines came the question of who would be the first official police president. The stakes were of course very large. Through the Viennese police system, augmented by the security forces of Eastern Austria, where Soviet control was unchallenged, the Communists could bring enormous pressures to bear on the government.

Franz Honner, the Communist Minister of the Interior, was anxious for the position to go to Hautmann, the provisional Chief of Police appointed by the Russians. The justification here was that Hautmann, as a Communist, would be better able to deal with the Russians, who at the time were the only occupation power. The Socialists, however, would not stand for it. As Adolf Schaerf, who was at the time the Socialists' representative on Renner's political cabinet, put it: "Under the Communists the police thought of themselves in the first place as the executive power of the [Russian] occupation power, in the second place as that of the Communist Party, and only last as Austrian police."[8] To Oskar Helmer, who at that time was the Socialist Undersecretary of the Interior, fell the task of preventing the Communists from exploiting this key position. Helmer took the tack with the Russians that the police president should be a professional, which Hautmann was not, and proposed a compromise candidate, Dr. Ignaz Pamer.

Pamer at the time was 78 years old, a man who had joined the police in 1892 and had in his time welcomed both Bismarck and Theodore Roosevelt to Vienna. He had retired from police work in 1930 after having served in many capacities including Vice-President of the Vienna Police Direction. Faced with Socialist resistance to the appointment of Hautmann at a time when the Communists were pressing for unity of the two parties, Pamer must have appeared to the Communists as a most desirable compromise candidate. Respectable, professional, and old, he had all the makings of a pliable figure-

head. Before agreeing to this compromise, the Communists secured
the position of Vice-President under Pamer for a party member,
Othmar Strobel, and that of Director of State Police for another Communist, Dr. Heinrich Duermayer. Rudolf Hautmann was named
head of the administrative division of the Vienna police.[9]

Dr. Ignaz Pamer was appointed to the post of President of the
Vienna Police Direction on May 23, 1945. On June 13, Pamer issued
a directive announcing that as of that date the Vienna Police Direction was assuming control of all Vienna. The police were to be organized in precisely the same manner as before the coming of the Germans in 1938. In addition, the Police Auxiliary (Polizeilicher Hilfsdienst) was to be incorporated into the police system.[10] The reorganization of the Polizeidirektion Wien proper was completed on July
31 with the establishment of the various departments. In the broad-
est outline the Viennese police system was organized along the following lines: under the President and Vice-President fell a number
of presidential offices, including a secretariat. The President directly
supervises a number of departments *(Abteilungen)*: Abteilung I was
the department of the state police (Staatspolizei) responsible for Nazi
questions, passports, the press, war criminals, and internal security;
Abteilung II was the criminal police department, including the "economic police" concerned primarily with black market operations;
Abteilung III was the administrative police.[11]

In the meantime, after prolonged negotiations between the pre-
1938 group of police officials headed by Dr. Heinrich Huettl and the
Communist faction, the "Registration Staff" or Erfassungsstab, a potential rival to the organization being built by Hautmann, became on
July 2 the Generalinspektorat der Sicherheitswache—Inspector General's Office—under the Socialist Ferdinand Linhart, with Huettl as
his deputy.[12] The major concern of this organization was the procedural functioning of the district police system, including discipline,
supply, and training. Furthermore, by the provisions of a bill approved by the Austrian Provisional Government on July 20, 1945,
the nation-wide General Direction for Public Security (Generaldi-
rektion fuer die oeffentliche Sicherheit) was placed immediately under the Ministry of the Interior, with the Police President of Vienna
serving simultaneously as Director of Security for Vienna.

The law of July 20 also called for the creation of militarily organized, armed, and uniformed police authority. This step, which provided a legal basis for the rebuilding of the police system, had been
anticipated on July 13, when an order was issued for the dissolution

of the Polizeilicher Hilfsdienst. This order carried the promise that these men would be incorporated into the new police system.[13]

By August 1945 the reorganization of the police and internal security system of Vienna and Eastern Austria was well under way. The reorganization was singularly centralistic in character, with the Minister of the Interior firmly astride the entire internal security system. Confidence in retaining control of the Ministry of the Interior is probably the reason why Honner and the Russians agreed to the inclusion of the Huettl group in such a sensitive spot in the organization. As long as the Communists could hold the top spot of minister, there would be no problem, and in July 1945 the Communists seemed very confident and sure of their future.

The Austrian Communists were not content with merely packing the police ranks with reliable party members, for there were other ways of gaining complete control of the security system. One was the use of the so-called Kulturreferat (Cultural Section) of the police for propaganda purposes. Under Communist direction the Kulturreferat opened a library and arranged lectures to develop within the police a "sense of democracy and Austrian patriotism."[14] Another technique was to gain control of the leadership of police trade union sections. In Austria the police are organized within the Austrian Trade Union Federation as a professional group (Fachgruppe Polizeiverwaltung) in the Public Services Trade Union. In 1945 this group was organized and led by one of the most intelligent and capable Communists in Austria, the Chief of the Economic Police, Moritz Fels-Margulies.* Margulies very ably used this organization as a sounding board for demands for more pay and privileges for the police, as well as for attacks on Oskar Helmer after Helmer became Minister of the Interior.

The Austrian Communists in their new capacity as the real power within the police establishment were most anxious to stress the difference between the "new" police and the "old." The deep-seated distrust many Viennese, particularly the Socialists, had for the police was well known, and the Communists were eager to exploit this fear of the old police system. Rudolf Hautmann keynoted the Communist approach when he told a crowd in June 1945 that "we come with clean hands; we will be a police force that thinks and feels as the

---

* Margulies had been appointed Chief of the Economic Police (Wirtschaftspolizei) by Honner in May 1945 (Austria, *Provisorisches Personal—Standesverzeichnis fuer das Jahr 1949*, p. 10). Margulies earned the name of Fels ("rock") during the Spanish Civil War.

people do, a police that is with and not against the people." Honner
followed this by stressing that "this time the Vienna police will not
be an enemy of the city, but in the truest sense of the word a Viennese
police—a people's police (*Volkspolizei*).* The Communist Party was
insistent in its promise that "never again will the Viennese police
dare fire on the Viennese. That is the objective of the Communist
Party.[15] The party pledged itself to the "complete purging of the
police and gendarmerie of Nazi, Fascist, as well as all other anti-
democratic elements."[16]

The results of Communist efforts to control the police were reflected in October 1945 at the Allied Council. The Internal Affairs
Quadripartite Committee of the Allied Commission had proposed,
on French and British initiative, that a special committee of military
experts be set up to work with the police and supervise their training
—a proposal that would mean considerable control of the police by
the Four Powers. The Soviet element suggested that such a system
would show "mistrust" in the Austrian internal security officials, and
the plan was dropped.[17]

The national elections of November 1945 dealt a serious blow to
Communist chances of consolidating their hold on the internal security system. As a result of the poor Communist showing, they lost the
Ministry of the Interior. The reorganization of the cabinet in December 1945 brought to the office of Minister of the Interior a Socialist,
Oskar Helmer. With Helmer's appointment the Communists began
a long and bitter struggle to preserve their gains in the police system
and to regain the initiative.

II

The Austrians tell the following story of Oskar Helmer. One day
when Helmer was on an official tour of internal security installations,
his automobile was halted by the Russians at the Enns checkpoint,
which divided the American and Soviet zones. A Russian soldier took
and carefully examined Helmer's identification. After a long pause
he stuck his head in the car window and stared at the bulky figure

---

* *Oesterreichische Zeitung*, June 3, 1945. In the same vein see *Volksstimme*, November 21, 1945, for Honner's claim that the police would never be used against
the people as they were on July 15, 1927, and February 12, 1934. (This was a reference to the two most notorious instances of what the working class considered
police brutality.) Nor would the new police ever welcome a Hitler, as was done
in 1938.

in the back. "Du Chelmer?" he asked. When the minister replied in the affirmative, the soldier responded in an exasperated tone of voice: "Du nix gut" and with a wave of the hand signaled the car on in the very best Viennese dialect—"Gemma, Gemma" (Get along).

Indeed, for the Soviets and Austrian Communists Oskar Helmer was decidedly "nix gut." There may have been one or two Austrian politicians who were more astute and perceptive in their dealings with the Russians, but there was none more fearless. Short of stature, almost massive in bulk, Helmer was a man remarkably articulate though uneducated, single-minded to the point of stubbornness, personally courageous to the point of bravado; all relieved by an unfailing cheerfulness and sense of humor. The very characteristic that earned him many critics—the tendency to see Austria's liberation in 1955 as a victory of the Austrian workers and the Socialist Party— served him well in dealing with the Communists. To Helmer the issues of the occupation period were remarkably simple—communism in all its forms and manifestations was a cancer that had to be cut out of Austria, and the working class, as led by the Socialist Party, was to be the surgeon. Communism in Austria never had a more implacable enemy.[18]

The task confronting Helmer in December 1945 was an enormous one. To purge the police system of Communist influence would be a difficult and dangerous chore. Schaerf put the issue most clearly when he wrote that in 1945, "in spite of the fact that there was a non-Communist police president, the Viennese Police Direction was in the hands of the Communists."[19] The Viennese police were the key to control of the city and perhaps ultimately of the country. Here, however, the Communists were most strongly entrenched; their position was backed not only by the Austrian Communist Party but, more important, by the Red Army. Furthermore, the Russians had unchallenged control of Eastern Austria. To press too hard would increase the growing fear that the Russians would seize on some pretext to split Eastern Austria away from the rest of the country.

Helmer's first blow was struck while he was still undersecretary to Honner during the six months before the first parliamentary elections. The suggestion Helmer made to Honner was simple enough, but as Helmer himself put it, "it exploded like a bomb" in the Ministry of the Interior. Helmer required that all the police, both regular and auxiliary, have a clean police record. This amounted to a stiff blow to Communist hopes of packing the police with their supporters

—a remarkable paradox, seemingly a contradiction in terms. Honner procrastinated but ultimately had to submit; to have refused would have been all but impossible.[20]

This device and other forms of pressure applied by Helmer after he took office probably accounted in large measure for the heavy turnover of personnel in the Viennese police system. In 1945 alone, out of an original 6,152 police officers (*Sicherheitswache*), 1,876 left voluntarily and 2,723 were fired—a total of almost 75 per cent. In the detective division (*Kriminalbeamte*) the turnover was 610 of 1,235 —almost 50 per cent. In 1946 the figures dropped to 26 per cent of the *Sicherheitswache* and remained around 50 per cent for the *Kriminalbeamte*. All this is in contrast to the average of a 1 per cent turnover for both departments after 1950.[21]

This is not to say that all those removed were Communists. Many, perhaps a majority, were incompetent; nor are Communists the only men in Austria with police records. Nevertheless, there were cries of outrage on the part of the Communists, after Helmer took office, over the destruction of Honner's "democratic police" organization.[22] The *Volksstimme* complained in 1947 that Honner's objective was "to build a new truly democratic police through the enlistment of new, and in their democratic convictions, proven forces." Helmer, however, through his purges was installing not young, like-minded Socialists but "former Wehrmacht officers."[23]

One of the most successful weapons used against Communist penetration of the police was the reestablishment of a police academy in Vienna that was securely under Helmer's control. With the help of the Western Allies, who were concerned at the time with the low police morale, resulting in large measure from overwork, underpay, and lack of training and proper weapons, a police training school was opened in Vienna on January 18, with 420 candidates attending. The initial training was for only three months, but the instructors were all veteran members of the police department and under the command of the ubiquitous Dr. Huettl. The first class of around 300 was graduated on March 25. Helmer now had a ready and continuing source of replacements after the recurring purges.[24]

Employees of the Austrian civil service, which includes the police, once they have received their *Pragmatisierung*, or permanent civil service status, can only be removed for such reasons as flagrant disobedience and moral turpitude. These charges are hard to prove, and once a man has reached this protected position, the most effective way to get rid of him is to transfer him or reorganize the department. And so it was in Austria after Helmer took charge. A man could not be removed simply because he was a Communist and, in Helmer's view, a threat to the very existence of a democratic Austria. If the present-day Viennese occasionally wonders why most of the remaining Communists in the police system can be found in the Verkehrsamt (Traffic Bureau) or the Buero zur Bekaempfung der Geschlechts- krankheiten und des Maedchenhandels (Vice Squad) and the prison system, the answer may be found in the imaginative and slightly sardonic mind of Oskar Helmer.*

First of all, the Polizeilicher Hilfsdienst was not incorporated into the police system as Honner had promised but redesignated, with the men now known as Sicherheitswachebeamten-Anwaerter (SWBA); a semantic distinction on the surface, but enough to place them in a probationary status whereby they could be weeded out gradually.[25]

Then Helmer began a process of centralization and reorganization which worked to the definite disadvantage of the Communists. The Fremdenbuero, which handled nonnationals and was in the days of the displaced-person flood an extremely important bureau, was redesignated as the Auslaenderamt in October 1946. The Communist Albert Schlesinger, who the Communists claimed was a Socialist, was replaced as chief of the new office by Dr. Josef Paul, whom the Communists described as a "Schober Police Official."† Simultaneously, the American and British occupation authorities quietly removed a number of Communist police officials in their districts of Vienna, including Commissioner Fronek of the Doebling District.[26]

In the spring of 1946 Dr. Pamer announced that he wished to retire as Police President. Helmer, whose prerogative it was to name a successor, nominated Major General Franz Winterer, a former officer in the German army, who had been the undersecretary for Heereswesen (military affairs) in the Provisional Government of Karl Renner. The Allied Council refused to approve the appointment of Winterer. Helmer contends that the reason for the action was that Winterer was a Socialist.[27] The charge is more a reflection of Helmer's

---

* Helmer's clever tactics were not without tragic consequences in at least one case. In 1962 a young Hungarian officer, Bela Lapusnyik, who was rumored to be in military intelligence, defected to the West. While he was being "safeguarded" in an Austrian prison prior to questioning, he was murdered by poisoning. The act was unquestionably the work of Communist guards.

† *Volksstimme,* October 8, 1946. Schober was a well-known and widely feared police chief of Vienna during the interwar period, whose action during the 1927 disturbances earned him the everlasting hatred of the Socialists.

ideological myopia than an explanation of the disapproval. More pertinent is the fact that Winterer's reputation with the Allied Council was permanently blackened in early 1946 when it was discovered that the Heeresamt he directed for the ostensible purpose of supervising the demobilization of the Austrian army was actually preparing statistics studies for a future Austrian army and registering manpower for possible mobilization.[28]

Ferdinand Graf, Helmer's undersecretary and member of the People's Party, backed Dr. Huettl for the post; the suggestion did not please Helmer, presumably because Huettl, although a professional police official, stood very close to the People's Party. In the absence of any agreement, Helmer finally suggested Dr. Arthur Klausner, a career police official.[29] Huettl was named Vice-President of the Viennese Police Direction, where he gradually took over the responsibilities and power of the Communist Strobel, who became, as the result of the fine hand of Austrian administrative magic, Second Vice-President.[30] Dr. Pamer left office on July 20, 1946, and Klausner took over. The very real threat that the Communists would use the aged Pamer as a figurehead was gone. But Helmer was soon to find that Klausner was also not the man for this most critical job. The circumstances surrounding Klausner's removal from office in September 1947 are closely interwoven with perhaps the most remarkable episode in Austria's ten-year struggle to regain its independence—the case of Dr. Heinrich Duermayer and the Staatspolizei.

III

The bitter and prolonged struggle between Oskar Helmer and Dr. Duermayer, the Director of the State Police, moved through 1946 and 1947 with all the deliberateness of a chess game. But this chess game was played with the most bizarre pieces imaginable—a young boy who allegedly plotted to build a new Nazi party in Austria, a police informer who specialized in tracking down Nazis although he himself was a former member of the Storm troopers, a monument built by the Russians to commemorate the liberation of Vienna, and finally an obviously disturbed girl who allegedly had a swastika tatooed on her breast. This collection of unlikely chess pieces was moved in a game of deadly earnest. Had Duermayer been successful in this game, Austria would have been faced with the establishment of a separate police force in Eastern Austria.

The story of Heinrich Duermayer and the Austrian Staatspolizei begins with his release in April 1945 from death camp Mauthausen —the most infamous concentration camp on Austrian soil. Upon arriving in Vienna, Duermayer contacted Franz Honner, who was then Minister of the Interior. Duermayer was made Director of Abteilung I—the Staatspolizei.*

Short, barrel-chested, with iron-gray hair, Duermayer has the worn, hard look of a man who has seen much death and suffering. Like many of Austria's postwar Communists, Duermayer was a young Socialist in 1934. Dismayed and confused by what he took to be cowardice and lack of conviction on the part of the Socialists in resisting Dollfuss, he became a Communist. During the next ten years he fought in Spain; he was interned by the French after the collapse of the Loyalist cause, and finally in 1940 he was handed over to the Gestapo by the French. His wartime memories are those of Auschwitz and Mauthausen, of the resistance groups within the camps, where he met such men as Joseph Cyrankiewicz, the present Premier of Poland.[31] Duermayer was not "Moscow-trained," with all the overtones of well-schooled subversion, as Richard Hiscocks suggests,[32] but a dedicated and very Austrian Communist to whom ruthlessness had become a way of life.

Under Duermayer's direction the Staatspolizei quickly became a powerful and widely feared force. Although the extent of its authority was theoretically confined to Vienna, the Staatspolizei by 1947 consisted of 1,000 officers operating throughout most of Austria.[33] The Staatspolizei did not procure its men through the normal channels of the overall police personnel section, but had complete freedom to select its own force. Since, as Dr. Duermayer himself has explained, Communists were "the only really reliable and implacable foes of fascism in Austria," the State police were at least 90 per cent Communist.[34] Duermayer was particularly anxious to recruit Communists who had spent time in the concentration camps. In this way a man such as Hans Marsalek, who was to write a chilling book about Mauthausen, giving every emphasis to the admirable role of the Communists there, was offered a top position in the Staatspolizei.[35]

* The principal source materials used in the following section were made available to me through the permission of both Dr. Duermayer and Oskar Helmer. These are the court proceedings, statements of supporting evidence, and appended documents of two libel suits brought by Dr. Duermayer, first against the publisher of Helmer's memoirs—*50 Jahre erlebte Geschichte*—and then against Helmer himself in 1958 and 1959. They are Akt zu 1603/57 and zu 1159/59, Landesgericht fuer Strafsachen Wien II. These portfolios include all the original investigation reports, correspondence, and testimony of all the principals. In addition, there are the court proceedings and all appended evidence of the trial of Karl Kocanda —the young man accused of plotting to blow up the Russian memorial. This may be found at the Landesgericht fuer Strafsachen Wien I, as Akt zu HV 1573/47–VglVr 4492/47.

One of the primary tasks of the Staatspolizei was rounding up dangerous National Socialists and war criminals. With the unqualified and enthusiastic support of the Russian military authorities, the state police exercised this prerogative in the widest possible manner. Completely without orders from his nominal superiors, Duermayer established a number of so-called *Anhaltelager*—detention camps—into which selected National Socialists or the "politically unreliable" were herded.[36] The political implications of such unrestrained police power were obvious.

Helmer was certainly aware of the danger to his control of security represented by the Staatspolizei. On March 11, 1946, when Helmer visited new state police offices on the Deutschmeisterplatz (safely within the Russian sector of the city), he pointedly remarked in the presence of Duermayer that "the individual elements of the police must work for the whole and dare not shut themselves off from one another. The police exist for the state and the people."[37]

Apart from a series of warnings to Duermayer to close the *Anhaltelager* because they were both unlawful and unauthorized, Helmer was presumably unwilling or unable to risk a direct confrontation with Duermayer.[38] He therefore limited his efforts to reorganizing those departments where the Communists were less well entrenched and to rebuilding the police training system to ensure that the police replacing the purged Communists were dependable. Helmer's severe illness in the spring and summer of 1946 also delayed any action against Duermayer.

We cannot know what action Helmer would have eventually taken against Dr. Duermayer's Staatspolizei because the initiative was taken away from him by Communists themselves. Why the Communists forced the issue, beginning in the fall of 1946, is not difficult to imagine. By this time Helmer's constant purges and reorganizations were bringing dividends, culminating in the appointment of Klausner as police president and Huettl as *de facto* vice-president. However, the Communists were still very much in control in the Russian sector of Vienna and in the Soviet zone. Here was their main strength, and time was proving that soon it would be their only strength. The last refuge of Communist strength in the fall of 1946 outside the Soviet-controlled zones was the Staatspolizei. The Communists thus had but one alternative to a complete erosion of their position: to split the internal security system of the country and create a Russian and Austrian Communist-controlled police establishment in the Eastern zone.

IV

Helmer received his first warning in early October 1946 that the Communists had shifted to the offensive in the struggle for control of the security system. At this time he was summoned to the Russian headquarters in the Imperial Hotel by Colonel General A. S. Zheltov, second in command of the Soviet occupation forces and responsible for political affairs. Zheltov told Helmer that a wave of Nazi reaction was in motion in Austria and that Helmer was hindering the efforts of the state police to control it. As a result of this obstruction the Soviet occupation authorities did not feel secure and would be forced to intervene if the situation continued. This was the first time the Soviets had leveled such charges and Helmer was deeply concerned.[39]

At approximately the same time Theodor Koerner, the Socialist mayor of Vienna, received an equally ominous letter from General Lebedenko, the Russian commandant of Vienna. Lebedenko wrote that he had heard reports that certain Nazi elements in Vienna were plotting to blow up the Russian War Memorial in the Stalinplatz (Schwarzenbergplatz before and after the Russian occupation). Koerner was warned: "When this monument in the year of its dedication was given over to the care of the City Government, I remind you, it [the city government] assumed the complete responsibility for the protection and maintenance of the monument."[40]

This memorial is a massive concrete structure, over 120 feet high, put up by the Russians immediately after the war. It was built by Soviet engineers and architects; construction began in the middle of May 1945 and took three months to complete. It is topped by the bronze figure of a Russian soldier with the Red Flag held high in his right hand, automatic weapon across his chest, and a shield held low in his left hand. The monument was dedicated on August 19, 1945.

An affront to the memorial, as the acknowledged symbol of the Soviet liberation of the country, would be a direct insult to the Soviet occupation forces.[41] Despite the fact that to the Viennese the figure atop the memorial was known as the *unbekannte Pluenderer* ("the unknown plunderer"), a plot to destroy the memorial could have been the pretext to declare the entire Austrian security system inadequate and establish a Communist police system in Eastern Austria.

Meanwhile Helmer had turned his attention to breaking Communist control of its last and most powerful citadel—the Staatspolizei. Deprived of any effective control of the state police, Helmer first built a cadre of his own state police within the Ministry of the

Interior. This section began with some 30 men under the direction of Inspector Anton Marek.[42]

Then in March 1947 Helmer was able to transfer into the state police a police official, Dr. Franz Mayer, who was loyal to Helmer and who was charged by Helmer with the review of all state police cases of importance. Mayer recalls that his reception in the state police was hardly friendly, with speeches made against him and every effort made to conceal from him what was going on.[43] With the placement of Mayer in the state police, the issue was soon to come to a head. It is at this point that the case of Karl Kocanda and his alleged "fourth party" crystallized the issue of control of the internal security forces.

During the first few months of 1947 the Communist papers in Austria—particularly the *Volksstimme* and the Russian military *Oesterreichische Zeitung*—were ablaze with headlines reporting one incident after another resulting from what was described as a resurgence of fascism in Austria. "Fascist Bomb Plot in Leoben," "Extensive Nazi Secret Organization Discovered," "20% of the State System—Nazi," "Prominent Nazi Criminal Spirited out of Prison"—these and similar headlines combined over the first six months of 1947 into a veritable flood of such stories.[44]

Perhaps it was mere coincidence that squarely in the middle of this campaign the Staatspolizei uncovered a plot engineered by a 19-year-old Viennese by the name of Karl Kocanda to destroy the memorial. In an extensive report to the State Attorney's office dated June 24, 1947, the state police submitted evidence of the fact that one Karl Kocanda and his two companions, 19-year-old Othmar Schwab, and 25-year-old Gertrude Sauter had plotted to blow up the Russian memorial. According to this report, Kocanda, during the first week of May, in the presence of Schwab and a police agent described only as "a certain Herbert," confided that he had a secret cache of explosives. Kocanda allegedly boasted that "the Stalin Memorial would be blown up with these explosives as a signal for renewed activity of Werewolf groups."[45]

Dr. Herbert Ernst, a senior official in the state police, who prepared the report, was a little hard pressed to make the Nazi relationship completely clear. Kocanda, Ernst reported, had been a member of the DJ (Deutsches Jungvolk) since 1939—i.e., since the age of 11— and furthermore "membership in the HJ [Hitler-Jugend] cannot be excluded." Moreover, Schwab's father and brother were members of the Nazi Party and Schwab himself was a member of the HJ from 1938 to 1943. Since 1946, in the company of Gertrude Sauter, they have been pursuing "anti-democratic conversations in cafes."[46]

The explosives in the possession of Kocanda were discovered by him while he was briefly employed by the French occupation forces. The explosives, according to the report, consisted of the following: 6 Italian and German hand grenades, 15 detonators, 3 dynamite sticks, including 2 damaged by dampness.[47] The report concluded by stating that "Kocanda possesses a certain intelligence and was completely aware of the consequences of possession of the illegal munitions" and that "he took the plan for the demolition of the Stalin memorial completely in earnest."[48]

Although the state police were aware early in May of the fact that Kocanda was in possession of illegal munitions—a particularly serious crime in the immediate postwar years—the suspect was not picked up until May 22 and his friends not until the 28th. With the arrest of the three suspects, all investigation of the case by the state police ceased.

Until the end of June, when the report to the state prosecutor from the state police on the Kocanda case was finally received by the Ministry of the Interior, Helmer had no idea of what was happening. However, in the first week of June he was called on the carpet by Colonel Ilychev of the Russian occupation command and confronted with the charge that Ilychev had information proving that there was a plot to destroy the monument. He then declared that the Soviet forces were unsatisfied with the security system under Helmer and demanded that a separate police direction be established in the Russian zone. Helmer stalled for time.[49]

Although Dr. Mayer, Helmer's watchdog in the state police, was later to claim that the first information he had on the Kocanda case came on July 7 as the result of a disclosure of the "plot" in the French information newspaper of Vienna, *Welt am Montag,* it is certain that Helmer and Mayer knew of it at least by July 1.[50] The problem was what to do about it. The Russians were anxious to use this case as a lever to establish a new police system in Eastern Austria, with—as Helmer was soon to learn—Heinrich Duermayer as its director.[51] All that was necessary, it would appear, now that the case with its damaging testimony was formally submitted to the state prosecutor's office, was for the Russians to coordinate a newspaper revelation of the facts of the case with a dramatic disclosure at the Allied Council. The Soviets could then claim that the rising tide of Austrian Nazism was not being checked by Helmer's inefficient security system and therefore the Soviet element felt it necessary to establish a more reliable security system in its own zone. At any rate, there seemed to be a very close connection between the alleged plot to destroy the Russian memorial and the rising demand for a separate police direction in Eastern Austria.

How it was planned to use the Kocanda case to gain a separate police organization in Eastern Austria is not known. Before the Russians could act, the initiative went over to Helmer; or more accurately to the Western Allies, who were backing Helmer against the Soviet contender for control of the Austrian internal security forces, Heinrich Duermayer. On Monday, July 7, the official newspaper of the French information service in Austria, *Welt am Montag,* ran the headline "Hitler Youths Wanted to Dynamite Memorial in Stalinplatz."[52] The story recounted that it had learned from "legal circles" that a certain young Austrian was a member of a conspiracy to blow up the memorial with a "great quantity of explosives." Had this plot been carried out, the results would have been disastrous for the population in the area.

With this article as an excuse, Dr. Mayer, under orders from the Ministry of the Interior, immediately launched a whirlwind investigation of the entire affair, claiming that a matter of such great importance should not have been brought to the attention of Mayer by the state police through a newspaper article. In a blistering and remarkably detailed report dated July 9, 1947, just two days after the article appeared, Mayer charged that the entire description of the affair in Dr. Ernst's report was a blatant distortion of the facts.

Mayer's report included the following interesting facts that were subsequently never denied by Duermayer at the post-occupation trials: Kocanda was a wild-eyed braggart who was never in the HJ, or any other Nazi organization, but was in fact a callow, emotionally unstable boy who was mustered out of the RAD (Reichsarbeitsdienst) —military work battalions—because of physical defects. In the absence of his father, who in 1947 was still a POW in the Soviet Union, Kocanda frequented the rundown nightclub Die Koralle, where he exercised his imagination by boasting of past Nazi connections and future party plans while characteristically playing with a loaded cartridge. Furthermore, Kocanda during the initial investigation had told Dr. Ernst that "Herbert" was the one who suggested the dynamiting, an accusation never mentioned in the final Staatspolizei report, which contended that Kocanda admitted the intention to destroy the memorial. Mayer's report also revealed that the "certain Herbert" was in fact a "certain" Alfred Papenheim, a former SA Ober-Truppenfuehrer (brown shirt or storm trooper) whose affiliation with the Nazis only came to an end when, as a result of the Nuremberg race laws, he was removed from the party. Papenheim had appealed the decision and was only finally removed from the rolls in December 1942. Now he was a nameless and apparently completely reliable informer. Among the innumerable contradictions in the reports, the most significant was that concerning the munitions. Mayer's report, based on the examination of an acknowledged explosives expert, revealed that among the explosives that the Staatspolizei contended were intended for the demolition of a massive 120-foot concrete monument "only the 15 No. 8 detonators could be described as true explosives, and that those detonators could have been used to set off other explosives but never could be used for blasting in themselves."[53]

Dr. Duermayer has dismissed these glaring contradictions in the report of his long-experienced and highly placed assistant, Dr. Ernst, as a matter of "clumsiness" and poor police work.[54] He has also contended that he was not aware that the investigation had been initiated until Mayer intervened in the case and accused Duermayer of staging a "provocation."[55]

In all probability the article in *Welt am Montag* on July 7, which gave Mayer the chance to conduct the investigation, was planted there by the forces in Austria favoring Helmer's unchallenged control of the police system. *Welt am Montag* was, after all, a paper controlled by the French Information Service, and all such news obviously was printed with the knowledge and approval of the French occupation forces. It should be noted that the paper comes out in the afternoon on Monday, Vienna's only paper that day, and by nightfall Mayer had the first report on the explosives. By July 9, a day before the Allied Council was scheduled to meet, the report was finished.

Duermayer's reaction to the investigation conducted by Dr. Mayer was to write to Police President Klausner accusing Mayer of pursuing the investigation in "an outrageously aggressive and excited manner," of charging his superiors with arranging the entire affair, and of actually investigating the Staatspolizei rather than the case at hand. He demanded that disciplinary action against Mayer be taken and that, in the meantime, he be suspended from all duties.[56] Failing to get immediate action from Klausner, Duermayer wrote again on August 28. This time Duermayer threatened that if Mayer was not immediately suspended he would be forced "to forbid the entrance of Section Councilor Dr. Mayer into the offices of Section I [i.e., the state police] as well as all activity connected with Section I."[57]

This letter was to prove Duermayer's undoing. Since Mayer was placed in Duermayer's organization on orders given personally by the Minister of the Interior, to bar him from the offices of the state police was an obvious and serious breach of discipline. But could Helmer actually fire Duermayer or even transfer him to an unimportant position somewhere in the Western zones? What would the reaction of the Soviet military forces be if Helmer attempted to crush this last important hold of the Communists in the police system, particularly now that the Russians apparently intended to use the Staatspolizei as the nucleus of a new police establishment in Eastern Austria? For Soviet intentions had become all too clear soon after the investigation conducted by Dr. Mayer, when the Russians again came to Helmer and demanded a separate police organization in their zone, adding that the man they had in mind to lead the new organization was Dr. Duermayer.[58]

A witness at the post-occupation trials called September 2, 1947, Austria's most decisive hour.[59] It was on this day that Oskar Helmer ordered Duermayer transferred. At the same time Dr. Klausner, the police president, was replaced by Joseph Holaubek, who became Vienna's first Socialist police president, something that would have been beyond imagination during the interwar period.

The official announcement of the reorganization came on September 3: Klausner was retiring "because of severe illness."[60] The next day the Viennese papers published a statement by the Director of General Security, Wilhelm Krechler, saying that "for official reasons" Dr. Duermayer, "the former chief of the state police section of the Viennese Police Direction, had been transferred in the same capacity to the Salzburg Police Direction. His former position has been assumed by Dr. Peterlunger."[61] The irony of the phrase "the same capacity" is obvious; in Salzburg, deprived of Russian support and separated from his carefully selected and trained force of 1,000 men, Duermayer would have been the chief of a section with fewer than 100 men and completely under the thumb of the Americans.

Much hard thinking had gone into the decision to remove Duermayer. One witness to the moment of final decision has said: "No one knew what consequences might be entailed. At the time the Min-

ister [Helmer] and the leading officials discussed possible consequences. The Minister held at the time that one must take on the
possible consequences, since it was a question of life or death of the
Austrian state."[62] He was not of course referring to the anticipated
outpouring of abuse and frustration from the Communist press. The
Volksstimme raged that Peterlunger was a Fascist and Helmer the
agent of the "reaction," and protest demonstrations were held in
many of the Soviet-controlled factories. However, this was of very
little concern to Helmer or to the Western occupation forces, whose
presses remained quiet on the subject during the first few days after
the announcement of the removal of Duermayer.[63]

Helmer's concern was centered on the reaction of the Soviet military authorities. They might have brought Duermayer into the Russian sector of Vienna with the bulk of the Staatspolizei and established the police direction they wanted. Short of a Soviet policy statement on the matter, there is no way of knowing the reason for the
lack of Soviet response to the transfer of Duermayer. This much seems
clear, however: the Soviet reaction to the Duermayer case was very
much in line with previous Soviet actions in Austria. They played
the game carefully, perhaps too carefully, until such time as it would
be necessary to recoup their losses through a demonstration of force.
Stripped of all pretexts in the Duermayer case, the Soviet military
backed off. Force, here as elsewhere during the struggle for Austria,
was a weapon the Soviet Union was apparently not prepared to use.
Faced with such a choice, they allowed the dismantling of the state
police and the transfer of Duermayer.

The imposition of control over the Staatspolizei by Helmer was
conclusively underlined in March 1948, when the offices of the state
police were unobtrusively removed from the Deutschmeisterplatz in
the Russian sector to the Zedlitzgasse in the international zone.[64]

The spring of 1948 also saw Helmer break the Communist hold
on the last important stronghold of the Communists in the police—
the Wirtschaftspolizei, or Economic Police, under the astute Moritz
Fels-Margulies. The pretext was provided by shakedown of a Hungarian merchant by two officials of the Wirtschaftspolizei. As a result
of the subsequent investigation, Helmer in May had Fels-Margulies
transferred to the traffic police, and the economic police reorganized.
With this reorganization, Helmer was able to put into effect a long-
standing order for the transfer of the entire economic police section
out of the Russian sector and into the Western sector of Vienna,[65]
an order that had been ignored until now.[66]

A final touch was then added with the transfer of the Traffic Bureau (Verkehrsamt) to the old offices of the Wirtschaftspolizei in the Russian zone along with its rather full complement of Communists (including Fels-Margulies). The Soviets now had unchallenged control of the traffic police—the Helmer faction was not without humor in playing the game.

Other Communist footholds in the police system were dealt with less dramatically. One of Helmer's first steps after taking office was to deal with those members of the Austrian battalion whom Honner had brought back to Austria and, as recounted, merged, weapons and all, into the Austrian police. Helmer's solution was to transfer small detachments to various sectors of the Austrian border and then gradually remove them from the police.[67]

The Communist control of the Kulturreferat was not so easy to break. Helmer ordered the dissolution of the Cultural Section in August of 1946, fully appreciating its propaganda possibilities.[68] To take the place of the Kulturreferat the Ministry of the Interior organized a similar organization—Kulturvereinigung der Polizeibediensteten—which was formally dedicated on February 14, 1947, with the police president, Klausner, as honorary president. The three leading positions in the society were given to representatives of the three parties; Margulies, as the Communist representative, became general secretary.

Much to the chagrin of Helmer, his own cultural society soon came under complete Communist control. The organization had its offices in the Russian sector, and he could not get them out of the government building they occupied. Helmer's frustration was to last until 1955, when the Russians left and the society was disbanded. Until that time he was left only with the feeble gesture of preventing the society from listing itself as the Kulturvereinigung der Polizeibediensteten in the Vienna phone book.[69]

This small Communist victory, however, did not change the general picture. With the removal of Duermayer in September 1947, the Communists had lost all control of positions of real power in the Austrian internal security system. From this point on, the objectives of Soviet policy in Austria with respect to the police system were fairly well defined. First, through obstructive tactics at the Allied Council and periodic dismissals of police officials in their own zone, they tried to prevent the rearming of the police and generally to keep the internal security system as weak as possible. Second, they developed the Werkschutz—the plant guards in the Russian-controlled industries, primarily in the oil fields—into a well-armed force which could also be used in riots and demonstrations. Third, they continued to obstruct tampering with the security system in the Soviet zone.

On the other hand, the objective of the Western Allies after September 1947 was to press for a gradual buildup of the numerical strength and armament of the police and gendarmerie, now that control of these forces seemed to be finally in Western hands. Failing this, owing to the consistent and successful efforts of the Soviets at the Allied Council to prevent the effective arming of the police, the Western Allies after 1948 secretly developed units of the Western Austrian gendarmerie into a well-armed, mobile fighting force which could be used during a Communist uprising (and was indeed so used in 1950), as well as providing the cadre for any future Austrian army.

V

The aftermath of war in Austria brought a wave of crime and violence of frightening proportion. In the spring of 1945 desperate men armed with abandoned weapons of war roamed the streets of Vienna. The task of the newly formed police was enormously difficult, because violence provoked by hunger and despair had become a sordid way of life for many in Austria. Against these men, who were very often armed with automatic weapons and grenades, the police had little with which to protect themselves. To arm the Austrian police adequately soon became a burning issue for the Austrian government. Unfortunately for the police, the issue soon went beyond the proper arming of the police against criminals and became a question of real importance for the occupying powers.

All the Allies were at first extremely cautious in the matter of arming the police. This was natural and not entirely a matter of waiting to see who gained final control of the internal security forces. Weapons in the hands of the police could be turned against members of the occupation forces with unpleasant results.

Initially, then, the Austrian police were armed in much the same manner as their quarry—with pickup weapons, all irregular and sometimes more dangerous to the police than to their target. After a prolonged discussion in the Executive Committee of the Allied Commission, it was finally agreed to permit the gendarmerie to carry carbines and the police to have revolvers. Forty rounds of ammunition were to be issued for each weapon, which could be replaced only with the permission of the occupation authorities. Both the police and the gendarmerie would be permitted to carry only two rounds while on duty. This measure was adopted by the Allied Council on April 10, 1946, as Chancellor Figl so announced the next day.[70]

The fact that an agreement was reached on what kinds of weapons should be given to the Austrian police did not mean that the police actually received these weapons or the ammunition. The original agreement did not indicate how and against whom the weapons could be used. The Soviets were soon to insist that the police be prohibited from firing on the nationals of any of the occupying powers, a regulation the Western Allies objected to because, as British Major General T. J. Winterton so aptly put it, "This regulation was one which would have been impossible to carry out because, first it was assumed that the Austrian police could see in the dark, and secondly, because thieves dress themselves in the garb of the occupying powers."[71] Since the Allied Council was never able to agree on this point, the police were never officially issued arms from the Control Commission but received them from the individual powers.

As it became increasingly clear to the Soviet forces that they were losing control of the internal security forces, opposition to arming the police and gendarmerie grew more intense. This effort was coupled with the demand after 1946 that the police and the gendarmerie be restricted in size and that some 3,400 police and gendarmerie considered by the Russians to be Nazis be purged.[72] The American position on this issue was to agree to a restriction of the size of the police, but to deny any attempt to fix the strength of the gendarmerie.[73] As with the matter of arming the police, no agreement was reached.

Deeply concerned about the deteriorating security throughout the country, Chancellor Figl wrote the Allied Council in May 1947, complaining of the dangerous situation.[74] Figl, in a letter to the Allied Council stressed the general decline of public security:

One must speak of general public insecurity. . . . The number of murders committed throughout Austria was 26 in August, 36 in September, and 41 in October. . . . The criminals possess almost without exception revolvers and automatic weapons, even hand grenades have been used, whereas the police and gendarmerie are inadequately armed with unwieldy carbines and insufficient ammunition. They are sometimes sent out to their dangerous service without any arms at all.[75]

All this was to no avail. The Soviets after 1947 were determined, with good reason, to keep the police and the gendarmerie as weak as possible. Finally, by 1948, an American statement to the Allied Commission on the condition of the Austrian police was forced to conclude: "Actually the sum total of quadripartite assistance to the Austrian law enforcement agencies over the last three years is contained in the

Executive Committee decision of 20th May 1947, which states that 'the Allied Council has no objection to the arming of all ranks of the police with truncheons of hard wood.' "[76] The Soviet Union, in stoutly resisting all efforts to arm the police, while simultaneously calling for one investigation after another of police and gendarmerie activities, had by 1948 come a long way from those days in the fall of 1945 when they chided the Western powers for a lack of faith in Austria's police officials. The reason for the change is clear enough. Denied the use of the police system as a positive force in Austria, the Russians after 1947 concentrated on neutralizing the police and denying the Austrian government and its Western backers the effective use of the internal security system.

Barely a month after the transfer of Dr. Duermayer, the Russians removed from office the police chiefs of Wiener Neustadt and St. Poelten and the representatives of the Director of Internal Security for Lower Austria in Baden. These were the three most important posts in the Soviet zone. The charges were vague: the officials involved had not fulfilled their police duties or followed the administrative directives of the Russians; nor were they "true fighters against fascism."[77] The connection with the Duermayer case is too apparent to ignore. The Soviet Union thus made it completely clear that all police officials in the Soviet zone, regardless of whether they were selected by Helmer, would be under the control of the Red Army or they would be dismissed or kidnapped.[78]

The Soviet counterforce to Helmer's police was the so-called Werkschutz, or plant guards. Little is really known about the size, function, and organization of the Werkschutz, a force trained by Soviet officers and organized along military lines for the avowed purpose of guarding the Soviet-controlled oil fields in Eastern Austria. In May 1948 the *New York Times* reported that the number of Werkschutz in the Soviet zone had been increased from 10,000 to 12,000.[79] But this figure is undoubtedly more a reflection of the high state of tension in Austria in the early spring of 1948 than of any hard evidence. Somewhere between 1,500 and 2,000 men is probably closer to the real figure. Perhaps more important than the actual numerical strength of the Werkschutz was the fact that these guards, many of whom were former members of Honner's Freedom Battalion, were armed with far superior military equipment than that issued to the Austrian police. The overriding fear was that in any attempted coup these guards would be turned loose and the Austrian internal security forces would be powerless against them.[80]

Rumors of the expansion of the Werkschutz intensified the grow-

ing concern of Helmer and the Western Allies over the situation on
the gendarmerie in the Soviet zone. Beginning in late March 1948,
the Soviet authorities ordered the closing of four of the eight gendarmerie schools in their zone. Furthermore, members of the gendarmerie in the Soviet zone were now required to have Soviet permission to travel to the Western zones for training, and this permission because increasingly more difficult to obtain.[81]

By 1948, therefore, the Soviet Union had effectively neutralized
most of the advantages won by the coalition government and the
Western powers in gaining control of the police system. Then came
the Berlin Blockade.

VI

Beginning in April 1948, the long shadow of the Berlin crisis spread
slowly across Austria. Vienna and Berlin, both located far within a
Soviet zone of occupation, were tactically indefensible, dependent
on narrow air corridors and limited rail and highway facilities for
supplies. As the tension in Berlin mounted and interference with
Western access to the city hardened into a complete blockade, the
echo was heard in Vienna, and by June 1948 there was open talk in
the city of Russian intentions to deny access to the city to the other
powers as a signal for a Communist coup. These fears initially seemed
well justified. The Communist takeover in Prague in February had
made a deep and frightening impression in Vienna—Prague was no
faraway capital, and now it had gone the way of Budapest. Vienna
wondered whether it was to be next.

All the signs were there. On April 12 the Soviet High Command
had placed barriers for a short time across the roads leading from
the British air terminal at Schwechat and refused to allow British
military personnel to pass through.[82] Moreover, prior to this action
the Soviets had raised, at the Allied Commission's Air Directorate
meeting of April 7, several issues which threatened to seriously restrict
Allied use of the air corridors. The Soviet element contended that
the existing "Interim Regulations for Air Traffic over the Occupied
Zones of Austria" were just that—temporary—and thus needed revision. Furthermore, the Western powers had violated the original
agreement by using the corridors for commercial and military aircraft
(bombers and fighters), whereas the original agreements—the July 9,
1945, agreement and subsequent decisions of the Chiefs of Staff of the
Occupying Powers on July 24–25, 1945—provided only for the use
of the corridors by transportation and communications aircraft.[83]

The Soviet representatives considered it imperative that these violations of the use of the two airfields controlled by the Western Allies —Tulln and Schwechat—cease at once.

At the Allied Council meeting of April 30, where this issue of access to Vienna was discussed at length, the United States representatives pointed out that the adoption of the Soviet proposal would mean the control and restriction of the Allied flights into Vienna. The U.S. element was also unable to understand why the Soviets insisted in their proposal that flight safety regulations be improved when simultaneously they insisted that all weather homing equipment be removed from the U.S. airfield. The British could only contend that the existing agreement did not "exclude" either military or commercial aircraft, nor did the July 9 agreement mention the issue of what kind of aircraft could use the corridors.[84]

This direct threat to Allied air access to Vienna, when taken together with the sporadic blockading of the roads to Tulln and Schwechat, the Soviet interruption of the interzonal telephone circuits between Upper and Lower Austria, and the Soviet demand that after April 11 all British personnel must show military identification when passing over the 50 miles of Soviet territory that separated the British zone from Vienna, had all the appearances of following the Berlin pattern. The question was whether Vienna would be subjected to the progressively tighter restrictions on rail and highway traffic which began in Berlin on March 31 and finally ended with the complete isolation of the city on June 24, 1948.

Many in Austria thought so. When the Soviet element, in an apparent reversal of form, proposed at the Executive Committee meeting of April 9 that the power of the Allied Military Police with respect to Austrian citizens and stateless persons be limited, the other powers were at first completely baffled. The Soviet resolution contained the following clause: "Beginning with 15 April 1948, the activity of the Allied Military Police and other Allied agencies in each zone of occupation as well as in the city of Vienna shall not extend to Austrian citizens or stateless persons who have resided in Austria since 13 March 1938, except for cases involving crimes against the Occupation Forces."[85] During the subsequent discussions of the proposal the Soviets strongly objected to the American amendment that the Austrians be allowed to call for Allied assistance in an emergency.[86] It may be that the Russians were only seeking clarification of the vexing question of jurisdiction of criminal matters, but the vigor of the Western rejection of the proposal seems to indicate that the Western Allies were suspicious that such an agreement would prevent the Western forces from intervening if a Communist-inspired uprising occurred in Vienna.[87]

As the pattern of Soviet pressure on Berlin began to emerge during the spring of 1948, the Western powers in Austria became acutely aware that a Soviet blockade of Vienna along the Berlin model would be disastrous. Unlike Berlin, Vienna had no airfield within the Western sectors of the city. Deprived of the airlift operation, the Western powers if challenged by a Soviet blockade would have been faced with a choice between direct military confrontation or loss of the city.

But, although all the indications were there, the Soviets never pressed their advantage, and thus the more vulnerable Vienna was spared the test of a blockade. The Soviet Union in blockading Berlin may have been responding to several important Western moves in Germany, such as the currency reform and the merging of the Western zones, which the Soviets clearly considered a threat to their interests. In Austria, on the other hand, there were no "provocative" Western initiatives to counter. Then too, as has been suggested, the Soviet Union's interests were not so directly engaged in Austria as in Germany. The prize was apparently not worth the military risk.

Whatever the reasons, Soviet actions, or the lack of them, in Austria during the Berlin crisis seem to be one more indication that the Soviet Union in its Austria policy was determined to apply the strategy of "peaceful transition" which had worked so well in Czechoslovakia.

For their part, there is little doubt that the Austrian Communists must have been disappointed by the Soviet Union's restraint in the spring of 1948. Nevertheless, the successful coup in Prague was the signal for the beginning of a period of renewed KPO militancy, which only subsided in 1950. Although Communist efforts to form "action committees" of workers and farmers along the Czech model were frustrated by the Socialists, the attempt to provoke a general strike came at a time when the Austrian forces were virtually disarmed.

Beginning with a transportation strike in Linz in March 1948, and culminating in a general strike in September 1948, the KPO sought to disrupt the Austrian economy and possibly to unseat the coalition government. Although there were domestic issues ripe for exploitation in 1948, particularly those of wage and price levels, and the Communists had an ominous threat in the Werkschutz forces, the 1948 strike effort turned out to be a dismal failure. Not only did the coalition government maintain its poise and unity, but Socialist trade union leaders were able to hold the workers in line. Two years later, however, the discipline and control would prove momentarily ineffective, thereby giving the Communists another, and far more promising, chance.

The Berlin crisis had dramatically raised the possibility that Vienna could be subjected to either a Communist putsch or a blockade of the city, or both. This experience seems to have convinced the Western powers that a good deal more than a loyal police was necessary in Austria. Although the evidence is not entirely conclusive, there is every indication that beginning in 1949 the Austrian coalition government, with the aid of the Western powers, began to train and equip a mobile regiment of the gendarmerie in the Western zones.* This regiment was divided into special shock battalions—*Alarmbataillone*—and had its headquarters in Linz, with units stationed in the three Western occupation zones. Moreover, there is strong evidence that after 1952 a cadre of officers and senior enlisted men (representing the future Austrian army) was built into the gendarmerie.[88]

In June 1948 Chancellor Figl addressed a letter on the subject of U.S. training for Austrian security forces to Lieutenant General Geoffrey Keyes, U.S. High Commissioner for Austria. Figl requested General Keyes to authorize U.S. instruction in modern weapon techniques for a number of Austrian police and gendarmerie and "to place an adequate number of weapons at their disposal in case of need." The request specifically asked for instruction for 200 men in the U.S. sector in Vienna and for another 200 to be trained either in Salzburg or in Upper Austria. General Keyes's reply, although stating that it was impractical "at this time" to give weapons to the Austrians, agreed that it was desirable for the security forces in U.S. occupied areas to "be familiar with American weapons." Therefore, Keyes approved the training of Austrians by U.S. forces and suggested that the Austrian Ministry of the Interior establish contact with the U.S. Army officials responsible for organization and training.[89] A beginning had been made. By the fall of 1949 the U.S. Army was transferring supplies, equipment, and vehicles to the Austrian gendarmerie.

* According to a conversation with Oskar Helmer on April 5, 1961, an Austrian committee composed of Helmer, Julius Deutsch, Ferdinand Graf, and General Emil Liebitzky was established in the spring of 1948 to plan for the formation of the new Austrian army.

This was apparently all done under the project code name of "Kismet."[90]

The building of a mobile gendarmerie force capable of dealing with Communist uprisings was a difficult problem for the Austrian government, since money for the gendarmerie had to be budgeted for both the Eastern and Western zones, and the Soviet element kept a sharp eye on the annual budgets. In the budget for 1949, for example, which was submitted to the Nationalrat in December 1948, the expenditure estimate for the gendarmerie rose 35 per cent over the previous year, while that of the police remained the same.[91] In explaining this significant rise in expenditure, the government reporter of the budget explained that the increase was the result of an effort to motorize the gendarmerie. The extremely high increase in training expenses was simply due to the fact that a modern gendarmerie required it.[92]

The Russians had another explanation. At the meeting of the Military Directorate on April 26, 1949, the Soviet representative charged that the Austrian government was increasing the number of gendarmerie schools. Moreover, the gendarmerie academy in Graz, opened in March 1949, was conducting "Special Courses for Leading Gendarmerie Officials," including instruction in military tactics as well as training in the dispersal of demonstrations and the breakup of meetings. The Allied reaction to the Soviet charges was simply to ignore them. At no time, either at the Executive Committee or the Allied Council level, did the Western powers offer to allow the Russians to conduct an investigation of the gendarmerie in the Western zones either alone or on a Four-Power basis. To challenge the Soviet element to an investigation was the normal Western response to such charges; in this particular case, however, the Soviets received only vague answers that the armament of the gendarmerie was a question to be dealt with by each occupation power independently.[93]

On April 12, 1950, the Soviets brought the charge to the Allied Council that the Austrian government, with the support and training of the Western powers, had organized a mobile gendarmerie unit with headquarters in Linz. The first battalion was stationed in Upper Austria and Salzburg, the second in Styria, and the third in Tyrol and Voralberg; in other words, one in each of the three Western zones. According to the Soviets, these men were specially trained shock troops—*Alarmbataillone*—of some 500 men per battalion, complete with signal units, armored vehicles, and two rifle companies. The Soviet representative on the Executive Committee demanded that the situation be investigated. As in the case of the gendarmerie schools, the U.S. element never took exception to the facts of the charge, but merely stated that such matters were the concern only of the respective high commissioners.[94]

There is little doubt that the Russian charges were well founded and that the Western powers, in 1949 and 1950, were supporting the Austrian government in the creation of an elite group of gendarmerie whose primary mission was dealing with Communist uprisings and demonstrations in the Western zones. The situation in Austria demanded it if Western interests, which included the continuation in power of the coalition government, were to be protected. The direct intervention of the Western powers in any Communist general strike or uprising would have been difficult at best, and could very well have provided the Soviet forces with an invitation to intervene more directly and deeply in their own zone. Austria now had a well-trained, mobile, and completely loyal unit capable of dealing rapidly with most internal threats to the stability of the coalition government. The sudden and total collapse of the Communist strikes in some of the Communists' most important industrial strongholds in the Western zones during September–October 1950 days was, as we will see, due in large measure to the use of these *Alarmbataillone.*

If the development of a mobile gendarmerie presented a ticklish problem for the Austrian government and its Western members, the formation of a cadre for an Austrian army carried the threat of an even more explosive issue. In a letter to the U.S. military authorities dated July 13, 1949, Austrian Vice-Chancellor Schaerf discussed the details of a projected provisional army plan which had already been the subject of broader consultation. Schaerf proposed that a land defense council be established within the Ministry of the Interior. This council would be charged with drawing up plans for the formation of a 20,000-man Austrian army of four brigades, the rank and file to be draftees.[95] Although no date is given when this force was to be formally organized, presumably it was to come into being immediately after the signing of an Austrian peace treaty. For at that moment the Western troops would be forced to leave Austria, and without a Western-oriented army that could be quickly organized, the Communists would have a good chance of taking over.

It was only in 1952, however, that hard evidence began to come to light that the Austrian government was actually proceeding with plans to build a cadre group which would form the nucleus of a future Austrian army.[96]

Evidence for this buildup may be found by examining the personnel registers of the gendarmerie for the years 1952 to 1958. Up to 1952 the upper ranks of the Austrian gendarmerie—that is, from captain up through general—included approximately 170 officers. Beginning in 1952, although the 170 figure for regular officers remained constant, two new categories were added to the upper ranks—"in excess" and "in addition for a time of temporary need." In 1952, 30 officers classified in the latter category were added to the register in the rank structure of captain. By the beginning of 1955 there were 260 officers in this special category, all at the captain level. In addition, there were three colonels, four lieutenant colonels, and 31 majors included in the "in excess" column. That is to say, in 1955 there were 298 officers in the gendarmerie under these special categories, while the number for regular officers remained at 170.[97]

In 1956, after the signing of the State Treaty, the number of regular officers was raised from 170 to 200, while 19 remained in the "in excess" column. If the additional 49 officers from the 1952 levels were taken from the special categories, that would leave 249 officers who seemingly disappeared between 1955 and 1956. Under these conditions it is hard to escape the conclusion that the Austrian army, which in 1956 had 11,315 officers and men, drew its cadre in large measure from the gendarmerie.[98]

In addition, it might be noted that the budget for the year 1955, submitted in December 1954, some months before a sudden reversal of Soviet policy brought Austria the State Treaty, which ended the occupation in a matter of a few months, contained an expenditure of 187.5 million Austrian shillings ($7 million) for the development of a so-called *Wachkoerper*.[99] This action particularly outraged the Soviet representative on the Allied Council. He said it was well known that this "guard corp" consisted of illegal formations in the Western zones. He said that the Russians considered it necessary that this appropriation be removed from the budget. The response of the Western representatives was characteristically evasive, and the Russians won neither the investigation they wanted nor removal of the item from the budget.[100]

But this is to go ahead a bit too far. By the spring of 1950 a rough balance sheet could be made out on the efforts of the two power factions in Austria to control the internal security forces. The initial Communist successes had been nullified by the results of the elections of November 1945, when Oskar Helmer was given the opportunity with Western assistance to purge those Communists not directly under Soviet control. The Soviet response was to neutralize the effectiveness of the police by stubborn refusal to permit the police to be properly armed, by periodic dismissals in their own zone, and by arrest of key police officials loyal to Helmer. Faced with this situation, the Western powers acknowledged the neutralization of the police, at least in Vienna, and then proceeded to arm and equip unilaterally both the police and the gendarmerie in their own zones. Emphasis was placed on the gendarmerie, presumably because it had the advantages of mobility, which the police did not, and because the gendarmes could be quartered and trained in relative seclusion.

The Russians, on the other hand, in the spring of 1950 still had control of the police system in their own zone, the loyalty of a majority of police commissioners in the Soviet-controlled districts of Vienna, and a counter to the *Alarmbataillone* in the Werkschutz. The events of September–October 1950 would reveal the comparative effectiveness of these two forces.

Soviet Industries in Eastern Austria

For all its concern with Austria's strategic position, the Soviet Union in 1945 was quick to exploit the economic advantages that occupation of Austria offered. In the wake of the Red Army came special units charged with dismantling and shipping to the Soviet Union, aboard expropriated rolling stock, factories, railway equipment, and anything else of known or suspected value. Particularly hard hit were the valuable oil-drilling and oil-processing installations of Eastern Austria where drilling rigs, diesel motors, and refining equipment were carted off.

After a few months of this haphazard and often senseless activity, Soviet military authorities sought to rationalize the process of exploitation by attempting to blend those sections of the Austrian economy in which the Russians were most interested into so-called "joint-stock" companies. Although Molotov was later to speak contemptuously of the "joint-stock" device because of the problems this particular form of economic exploitation caused the Russians in Yugoslavia and Communist China, the Soviet Union used this technique of joint ownership of important economic assets quite successfully in those former "enemy countries" overrun by Soviet armies.[1]

The arrangement was remarkable simple, but it served Soviet interests in two important ways: it provided raw and finished materials for the rebuilding of the Soviet Union while simultaneously giving the Russians a powerful lever within the "host" country. The Potsdam Agreement had given the Soviet Union possession of the German assets in a number of former enemy countries such as Rumania and Hungary. The Soviets later used these assets as their contribution to the formation of a series of joint-stock companies within the country concerned. For example, in 1945, the Soviet Union and Rumania formed an oil company—Sovrompetrol—in which the Russians contributed, as their share, the German holdings in the Rumanian oil companies. With Sovrompetrol, the Russians had a significant share of the most important single export of Rumania. Once established, the company with its extraterritorial privileges applied constant and intense pressure on its less fortunate competitors in Rumania and on the Rumanian government. This constant drain on the Rumanian economy contributed to the collapse of the government. In June 1948, a now politically reliable Rumania nationalized the entire oil industry.[2]

The Austrian counterpart of Sovrompetrol was to have been Sanaphta. And, as events would show, Sanaphta was intended to be only the first of a series of such companies embracing most of Eastern Austria's heavy industry.

The first sign of Soviet interest in binding the Austrian fields into a joint-stock company came in July 1945. Until this time the matter was one of delivering oil to the Russians, not ownership of the fields. It was not until August 30, a month after Potsdam, that the Russians came to the bargaining table with concrete proposals. The Austrian delegation at the meeting was headed by Julius Raab, who was at the time the Minister of Trade and Reconstruction in the Renner government, and Eduard Heinl who succeeded Raab in this post with the formation of the Austrian government after the November elections. Sanaphta, according to the Russian proposition, was to have had a Russian director and retained its concessions for 50 to 60 years. The financial arrangement called for a total capitalization of $27 million "equally" divided. The Soviet contribution was to have been the German-owned oil properties (which included British, American, and Dutch assets acquired by the Germans after 1938, mostly under duress, but purchased nonetheless). These properties the Russians assessed as having a value of 12 to 13 million dollars; to this they would add the rest of their capital in cash. The Austrians were to have provided as their cash contribution 13.5 million dollars over a period of five years—all this, it should be remembered, for the use of an Austrian natural resource.[3]

The Russian proposal was brought to the Political Council of the Provisional Government on August 29. Schaerf writes that Chancellor Renner felt obligated to recommend its acceptance, considering Austria's unfavorable bargaining position. Koplenig, of course, was championing the Soviet proposal and Figl also approved of it. Schaerf strongly opposed the measure, first, because he saw it as a partner-ship, in which "the one has only rights and the other only obliga-tions,"[4] and second, because he was "naïve enough" to believe that the Allies would not take "German property" without coming to some understanding with the country concerned—in this case Aus-tria—as to what a "German asset" was.[5] On the basis of Schaerf's objections, the Sanaphta proposal was turned down by the cabinet and the issue returned to conference.

This first rebuff of the Soviet proposals was followed by intensive negotiations, which went on until the middle of September. There is little doubt that the Austrians would have accepted a reasonable offer, but not one that would have meant the mortgage of this impor-tant natural resource for such a long and uncertain period.* On Sep-tember 4 the issue was again before the political cabinet, with the Russian delegation as well as Raab and Heinl just outside the con-ference room. This time Koplenig found that his motion to accept the Soviet offer was opposed by both Schaerf and Figl, although Renner still reluctantly favored the agreement.[6] Figl remembers that Koplenig, in one last futile attempt to win approval for the agree-ment, complained that the luncheon to celebrate the signing had already been arranged. The Russians got neither the luncheon nor the agreement.[7]

The fact that formal negotiations were suspended in September did not mean that interest in reaching an agreement had waned. Feelers for resumption of serious negotiations were put out by both sides until the late spring of 1946, and at one point Figl, who became chancellor in December 1945, was willing to agree to allow the Rus-sians to maintain their concessions for five years after the peace treaty was signed.[8]

In these negotiations the Soviets were in a powerful position. How-ever, their inflexibility, combined with the firm resolve of the Aus-trians not to bind the Austrian economy to Russian interests, de-prived the Russians of the joint-stock arrangement they so earnestly sought. There may have been one additional reason for the Austrians'

---

* Heinl (p. 311) speaks of "days and weeks of uninterrupted negotiations," when the Austrian delegation attempted to reconcile Russian demands with the reser-vations advanced by the Austrian side, which Heinl and Raab felt necessary to the very existence of Austria. The Austrians demanded that the preamble include a Russian guarantee that the Austrian partner would be free of all claims that might be raised by the foreign oil companies. This reservation and the Russian insistence on concessions for 50 to 60 years seem to have been the main points of contention.

refusal. According to Molotov, the agreement would have been signed in early September if the United States and Great Britain had not told Dr. Renner on the eve of the formal ceremony that, if Renner signed, they would not recognize the Provisional Government.[9] Whatever the cause, however, the joint-stock device, which was proving so successful in Rumania and Hungary, had failed in Austria. But the "German assets" could be used in other ways—less subtle but nonetheless effective.

During the first few months of the discussions on the joint-stock proposal, the Russians were most discreet on the meaning of the Potsdam decision on "German assets." The "Proclamation to the Austrian people," issued by the Allied Council when it assumed supreme authority in Austria on September 11, 1945, was very explicit when it stated: "The most urgent task is the unification and economic rehabilitation of the country, the elimination of the aftereffects of the war and Hitlerite misrule, and of German influence in the whole life of Austria."[10] This was a hopeful start, or so the Western Allies thought. The virtual collapse of the Austro-Soviet negotiations on September 15 broke the Soviet silence on the subject of the Potsdam concessions and how they chose to interpret them.

Following a number of unsuccessful efforts on the part of the Western Allies to reach some agreement with the Soviet element on a definition of "German assets" which would be acceptable to all the occupying powers, General Mark Clark, the American Commander in-Chief, pressed the issue at the Allied Council meeting of January 10. General Clark said that the United States considered this question of greatest importance and followed his remarks by introducing a resolution that called upon the members of the Council to agree that "until decisions are reached by the four governments concerning the interpretation and implementation of the general provisions of the Potsdam Protocol relating to German foreign assets in Austria, no attempts will be made to implement those provisions by unilateral action."[11]

The reaction of the Soviet member of the Allied Council, Marshal I. S. Konev, to General Clark's motion keynoted the position that the Soviet Union would consistently maintain on the jurisdiction of the Allied Council over the German assets: it had no jurisdiction, and he, Konev, was not empowered to reverse the decision made at the Berlin Conference. Konev made the concession, however, that the Soviet element did envisage the possibility that the Allied Council would discuss certain specific cases, if branches of the company involved were situated in different zones, or if there was some real doubt as to ownership.[12] At the January 30 Allied Council meeting a resolution was actually approved directing the Quadripartite Reparations Division to make such a study of specific cases where the property in question was situated in different zones and doubt existed as to ownership. This committee was to report back by February 6, 1946.[13]

Perhaps driven by a realization that the Austrian government was growing increasingly wary of Soviet attempts to force agreement on the joint-stock companies, the Russians took a step on February 2, a few days before the report was due, which made a mockery of the efforts of the Reparations Division. On that day a Soviet delegation appeared at the office of the Danube Steamship Company (Donau Dampfschiffahrtsgesellschaft, or DDSG) and announced that the company was now the property of the Soviet Union and the employees would henceforth take orders from a Soviet representative.

On February 14, the Austrian Chancellor, Leopold Figl, addressed a letter to the Allied Council questioning the Soviet action. As a result, the issue was raised by the Western Allies at the Allied Council meeting of February 11. Here Konev strongly contended that his actions followed the instructions of his government and were based on the Potsdam decisions. When the American representative raised the objection that the DDSG fell under the January 10 decision to discuss those companies of doubtful origin whose assets were in more than one zone, Konev replied:

The question of the DDSG is not doubtful. . . . Austria fought with Germany. In the record of the Moscow declaration is a statement that Austria is responsible for this participation in the war. . . . Our Governments at Berlin took all this into account. Anybody who wants to know anything about Berlin should ask his government.*

Frustrated in their efforts to achieve a Soviet-Austrian company for the control of the Austrian Danube, the Soviet Union had thus resorted to its trump card of the Potsdam Protocol. This action not

* Proceedings of the Allied Commission, ALCO/M(46)16, pp. 24–25, Meeting of February 11, 1946. The Danube Steamship Company, the first major Soviet acquisition under the terms of the Potsdam Protocol, is an excellent example of a "German asset." First organized in 1830, the company soon had a complete monopoly on Danubian commercial traffic—a situation that lasted until the settlement of the Russo-Turkish War in 1856. After enjoying a period of great growth in 1900–1914, DDSG suffered heavily from the results of the First World War, when the succession states, particularly Czechoslovakia, confiscated all the ships they could get their hands on. In 1938, the company, like most of Austria,

only assured the Soviet Union of complete control of the Danube from Linz to its mouth but served as a warning to the Austrians as to what might happen if they continued to resist the creation of a Soviet-Austrian oil company.[14]

There is little doubt that the seizure of DDSG and the subsequent confiscation of the oil fields, refineries, and business concerns under the terms of the Potsdam agreement were not carried out in the way the Russians would have preferred to acquire these properties. The joint-stock companies offered the advantage of legitimacy and local government support, whereas confiscation was awkward at best. From the moment the negotiations were first broken off, in September 1945, the Austrian Communists waged a tireless campaign to convince the Austrian people that these business seizures could be avoided if their political leaders would agree to formation of the proposed Soviet-Austrian joint-stock enterprises and send a trade delegation to Moscow. Johann Koplenig, the leader of the party, and one of the four Communists elected to the Austrian parliament in 1945, made the choice very clear. While speaking in parliament on May 22, 1946, he contended that, with "direct and friendly negotiations," complete clarification of the issues could be reached. Koplenig charged:

There is no doubt that it would be possible with good will to reach an agreement with the Soviet Union in all these questions, as other countries have already done. A typical example is Zistersdorf [a major oil field]. The Soviet Union, which on the basis of the Potsdam decisions can claim these oil resources, has offered to us a joint company, in which half the property would have been Austrian, the other half Russian, whereby the Soviet Union obligated herself to provide the entire technical equipment, to meet the needs of the Austrian economy in petroleum and petroleum products, and in addition to permit the income from the export of the Zistersdorf oil to flow into Austria. This suggestion was turned down in the interest of foreign capitalistic circles and their domestic cohorts.[15]

On March 22, the *Volksstimme* printed an open letter signed by the four Communist members in the Nationalrat. This letter called for renewal of the negotiations with the Soviet Union. According to

---

was in very poor financial shape—26 per cent belonged to the Credit-Anstalt (Austrian), 46 per cent belonged to an Italian-controlled banking firm, and the rest was scattered among private owners. With the Anschluss, both the share of the Austrian government and that of the Credit-Anstalt fell to the Germans, and thus the DDSG became a part of the Reichswerke Hermann Goering. Finally, in 1939 the Italian and private interests were eased out. The DDSG, then, by 1945 was certainly in unchallenged German possession. And if one ignores the circumstances of the German acquisition, the Russians were justified under the terms of the Potsdam Agreement in claiming it as a German asset.

the Communists, such action would alleviate the serious food situation and solve the oil shortages.[16]

Despite the DDSG seizure, or perhaps because of it, the Austrian government continued to hope for a negotiated settlement that would protect Austrian interests. On April 4, Austrian Foreign Minister Karl Gruber wrote to J. D. Kiselev, the Soviet political representative in Austria, asking on what grounds the DDSG was confiscated. Kiselev's reply of May 10, although stressing the fact that the Soviet Union was not prepared to renounce its general claims as specified at Potsdam, implied that he was willing to discuss individual cases. Encouraged, the Austrian government expressed its willingness to begin discussion on the DDSG, both as to ownership and future cooperative management. The Soviet reply to this proposal, dated May 24, said that the Soviet government was ready to begin negotiations on this basis.

Hardly had the Austrian side received this reply, and before they could properly prepare their case, the Austrian delegation was summarily called to begin the talks. At the first meeting the Soviet delegation showed scant interest in limiting negotiations to the specific problem of the DDSG. With little ceremony they raised the question of an Austro-Soviet trade agreement and the Zistersdorf joint-stock company. The Austrian delegation immediately broke off the discussion.[17]

To this last determined effort of the Soviet Union to force Austria into the trade agreement joint-stock mold which would have given the USSR the same economic levers in Austria that she had so carefully forged in Hungary, Bulgaria, and Rumania, *Volksstimme* added a chorus of threats alternated with inducements. On June 5, for example, *Volksstimme* reported that the Soviet Union was willing to resolve the Potsdam decision on German property in such a way as to guarantee that everything that was Austrian property before 1938 would so remain and that Austria would pay no reparations (the fact that the Potsdam Protocol had lifted all reparations demands from Austria was still officially unknown). Those installations erected by the Germans during the occupation, consisting mainly of war industries, would in principle be confiscated. The Russians, however, were willing to see their claims become part of the capital necessary for the formation of Austro-Russian companies. In this way, it would be assured that the properties would not fall into the hands of "Fascists or foreigners."[18]

Both the pressure of the Soviet negotiators and the ragings of the

Communist press were to no avail. The Austrian government stood firm in its decision to resist all efforts to force Austria to be a willing signatory to the economic exploitation of the country.

Finally General L. V. Kurasov, the new Soviet High Commissioner for Austria, issued General Order No. 17, dated June 27, 1946, ordering the confiscation of all German properties in Eastern Austria.[19] This order was the basic authority for the confiscation of a vast network of oil fields, mines, and light and heavy industry that were to form the basis of a Soviet extraterritorial enclave in the Russian-occupied zone of Austria. This sprawling complex, employing thousands of Austrian workers, consisted of three organizations: SMV (Sowjetische Mineraloelverwaltung), which exploited the oil fields in Eastern Austria; USIA (Upravlenye Sovietskovo Imushchestva v Avstrii), a diversified group of concerns engaged in all aspects of commerce and industry, including agriculture; and DDSG (Donau Dampfschiffahrtsgesellschaft), a company controlling transportation on that portion of the Danube within the Soviet zone.

On July 9 an interview with General G. K. Tsinev by a Tass correspondent was published in many of the Austrian papers, in which Tsinev sought to clarify the order. Tsinev began by recounting the terrible Soviet losses during the war. The German assets, he said, were awarded to the Soviet Union to help cover these extensive losses. To the question of which properties were to be considered German, he replied that the order would include the property of all Germans in Austria up to 1938, all property brought to Austria since 1938 by the Germans, and all property erected by the Germans since 1938, including those enterprises reconstructed by the Germans. In addition, the order would affect all property purchased by the Germans after 1938, provided a fair price was paid. Tsinev contended that the property seizure would affect "not more than 10 per cent of the industrial capacity of Austria."[20]

The American reaction to the Soviet order was well timed, coming on the next day, July 10, when the Austrian parliament met to debate the Soviet action. General Clark's letter to Chancellor Figl made it clear that the United States would recognize no transfer of property not in accord with the spirit of the Moscow Declaration. Furthermore, in a gesture that helped to establish his reputation as one of Austria's most outspoken supporters, Clark expressed the willingness of the U.S. government to enter into negotiations with the Austrian and the other Allied governments with the objective of reaching a general settlement on the German assets question. He said further that while these negotiations were in progress, the United States would be willing to give over in trust to the Austrian government all such properties then held by the U.S. occupation authorities.[21]

Chancellor Figl's speech on the confiscation order to the Austrian parliament on July 10, 1946, was delivered in an atmosphere of intense bitterness. To Figl, as to most of the members, the Soviet order threatened the very existence of Austria. The Chancellor protested that the Moscow Declaration had promised that the Austrian people would be given the opportunity to create within Austria a framework of political and economic security that would serve as the only practical basis of political freedom. Now, by virtue of the Potsdam decisions, the text of which was never given to the Austrian government and had to be gleaned from newspapers and unofficial sources, crippling reparations were demanded. As far as the Austrian government was concerned, Figl continued, "German assets" in Austria concerned only those properties held by Germans before 1938. Figl ended his speech with a dramatic appeal to the occupying powers:

The Austrian population has endeavored honestly and diligently to again create the foundation for the rebuilding of the country. We know only too well that we are only at the beginning and we must accomplish much more. A prerequisite of this is that they must not take from us the hammer, the shovel, and the plow. We ask nothing more than this: Let us Austrians work![22]

The plea went unheard and the confiscations proceeded unchecked.

In the months following the general confiscation order, the Russians went to great lengths to demonstrate the complete legalities of the seizures. Beginning in July with two notes to Chancellor Figl, the Soviet authorities described in great detail the type of concern that would be affected and on what basis the companies were being confiscated.[23] The Soviet officials, for example, continually expressed their willingness to make up the difference between the actual price paid by the Germans for certain concerns and the fair price. In an article in *Pravda,* written in 1947, the Russians, in justifying the confiscations, had made extensive use of both Austrian and German materials to disprove the contention that the German assets were built by Austrian labor and materials.[24]

Such legal refinements meant little to the Austrian people. Their resentment was aptly expressed by Ernst Molden, editor of the independent newspaper *Die Presse,* who commented that "in spite of the Moscow Conference and a vast array of other statements, 'this liberated state,' this 'first victim of Fascist aggression,' is burdened with unofficial reparations, the extent of which cannot be measured."[25]

I

Of all the areas of Eastern Europe where the Soviet Union organized and controlled important sectors of the economies of occupied countries, the Austrian case is perhaps the richest in background material. After the Soviet Union gained an economic foothold in Austria, its managerial techniques developed, and a study of this evolution provides useful clues on why the Russians finally abandoned Austria.

Overall direction of the USIA/SMV complex came from the Soviet State Administration for Property Abroad (Gusimz), which operated in close connection with the Ministry of Foreign Trade. Financial supervision of the Soviet properties was provided by a Soviet military field bank located in Vienna. The major accounts of the individual plants were held by this bank, although the Soviet military bank maintained accounts in banks throughout Austria where Austrian firms could pay their bills to the Soviet complex. The individual firms were held to an absolute minimum of working capital and all profits transferred immediately to the Soviet military bank. Very little capital was allocated for reinvestment in the USIA concerns, in contrast to the substantial investment made in developing the oil fields. This lack of reinvestment capital contributed heavily to the general deterioration of the USIA firms and their gradual inability to compete with Austrian-owned business. The overall operation of the USIA complex was clearly directed toward maximum short-term profits and the exportation of such profits.

On the working level, once a firm was confiscated by the Russians, a Soviet general director, a Soviet management engineer, and a Soviet chief accountant were placed in charge. The bulk of the administrative positions, however, were held by Austrians, often Austrian Communist Party members. Placing local Communists in these positions contributed not only to the security of the firms but to the solvency of the party.

Sowjetische Mineraloelverwaltung (SMV)

From the very first moment that the Russians pressed for a joint-stock petroleum company, it was apparent that their prime economic target in Austria was oil. In recent years the Soviet use of oil surpluses as a weapon in the cold war has tended to obscure the fact that in 1945 the Soviet Union was desperate for oil. The production of Soviet domestic oil was well below the 1940 production level. During the war many of their fields had been badly damaged, and they suffered as well from a lack of exploration and development.[26] By 1945, then, the Russians were seeking a ready source of oil. In this connection, it should be noted that in March 1946 the Soviet Union was forced to withdraw from northern Iran, which it occupied under the terms of the Anglo-Soviet-Iranian Treaty of 1942. The Soviet Union had announced in early 1946 that it intended to remain in this oil-rich area. Nevertheless, pressure from the United States and Great Britain through the United Nations caused the Soviets to reverse their decision and remove their troops.[27] Stymied in Iran, the Soviets scarcely a month later stepped up their efforts to get control of Austria's oil. When they failed to establish a joint-stock company with Austria, Order No. 17 provided the answer. The fields were confiscated and organized under the direction of the SMV.

The SMV had its main distributive office in Vienna's First District, including a security section and an office for geological exploration. The distributing agent for the petroleum products that remained in Austria was OROP (Osterreichische-Russische Erdoelprodukte), organized in October 1946. OROP grew to have some 800 employees and hundreds of service stations throughout Eastern Austria.[28] When it was returned to Austria in September 1955, SMV embraced the bulk of Austria's oil industry, consisting of 24 concerns and 9,206 employees, with a gross production worth almost three billion Austrian schillings ($115,000,000).[29]

The seizure of the oil fields and refineries by the Russians was immediately applauded by the Communist Party of Austria. In justifying the Soviet action, they held that the facilities belonged either to the Germans or to other foreign interests, and they emphasized that Austria's share was actually less than 5 per cent.[30] But this argument convinced few Austrians, and Soviet control of the oil fields continued to be a sore point and a source of embarrassment to the party.

The Austrian government and the Western Allies were soon to discover the meaning of Soviet control of the fuel supply. On July 20, 1946, Eduard Heinl, the Austrian Minister of Trade, informed the Allied Council that he had received notification on July 12 that for the month of July, Austria would receive 3,500 tons of gasoline. Heinl maintained that the minimal requirements for July would be 6,000 tons. He asked for information on this and further requested that Austria be given the power to take over control and distribution of the petroleum products.[31] At the Executive Committee meeting on July 23, the British members protested that Soviet control of the production and distribution of oil products violated the promises made by the Soviet government's representative himself. General Tsinev abruptly replied to these protests: "I would like to recommend one measure. Minister Heinl should have sent this letter to the Soviet element, then he would receive an answer."[32] The Allied Council took up the issue again briefly on July 26. The discussion was brief; General Kurasov was blunt in expressing the attitude of the Soviet government on the Austrian refusal to come to terms on the joint-stock company and in showing how the Soviet element intended to operate the fields. Kurasov, in responding to Western attempts to place the issue on the agenda, stated:

The policy as regards POL [petroleum and its products] is quite clear. This may be settled by the two parties—the Soviet element which has some authority to deal with this question, and the Austrian government. But as the negotiations on this subject were interrupted by the [Austrian] Government, now the control and production of POL is exercised by the Soviet Element. The Soviet Element is determining the POL policy and there can't be any other source. I refuse to discuss this item on the agenda and I move this item be deleted.[33]

When pressed on when he might discuss the issue, Kurasov ended Soviet participation in any discussion of the oil question firmly and permanently when he replied: "Not today—not later—never."

By 1948 the Western Allies, driven by critical shortages of fuel in Western Austria, were importing considerable quantities of fuel for themselves and the Austrians. Meanwhile, the SMV, through extensive exploration of new fields and installation of new equipment, was raising the oil production of the Austrian fields from 950,767 metric tons in 1947 to an average of 3,000,000 tons beginning in 1953. The new fields in Matzen, Bockfliess, Auersthal, and Aderklaa, developed in 1949–50, accounted for much of this significant rise in production.[34]

This increase in production, however, did not increase Austria's share of her own oil. From 1947 to 1955, 20,084,585 tons of crude oil were produced in Austria. Of this total, 34.2 per cent went into the Austrian market, 2.5 per cent was officially exported, and the remaining 63.3 per cent of the entire Austrian production from 1947 to 1955 was the exclusive property of the Russians. To cover its oil deficit, Austria was forced to import.[35]

With the production of oil under their control, the Soviets needed only a convenient system of export. The Second Allied Control Agreement provided the pretext. The agreement gave the Austrian authorities custom and control functions "which do not interfere with the

military needs of the occupation forces."[36] It was this last innocent
provision that gave the Soviets the legal right to import and export
any amount of goods. This normal prerogative of an occupying power
soon became the authority for the Soviet Union to export 11,000,000
tons of oil and tons of equipment and machinery.[37] In 1954, for
example, 76,900 tons of goods were shipped over Austrian rails to
the Soviet Union. Of this total, only 3.5 per cent was registered with
the Austrian Custom Control; the other 96.5 per cent went under
the immunity of occupation supplies.[38]

The cost to the Austrian economy of this wholesale pirating of
an important natural resource has been enormous. Granting the
many variances in exchange rates and petroleum prices and the actual
ratio of crude oil to petroleum products affecting the value of the
20,000,000 tons of crude oil produced in the years 1947–55, a reasonable estimate would run to at least $225,000,000 lost to Austria.[39] This
figure does not include the petroleum products taken in 1945 and
1946.

It is certainly ironical that this sum of $225,000,000 is so close to
the $250,000,000 in reparations that the Russians renounced at Pots-
dam. But this sum was not the only payment on the mortgage. By the
terms of the State Treaty in 1955, which ended the occupation, Austria was required to pay the Soviet Union an additional 10 million
tons of crude oil over a ten-year period.*

Upravlenye Sovietskovo Imushchestva v Avstrii (USIA)

Most of the enterprises seized by the Russians as German assets
were administered by one central organization—USIA—the initials
of the Russian title meaning the Administration of Soviet Property
in Austria. The central office of USIA was located at Trattnerhof 1
in the First or International District. Structurally, USIA was divided
into a number of production units, ironically enough called Aktsi-
onernye Obshestva or joint-stock companies. For example, the office
or component directing the leather and textile concerns was called
Letex; heavy machinery, Podyemnik, electrical machinery, Kabel. A
sales organization, an agricultural and forestry administration, and
offices for the sale of chemical and metallurgical products completed
the management of USIA.

On August 13, 1955, the Soviet Union returned to the Austrian
government 454 concerns confiscated under the terms of the Potsdam

* The requirement was amended in 1960 during Khrushchev's visit to Vienna.
Khrushchev, in a gesture of good will, cut the requirement of 1 million tons of
crude oil a year in half, and canceled the final year.

Protocol. Of this number 420 (including 109 agricultural and timber properties) were administered by USIA, 34 by SMV. The total number of Austrians employed by the Russians was approximately 63,000.[40] The number employed by USIA and SMV from the industrial sector of the Austrian economy was some 51,800 in April 1955, that is, 10 per cent of all industrially employed in Austria.[41]

The German assets taken over by the Russians can be divided into three large groups: German property in Austria owned before 1938, the so-called Deutsches Reichseigentum, and property acquired by the Germans in Austria between 1938 and 1945.

The first group would include such companies as Boehler, an important special steel works, and the Austrian branches of large German concerns such as AEG and Siemens-Schukert. In the second group, the Deutsches Reichseigentum, would fall most of the Herman Goering Werke in Austria, with its vast network of mines, transportation facilities, and plants (including the huge iron and steel works now known as VOEST). These were either built by the Germans from the ground up or developed from an Austrian base. The last group included the most questionable kind of German property—that acquired after the arrival of Hitler, including a good deal of property taken from the Austrian Jews.[42]

The question of ownership of the USIA concerns is immensely complicated. Many concerns, such as the J. M. Voith plant (heavy engineering, such as turbines and machinery for paper mills) were the property of German citizens who had lived in Austria since the beginning of the twentieth century. During the long and severe depression in Austria, others had gone into the hands of banking concerns—financial institutions which were often internationally owned —or to the Austrian government itself.[43] If we divide 210 of the most important USIA concerns into categories showing ownership in 1938 and 1945, the following pattern emerges:

German ownership in 1938 and 1945.................... 62
German firms founded after 1938....................... 35
Austrian property in 1938, German in 1945............... 36
Diverse ownership (German, foreign, Austrian) in 1938, German in 1945 10
Foreign property in 1938, German in 1945............... 9
Jewish property confiscated in 1938..................... 41
Foreign and German property in 1938, Austrian in 1945..... 3
Diverse ownership (German, foreign, Austrian) in 1938 and 1945 2
Austrian property in 1938 and 1945..................... 8
Foreign property in 1938 and 1945..................... 4

These figures indicate that of those properties seized by the Soviet Union and administered by USIA, some 90 per cent could certainly be considered "German assets" and subject to confiscation under the terms of the Potsdam Protocol.[44] In the absence of any specific definition, as might have been insisted upon by the Western Allies at Potsdam, the Russian definition of all property in German hands in 1945 was as good as any.

The desire of the Russians to demonstrate the legality of their actions and their avowed concern for Austrian interests are shown by the ritual they followed when taking over the plants. A Soviet military party would arrive, and papers ordering the transfer of the property would be produced. A Russian officer, invariably with the appropriate technical training, would assume the position of general director. Russian officers also normally took over as director of personnel and head bookkeeper. With the larger concerns this action was followed by a detailed newspaper account of the process. In these articles the emphasis was placed on the legality of the confiscation (always quoting the precise section from the Potsdam Protocol), on assurances that these plants would be producing primarily for the Austrian market, and on how markedly the conditions of the workers had improved since the transfer.[45]

This routine was then followed by a determined effort on the part of USIA to force the Austrian government to record the confiscated concerns as Soviet property in the registers of landed property. In August 1946, for example, the District Court of St. Poelten (Russian zone) approved the application of the Administration of Soviet Property in Austria to change the record ownership of the huge iron and steel works of J. M. Voith. The matter was referred to the Austrian Minister of Justice, who reversed the decision, contending that the matter of German property was the responsibility of the Allied Council. Angered by this and other refusals of the Austrians to confirm the legality of the transfers, the Russians maintained a steady and often threatening pressure on Chancellor Figl to reverse the decision of the Minister of Justice. In this they failed.[46]

In addition to the heavy machinery and electrical equipment sent to the Soviet Union, the USIA exports of timber, paints, and margarine to the satellite countries brought back, in addition to a certain amount of raw materials, a remarkable amount of consumer goods, such as tobacco, sugar, and kitchenware. These goods were then sold to the Austrian public through the so-called USIA-Laeden or retail shops. The existence of these shops was one of the most vexing problems the Austrian government had to face during the occupation. Here one could buy almost anything that is normally available in an American post exchange—typewriters, watches, clothing, nylon stockings, bicycles—all drawn from various parts of the new Soviet economic community. Especially galling to the customs officials and equally enticing to the Austrian public was the abundant supply of cigarettes and liquor. Foodstuffs, particularly scarce items such as sugar and butter, were available and cheap. The quality of goods was not always the best, but it was as good as anything else one could get in Austria. Few Austrians of modest means did not frequent the USIA shops in Vienna and Lower Austria.

The competitive advantages of the USIA shops over the Austrian retail store were overwhelming. The main advantage was that no customs duty was paid on any item sold—in the case of cigarettes and liquor the Austrian duty was, and is, extremely high—nor were taxes of any variety paid on the goods sold or the profits derived.

In 1950 the number of these shops began to increase markedly.[47] In 1952 it was reported in the Nationalrat that there were then 147 (92 in Vienna, 48 in Lower Austria, 3 in that part of Upper Austria held by the Russians, 4 in Burgenland; all the USIA shops were, of course, in the Russian zone). By 1955 the number had grown to some 200, with 100 in Vienna alone.[48]

The existence of these shops seems to have been embarrassing to the Russians, who endeavored to underplay their importance and to justify their existence. The Communist Party paper, *Volksstimme,* maintained that it was because profit went to the people that the prices were so low. Furthermore, it maintained, the refusal of the Austrian government to allow USIA goods to be sold elsewhere necessitated their sale in these outlets.[49]

The real reason for this expansion of the USIA retail store system can best be found in a Russian attempt to cover the mounting deficits of the USIA concerns through the sale on the Austrian market of tariff-free items. As the USIA firms became increasingly less competitive in the Austrian market, the Russians found it difficult to accumulate Austrian currency with which to pay the USIA employees. "Uncle Joe's Junk Shops," as they were called in Vienna, helped provide the Austrian currency to maintain the factories, to pay the workers, and to permit the most valuable products to be shipped to the Soviet Union and its satellites.

The Soviet Military Bank

The finances of the USIA industries, as well as the SMV and the Danube Steamship Company, were managed by a Soviet military field bank located in Vienna. On July 4, 1946, the Chief of the Administration of Soviet Property in Austria (USIA), Major General Borissov, ordered all credit institutions in the Soviet zone to transfer all German savings accounts and current accounts to Branch No. 2111 of the USSR military field bank in favor of the account of USIA. A further step was taken on July 25, 1946, when a circular was sent to the administrators of all concerns in the Russian zone, stating that from this date all financial operations affecting the Soviet military occupation of Soviet property, i.e., USIA, SMV, and DDSG, would be handled through the same Vienna office of the Soviet military bank.[50]

This Soviet military bank was a member of an extensive system of similar banks throughout the satellite countries and was probably directly responsible to the Soviet State Bank (*Gosbank*) in Moscow. It operated independently of Austrian law. All accounts of the concerns within the USIA complex, as well as those of SMV and DDSG, were held by this bank. Any financial dealings affecting the Soviet occupation were handled here as well. In addition, the Russian military bank advanced short-term credit to the USIA concerns.

The financial operations of the USIA concerns were run on a day-to-day basis. The head bookkeeper, always a Russian citizen, would transfer all receipts of the concern immediately to the Soviet military bank. The result of this was that the USIA concerns never had cash or credit on hand, and in 1955 practically all were in deficit to the bank. The lack of investment capital brought the USIA concerns ever closer to bankruptcy after 1950.

The Western Allies attempted to make the Soviet military bank an issue at the Allied Council, but the Russians consistently refused to discuss the matter. In the absence of any agreement on the transfer of frozen German accounts, the Austrian government could not prevent the transfer.[51]

With the establishment of the Soviet military bank the chain of extraterritorial prerogatives was complete. The entire production cycle was now firmly in the hands of the Soviet Union—raw materials, labor, plant facilities, transportation, marketing, and now banking.

II

The Soviet-administered concerns were a grave danger to Austria's economic life, retarding all efforts at reconstruction. As an occupied country, Austria had few weapons to combat the Soviet economic complex. In the Allied Council, the Soviet element refused to dis-

cuss it. Two lines of attack were devised by the Austrians themselves
—nationalization of some of the key industries seized by the Russians
and legislation prohibiting business with USIA. Both efforts failed,
and for reasons worth describing.

It would not be accurate to describe the Nationalization Acts of
July 1946 and March 1947 as purely a response to the Soviet confiscation orders. The Socialist members of the Provisional Government,
in harmony with long-standing Austrian Socialist ambitions, were
pressing for nationalization of many of the former German properties and other key industries as early as the summer of 1945. On September 5, 1945, a proposal nationalizing the power industry, the
mines, and the oil industry was approved by all three parties. Much
to the surprise of all concerned, the Russians refused to approve the
legislation.[52]

Up to this point the most outspoken champion of nationalization
in Austria was the Communist Party. Johann Koplenig put the issue
very clearly at a conference of Viennese Communists early in August
1945:

I come now to a further, very essential demand of our program, the demand
for confiscation and nationalization of German property and the property
of Nazi industrial barons, who have substantially contributed to bringing
Austria under the German yoke and leading her to destruction. Nationalization of the key industries and of those large concerns that have been
abandoned through the flight of the Nazis is one of the most pressing demands [*Lebensforderungen*] of our people and our new state.[53]

The September 5 decision of the provisional cabinet to nationalize
certain industries brought the enthusiastic response from the Communists that the first step had been made but that "the next ones
soon must follow."[54]

In any conflict of interest between the Soviet Union and local
Communist parties, the Soviet Union has invariably put its national
interest first—and so it was in Austria. The Russians were seemingly
indifferent to the never-ending barrage of KPO demands for nationalization. Until such time as the country was politically reliable, i.e.,
economically dependent, the Soviet Union was not interested in
nationalization of industries in Eastern Europe. The economic rehabilitation of Russia was paramount, and all ideological theories
of "socialization" were subordinated to this drive for recovery. This
the democratic parties and the Communist Party in Austria were to
learn.

The People's Party, representing the conservative interests, was the natural opponent of nationalization. Nevertheless, Chancellor Figl, a member of that party, in his acceptance speech at the Nationalrat after the formation of his government in December 1945, expressed a well-qualified support of nationalization. Figl conceded that, although "the overwhelming majority" of the Austrian people were for private industry, where private industry fails economically and socially, "appropriate measures" should be taken.[55]

The growing number of confiscations by the Russians, beginning with the DDSG in February 1946, however, was enough to stir up the most reluctant of nationalizers. By May 1946 both parties formulated bills nationalizing most of the key industries.[56] There is little doubt that any hesitations on this step, particularly by the conservative party, were stilled in the hope that nationalism would appeal to the "Motherland of Socialism" and that the confiscations would cease. Such hopes soon faded as the Soviet authorities increased the pace of confiscation during the period when the various bills were still being prepared.

Whatever difference existed in the party proposals fell away with the news of Soviet Order No. 17. On July 26 the Nationalrat met and passed the first nationalization law.[57] No longer were Austria's leaders naïve enough to believe that nationalizing the key industries would appease the great Socialist nation of the Soviet Union; their objectives now were simply to establish a legal claim on the industries in order to hold them for the Austrian people. The attitude of the Soviet military authorities toward the pending legislation was made perfectly clear immediately before the Nationalrat took up the issue. On both July 23 and 24, General Kurasov had sent sharp letters of protest to the Austrian government protesting the bill and charging that it was a blatant attempt to circumvent Order No. 17.[58]

Despite this protest the bill was passed. The decision was a painful one for the People's Party, and the speech of Dr. Eugen Margaretha, who represented the party, reads like the text of a funeral service.[59] The Communist delegates were in such an awkward position by this time that their only response to the proposed nationalization bill was to demand that the Nationalrat nationalize everything in sight.[60]

The First Nationalization Act nationalized the three largest banks, all principal mines, the largest steel, iron, and aluminum plants, the bulk of the petroleum facilities, the chief electrical plants, the auto, locomotive, and shipbuilding industry, and DDSG. The Second Nationalization Act, in 1947, placed all power facilities under state control. One must compare the list of USIA and SMV concerns with the list of enterprises nationalized in 1946 to understand what was going on and why the Soviet Union was so angered by the Austrian action. At least 60 per cent of the concerns affected were controlled by the Russians, including plants that employed 14,000 of roughly 63,000 in the entire USIA-SMV complex.[61]

The Austrian Socialists have long contended that it was their leadership in 1946 that eventually gained realization of their long-standing public ownership policies. This is only partially true. Karl Waldbrunner's contention that the principal credit for their success must go to Karl Renner and Otto Bauer is perhaps wide of the mark.[62] It would be more accurate to describe Marshals Kurasov and Stalin as the real architects of Austrian nationalization.

The Soviet Union chose to disregard the law, thereby delaying the entire nationalization effort until 1955. Thus the Austrian efforts to rescue the industries from the Russians through nationalization was a decided failure. Nevertheless, in the attempt, Austria had established a claim, however tenuous, on the German assets which it had not had before, and in the process gained a minor psychological victory not to be underestimated.[63]

Efforts to combat the flow of USIA products into Austria were as unsuccessful as the attempt at nationalization. But while Austrians may look with pride on the nationalization issue, the abortive attempt to boycott USIA and USIA products is a painful memory. USIA operations from 1946 to 1955 undermined not only the economic life of Austria but also the moral fabric of the country, for despite a series of halfhearted efforts to boycott USIA, the general response to the existence of this economic enclave with all its extraterritorial privileges was, quite simply, "business as usual."

Dr. Ernst Koref in 1952 was simultaneously mayor of Linz, in the American zone, and a member of the Nationalrat. In March 1952, Dr. Koref accused three citizens of Linz of doing business with USIA firms and thus contributing to tax evasion. Immediately a slander suit was brought against him. In the Nationalrat debate that followed, Julius Raab said in defending Koref:

I say here, not only must we recognize the fact that many concerns—and I say explicitly also in the Western provinces—have made themselves a party to delivering material to the USIA enterprises, but, furthermore, it is our duty to make known, as the Mayor of Linz has done in the legislative chambers, all those concerns that, for the pursuit of profit, strike down the Austrian economy. . . . You [who support the USIA concerns] are traitors to Austria's freedom.[64]

Brave words indeed, but hardly reflecting the realities of the situation. To act against the USIA concerns directly was, of course, impos-

sible, since they enjoyed the protection of the Russian military occupation. Action had to be limited to suppressing distribution of USIA
products and the goods imported from the satellite countries. This
could have been done by boycotting the USIA firms and retail stores,
legislating against those who did business with USIA or SMV, and
making public appeals. Whatever attempts were made along these
lines were totally unsuccessful. Austrian businessmen, consumers, and
even the government itself soon found themselves in the awkward
position of supporting the very system that was draining Austria's
economy.

In March 1954, at the Vienna Trade Fair, 79 USIA concerns were
represented. This annual affair is sponsored by the Austrian government, and the USIA concerns could have been barred. Very revealing is the fact that cartels were formed between Western Austrian
concerns and those of USIA with the objective of holding prices and
ensuring markets on both sides of the Iron Curtain.[65] The steel roof
for rebuilding of the Cathedral of St. Stephen, paid for in large part
by the government, came from a USIA firm (Waagner-Biro), as did
the steel curtain for the Burgtheater. At one point the Austrian government found for USIA 25 lessees to manage a number of large
agricultural concerns. Of the 25, 22 signed agreements with USIA
running anywhere from six to 20 years. The Austrian government
then proceeded to advance 5,000,000 AS in credit guarantee to get
the farms started.[66]

Legislating successfully against an organization as diverse and
pervasive as USIA would not have been easy. Could the Austrian
government have made it unlawful for a person to patronize the
Dianabad, one of the largest public baths in Vienna, because it was
controlled by USIA? In those hard times could one penalize the
harassed and often impoverished housewife for buying food at the
lowest available price, regardless of its origin?

III

By 1950, then, USIA and SMV were thoroughly integrated into
the general Austrian economy—much like a gigantic cancer whose
removal might kill the patient. From a purely economic point of
view the Soviet Union in Austria could be compared with the eigh-
teenth-century New Englanders who became wealthy from the cele-
brated "triangle" trade—West Indies molasses to New England, rum
to Africa, slaves to the West Indies. Similarly, the Russians employed
an endless variety of such triangles throughout Eastern Europe, with

great success. The Soviet Union had suffered cruel and staggering damage during the war; the land was bled white, and its peoples exhausted from years of turmoil. USIA and SMV were part of a highly organized system of export-import traffic that furthered the economic rehabilitation of the Soviet Union while simultaneously serving its political interests.

Despite the efforts of the Austrian coalition government to prevent the expansion of Soviet economic interests in Austria by refusing to accept the principle of joint-stock ownership, USIA and SMV became the only really permanent foothold gained by the Communists in Austria. The significant development of Communist trade union strength within the USIA/SMV complex remained one of the Austrian Communists' most important trump cards in combating and pressuring the coalition government. It was not until the fall of 1950, however, that they were forced to play it.

The Struggle for the Trade Unions

From 1945 until at least the fall of 1950, the Austrian Communists heavily invested time and effort in the Austrian trade union movement. They sought and finally won organizational parity with the Socialists and the People's Party in a nonpartisan and extremely powerful organization—the Oesterreichischer Gewerkschaftsbund (OGB). The OGB has a highly centralized structure and a membership base that is extremely impressive by Western standards, embracing all industrial workers, public servants, clerical workers, and even those in the professions. The membership in 1957, for example, included approximately two-thirds of those employed and more than 20 per cent of the entire population of Austria.[1]

This high degree of centralization that characterizes the OGB is in marked contrast to the almost complete lack of cooperation and coordination between the trade union groups, which hampered the effectiveness of the movement during the interwar period. The Free Trade Unions, for example, were the Socialist trade unions before World War II. Despite the fact that this federation in 1921 could boast of over a million members out of a total Austrian population of some 6,000,000, the federation itself was actually made up of 57 separate units, which, in the absence of a powerful central organization, often pulled in different directions. At the same time, a number of other wage earners and workers were organized either in a Christian Social Party trade union organization or a pan-German group.[2]

Moreover, the various factions of the trade union movement were controlled by the leading political parties, and the unions were often used purely for political purposes. From 1934 to 1938, during the period of Dollfuss and Schuschnigg, all unions, except for a single state-supported labor federation, were banned. In spite of this prohibition, however, the Socialist trade unions went underground, transferred a good part of their funds abroad, and under the flabby dictatorship of the Dollfuss regime continued to exercise considerable influence in Austria.

After the Anschluss the Germans abolished all unions and compelled the industrial workers to join the German Labor Front (DAF). Having been issued an *Arbeitsbuch,* the Austrian workingman spent some seven years without collective bargaining privileges or a voice in the formation of labor policies.

During the war many of the leading trade union officials of all political persuasions were imprisoned. The toll of those executed by the Nazis ran to at least 240. The most severe losses were suffered by the Railwaymen's Union, with 96 officials put to death, and the Engineering Workers' Union, with 48 executed. Most of these were Communists. The Communists gained considerable and well-deserved credit for their actions in the underground of the trade unions during the German occupation. Despite such individual acts of resistance, however, the Nazis soon stamped out all visible signs of an independent Austrian trade union movement. And so it remained until the spring of 1945.

I

As the field of battle moved slowly through the city of Vienna during the second week of April 1945, among those who emerged from the cellars in its wake was Johann Boehm, one of the most notable leaders of the pre-1934 trade union movement. Boehm made his way to the home of Josef Battisti in the First District, where he had heard that former trade union officials were assembling in the hope of pulling something from the ashes. On April 13, 1945, representatives of the three major trade union groups (Socialist, Communist, and Christian Social) met in Battisti's home. Here all three groups expressed interest in organizing a new, and this time unified, trade union. On the suggestion of Boehm a committee was formed.

After a series of conferences and discussions, the representatives of the three groups met finally in the administration building of the Austrian railway system opposite Vienna's West Railway Station. Boehm has written of this meeting: "While on the other side of the Danube heavy fighting continued, the trade union federation was founded. One can claim with justice that it was born under the thunder of cannon."[8]

Under the chairmanship of Boehm and Battisti the conference adopted the name of Oesterreichischer Gewerkschaftsbund (OGB)—Austrian Trade Union Federation—for the unified organization. The federation was initially to consist of 14 affiliated unions, with voluntary membership open to all wage and salary workers employed in Austria. The provisional leadership consisted of a representative from each of the affiliated unions, with Boehm unanimously elected chairman.[4]

The question must arise at this point why the Socialists and People's Party were willing, even anxious, to have the Communists represented in the new federation. After all, the last free election before Dollfuss became Chancellor demonstrated that the Communists represented not more than one per cent of the electorate. Moreover, Communist influence in the prewar trade union movement was negligible. Part of the answer is given by Lois Weinberger, a People's Party leader, who shared with Boehm and the Communist Gottlieb Fiala the triparty direction of the trade union federation. Weinberger later wrote of these first days:

[Like Boehm] Gottlieb Fiala seemed to be honestly concerned with the situation of the worker. . . . It was a great beginning. For the first time all employed workingmen were in a common, free and nonpolitical organization. . . . Who knows what would have happened in that confusing time if the Trade Union Federation had not organized the workers and, without religious or party prejudices, called them to participate in the rebuilding of Austria.[5]

That this common bond, this effort on the part of the democratic parties to form ranks with the Communists, soon broke tends to blur the memory of those first months, when Weinberger and others thought cooperation with the Communists was possible.

Part of the motivation for cooperating with the Communists came, of course, from the presence of the Red Army. Any reestablishment of the trade unions that did not please the Communists would not please the Russian military authority. On April 27, Boehm told a meeting of the trade union officials that a delegation headed by the Communist Fiala had gone to the Soviet army headquarters to discuss the question of recognition of the authority of the OGB by the Russians. The delegation was refused admission. Boehm also admitted that the negotiations between the three elements within the OGB on organization and representation had come to an impasse even before the delegation went to the Russians.[6]

Klenner's history of the Austrian trade union movement makes no mention of what the issues in question were, and he himself has also denied that there was any connection between the deadlock on organization and the refusal of the Russians to receive the delegation.[7] Nevertheless, the connection seems to be there. The Communists had at least two major demands during the formation of the trade union federation: they wanted the organization formulated along purely trade union lines and they pressed for complete parity with the other parties in the control of the federation.[8]

The first demand must have brought the Communists in sharp conflict with the People's Party, whose greatest strength in the labor movement came from those who would have been excluded from the OGB under the Communist proposal. Moreover, the Socialists' original plan would have made Boehm the sole chairman of a board made up of the elected representatives of the affiliated unions. From the Communists' point of view, this could hardly be described as parity of control. For at this stage, the Communists had no illusions on the ability of their party to win the support of one-third of the workers. If equality in the leadership of the OGB was to be achieved, better to do it before the workers themselves had a chance to decide.

During a special meeting, called on the initiative of Communist Party Chairman Koplenig, the two Communist representatives, Minister of the Interior Honner and Fiala, hammered out their differences with the Socialists.[9] Then on April 30, a new delegation consisting of Boehm, Weinberger, and Fiala went to the Russian headquarters and this time received permission to organize the workers.[10] The same day Boehm announced to the provisional representatives of the union that the original plan by which Boehm was to have been the sole chairman of the unified trade union had been altered and now there would be three chairmen: Boehm, Fiala, and Weinberger.[11] As a result of further bargaining, the first provisional executive council consisted of 27 members—15 Socialists, six Communists, and six Conservatives.

Finally, on May 8 the foundation of the Oesterreichischer Gewerkschaftsbund was officially announced and the long and extremely difficult task of organizing workers began.[12] The general confusion and lack of a cohesive common front, which was the lot of the labor movement during the prewar period, had convinced the Austrian trade union leaders that a change was needed. In the organization of the OGB, every effort was made to restrict the number of affiliated unions and keep the tightest possible control in the hands of the central organization. Owing presumably to the pressure from the

People's Party faction, the number had been raised from 14 to 16 unions. Both of these additional groups were made up of government employees. Nevertheless, the proliferation ended here, and there have been 16 unions in the federation ever since.

In addition to a strong central authority bolstered by membership dues ranging from 1 to 2 per cent of a man's earnings, the OGB soon developed a strong and vital press. By the end of 1947, for example, the OGB was distributing 29 different publications with a total monthly average of a million pieces.[13]

At first the presence of the occupation powers with their zonal restrictions impeded the growth of the OGB. In August 1945 the federation could count but 128,770 members.[14] The French occupation authorities, for example, refused to allow any trade union activity in their zone until September 17, 1945.[15] Finally, on October 8, 1945, the Allied Council approved a statement on labor policy which permitted the organization of trade unions "so long as their associations are not cloaks for Pan-German, Fascist, or militaristic purposes."[16]

Very shortly thereafter the British and American occupation authorities were to recoil from their initial approval of the new OGB and become increasingly suspicious of the rigid centralized authority of the federation. Johann Boehm was probably right when he suggested that the occupying powers, perhaps subconsciously, wanted to rebuild the trade union organization in the image of their own domestic trade union movement. Boehm also complained that "certain occupation powers" were opposed to a single trade union federation and the limitation of the participating unions to 16.[17] Boehm was undoubtedly referring to the United States and Great Britain. In contrast, the Russians were the champions of the strong centralized federation, with the finances controlled exclusively from the center.[18] At one point, the American authorities complained of the "monopolistic character" of the federation and strongly questioned the intention of the federation to limit membership to 16 unions.[19]

As was so often the case in occupied Austria, a change in circumstances was soon to produce a complete reversal of policy on the part of the occupying powers. The Western Allies would soon find themselves in the position of championing the right of the OGB to construct a rigidly centralized organization, while the Soviet Union became a strong advocate of "democratic" decentralization. However, for the moment both sides watched with increasing respect as the federation raised its membership from 128,000 in August 1945 to 625,000 in 1946 and again to 1,279,000 in December 1949.[20] The stakes were growing larger; control of the trade unions could mean control of Austria.

II

The very monolithic structure of the OGB tends to overshadow the fact that there are in Austria two other organizations designed to represent the interests of the working class. These are the Chambers of Labor (Kammer fuer Arbeiter und Angestellte) and Works Councils (Betriebsraete). Legally these bodies are separate and independent of the Federation of Austrian Trade Unions. In practice, however, they most often work together, although the very independence of the bodies, particularly the Works Council, is often a source of very real concern to the OGB. Both organizations were of great interest to the Communists. Winning control of them would have brought the eventual conquest of the entire trade union movement a great deal closer.

The Chambers of Labor were established in 1920, coming as the realization of the long-standing ambition of the working class to have a balance to the Chambers of Commerce and Industry. These chambers, with the national chamber located in Vienna, serve as the representatives of the working class on all administrative and legislative proposals directly affecting the working class. Reestablished in 1945, the chambers were given an extremely important function by the Austrian Nationalrat through the Collective Agreements Act in February 1947. By the provisions of this act the affiliated trade unions won collective bargaining rights in certain areas. These agreements are negotiated between the individual union and the industry concerned and relate to such matters as overtime and rest periods. The role of the Chambers of Labor is merely to provide advice and technical information. However, when it comes to negotiating wage agreements, the OGB is the sole representative of the workers.[21]

Communist hopes in the Chambers of Labor were quickly dashed. Their lack of success with the Vienna Chamber of Labor is a good example of what went wrong. The Wiener Arbeiter und Angestelltenkammer was reorganized in August 1945. True to the general Eastern European pattern, the Communists pressed for a unified chamber, with the members discarding all party labels. Here they encountered probably the most decisive force in the Communists' defeat within the trade unions, a fiercely proud and self-conscious Socialist faction which, despite all due deference to the principle of a nonparty trade unionism, refused to lose its identity.

Ignoring Communist protests that party labels would undermine economic recovery, the Socialist majority brought into being on August 25, 1945, a provisional Viennese Chamber of Labor consisting of 74 Socialists, 40 Communists, and 30 from the People's Party.* Over all Communist objections, the division of mandates along purely party lines soon became the pattern throughout Austria: after a good deal of horse-trading, the three factions decided, on the basis of area strength, how many provisional mandates or representatives each party would get. Thus, the first nationwide division gave 426 mandates to the Socialists, 155 to the People's Party, and 133 to the Communists. This division, although perhaps numerically favoring the Communists relative to their prewar strength in the unions, was clearly a defeat for the party. Deprived of the advantages of party unification, the Communists were subsequently forced to run entirely in the open. The results were disastrous. In the first national elections for the Chambers of Labor, in October 1949, the Communists feebly masqueraded as the Linksblock, or Coalition of the Left. Despite the cover, the number of Communist mandates fell from 133 to 56, while that of the Socialists rose from 426 to 508.[22]

Frustrated in their designs on the Chambers of Labor, the Communists could also find little comfort in the state of affairs in the OGB. Theoretically the OGB was above party; in practice the OGB became increasingly an appendage of the Socialist Party and, after the November elections, a staunch supporter of the democratic coalition. From the smallest organizational unit of the federation—the factory group —up through local, district, and provincial units, and finally to the trade union congress, which elects the presidium, the organizational skills of the Socialists paid increasingly handsome dividends. The Communists soon found that neither on the provincial conference level, which elected delegates from all the affiliated unions to the Trade Union Federation Congress, nor in the individual unions could the party find working majorities. The highest percentage of Communist supporters found at any time during the occupation period in any of the 16 affiliated unions was in the union of chemical

* The Communists were extremely disturbed by this turn of events, and the Central Committee of the KPO called a special meeting of the party trade unionists to discuss what to do about it. Nevertheless, the chamber, which met on August 25 for the first time in seven years, was constituted as the Socialists had demanded. The very audacity of this stubborn position is highlighted by the fact that the first meeting was held in the presence of three Russian marshals, including Konev. The Western Allies, it will be remembered, were not as yet in the city in force, and there was no particular assurance that they would ever be. *Volksstimme*, August 25, 26, 27, 1945; *Arbeiter-Zeitung*, August 26, 1945.

workers (Arbeiter der chemischen Industrie), where approximately 16 per cent, figured on a national basis, followed the party line.[23]

Certainly by early 1947 the Communists were fully aware that the tide was running out on their efforts to gain control of the trade unions. The Communist faction in the OGB was never able to improve its position in the upper levels of the federation. Representation in the presidium, aside from its value as a listening post, was of little practical advantage. The Communists were excluded from the propaganda media and were greatly outnumbered in the federation's hierarchy. Ironically enough, the very centralized system, with its strict discipline and rigid national structure—for which the Austrian Communists had joined with the Socialists and the Soviet military authorities in winning from the suspicious Western Allies—was now turned against its most outspoken champion. The Socialist faction, by virtue of this highly centralized structure, now had complete control of the finances of all the trade unions and could as well remove any trade union official found guilty of insubordination.[24]

By the end of 1946, then, the Communists could see about them only the ruins of their initial policy of infiltration and subversion of the Austrian trade unions. It was at this point, I would suggest, that they turned their full attention to the last of the Austrian trade union organizations—the Industrial or Works Councils (Betriebsraete). Routed in their attempts to take over the OGB from within, the Communists saw in the Works Councils a means of recouping their losses and eroding the dominant position of the OGB. Over the next two years, the Communists came remarkably close to their objective of winning control of the trade union movement from "below."

Fritz Klenner has very wisely observed that to the factory worker the Works Council is the "mediator and mouthpiece of socialism."[25] The Austrian Socialists after World War I were anxious to organize the workers at this critical factory level. Consequently, the first Works Council Act was passed on May 15, 1919. The law provided Works Council representation for all workers and employees, except those in agriculture and government service, employed in a firm or factory where there were more than four workers 18 years of age or older. In firms where fewer than 20 were employed, the employees were represented by one or two of their number, known as a *Vertrauensmann*. In those firms with 20 or more employees a Betriebsrat, or Works Council, was organized, with the number of representatives depending on the size of the firm. To support this council the employees were assessed one-half of one per cent of their salaries. In the case of a large concern, this would often amount to a great deal of money. Intimately involved with the everyday problems and thoughts of the workers, the Works Council became the point of most effective contact with the workers as the trade unions themselves grew more distant under the burden of a rapidly expanding membership.

According to the law itself, the purpose of the Betriebsrat was "to look after and advance the economic, social, and cultural interests of the workers and employees."[26] The Betriebsrat had the responsibility of representing the workers' interests in the implementation of the various collective agreements made between the trade unions and the industry. If the agreement did not cover all points relevant to a particular firm, the Works Council, with the cooperation of the trade unions and the management, adjusted the agreement. In addition, the Works Council was charged with the responsibility of working out local problems of overtime, work rules, discipline, and welfare programs. The council had the right to inspect all wage lists, examine the company's books, and to be consulted before a man could be fired.

Afterthoughts on the wisdom of granting a legally independent body so much power were not long in coming. In November 1919 the first Austrian Trade Union Congress was held in Vienna. Here a representative of the trade unions voiced the fear that the members of the Works Councils were no longer the representatives of the trade union movement but potentially a parallel force.[27] Such fears, however, were soon stilled, since the potential power of the Works Council to operate outside the interests of the general trade union movement and to participate in the management of the concern never developed. The long series of economic crises culminating in the depression of the 1930's so weakened the Austrian trade union movement that the capricious use of power by the Works Council during the interwar period never seems to have become an issue. With the reestablishment of the trade union movement in 1945, the re-creation of the Works Councils became a very natural step. On September 15, the OGB issued a directive calling for the reorganization of the Works Council in the spirit of the 1919 law and provided information directly out of the 1919 law on how it was to be done.[28] Oddly enough, there was absolutely no clear legal basis for the reorganization of the councils. Nevertheless, the project was pushed by the OGB, and one way or another the firms accepted their existence on a temporary basis. Elections to the councils, according to the directive, were to be completed by December 15, 1945.

Thus, in a rather willy-nilly fashion, the Works Council returned to the Austrian scene. However, as a result of the immediate postwar confusion, the first elections to the Works Council attracted little attention. What was important was the considerable effort required in just getting the factories back in operation. Precisely how the workers were organized was a secondary consideration.

This is not to say that the Communist Party was not initially vitally interested in the Works Councils. In terms more honest than those used after 1945, the KPO, as early as 1921, had made its intentions with respect to the Works Councils quite clear. To the Communists, "the question of the trade unions and the Works Councils is important not only for the Communist movement in Austria but for the entire Communist International because they form the basis and the departure point for the coming proletarian revolution."[29]

After 1945 it was more a question of emphasis. The inability of the Communists to turn the OGB into a true united front movement was a hard blow, and the Communists knew it. Time was working against them as the Socialists boldly consolidated their dominant position in the OGB.

A most significant change in Communist trade union tactics was revealed at the 13th party day of the Austrian Communists, in May 1946. Up to this time the basis of the party's organizational structure had been the city block cell and the factory cell. The cells elected the section leaders, who in turn elected the city district leaders. The chain then continued through the city organization all the way to the national central committee. To the Communists then, the cell was the "finger on the pulse of the population . . . the ears of the party."[30] At the May meeting, however, a radical change in its organization was announced. Henceforth, the most basic unit of party organization would be the *Betriebsorganisation* (factory or firm organization), that is to say, the organization into individual units of those party members who were employed by a particular factory, office, shop, or mine.[31] As a result of this reorganization the block cells were completely eliminated. All unnecessary duplication was avoided. The success or failure of the Communist Party in Austria's trade union movement was firmly tied to its ability to make the *Betriebsorganisation* a center of party strength.[32] The *Betriebsorganisation* was placed under the *Ortsgruppe* (section group). Then came the *Stadtorganisation* (city), and above the city a *Bezirk* or district organization. This vertical chain of command continued right up to the party congress. The call soon went out to the entire party:

"Look to the *Betriebe*—make the *Betriebe* an indestructible bastion of our party."[33]

The first objective of the Communists, after deciding to concentrate on the Works Council, was to increase the independence of the councils. Franz Honner keynoted this tactic when he demanded, in the name of the party, a new Works Council law—a law that "above all guarantees the immunity of the Works Council representatives and their officials."[34] He also called for a change in the *Gewerbeordnung*, or industrial code, which would have removed the district discipline applied to workers who incite wildcat strikes.[35]

The beginning of 1947 brought the long awaited new Works Council legislation to the Nationalrat. The Communist parliamentary faction, which had long supported what it termed "democratic centralism" in the trade union movement, suddenly became the champion of an advanced form of democracy in the Works Council. During the debate on the bill to legalize the reorganization of the Works Council, the Communists fought a hard but ultimately unsuccessful battle for the right of *Mitbestimmung*, or codetermination, to be given to the Works Councils. Such a provision would have given the Works Councils the right to participate directly in the management of the concern.[36]

The other 161 delegates in the Nationalrat, however, were not impressed by the Communists' arguments, and *Mitbestimmung* proposals fell on barren ground.

On March 28, 1947, the new Works Council law was passed by the Austrian parliament.[37] The law was essentially a reenactment of the 1919 legislation. Despite Communist protests, the right of "codetermination" became, in the language of the law, an innocuous *Mitwirkung*, or cooperation with the workers in the management of the concern.[38] The Works Councils, however, retained their legal independence and responsibility for the adjustment of such local issues as overtime wages, working conditions, and welfare programs. The new measure also provided that the Works Councils would assume their old prerogative of negotiating with the concerns when a particular collective agreement did not cover local conditions.

It was not until May 29 that the issue of the Works Councils was brought up by the Soviet element at the Allied Council. Reflecting the deep chagrin and frustration of the Austrian Communist Party, the Soviet representative strenuously objected to the bill and demanded its rejection. The Soviets maintained that the law in its proposed version violated the basic principles of democracy. Inasmuch as the 31-day period of examination had already expired, the

Russians proposed that the Allied Council order the Austrian government to draft a new law. According to the Soviet representative, "By this law, the industrial [Works] councils are transformed from a public organization of toilers to a government appendage; by this law the basic principles of democracy which public organizations should enjoy are undermined."[39] The Western Allies refused to take any action on the bill and therefore the Soviet objections came to nothing.

The implications of the Communist program to win for the Works Councils the right to participate in the management of firms and factories are clear enough. If the Communists could gain control of a significant number of Works Councils, they could, by wielding the club of *Mitbestimmung,* disrupt the entire economic life of Austria. Under such conditions the economic recovery of Austria and her capacity to successfully resist the many-faceted pressure of communism would have been brought into serious question.

As it was, the Works Councils, even without the right of *Mitbestimmung,* were still a powerful force. Years after the threat of a Communist takeover had receded, Fritz Klenner, a leading figure in the Federation of Austrian Trade Unions, expressed misgivings about the wisdom of putting so much power in the hands of the Works Councils and warned of the dangers of *Betriebsegoismus* (company self-centeredness) when he wrote:

The Works Council Representatives in many large concerns are today men who are in no way willing to maintain the necessary contact with the trade union. The Works Council law gave to them a great deal of independence, which, if need be, they use against the trade union. . . . The representative [*Vertrauensmann*] in the concern was formerly the representative of the trade union. Today the trade union is practically more dependent on the Works Council than the Works Council on the trade union.[40]

The point should be clearly understood that Klenner was not talking specifically about Communist Works Councils, for the influence of the KPO in the Works Councils by 1956 was very small, but about Works Councils in general. In Klenner's view these men were damaging the entire trade union movement by taking a narrow view of their situation. They often used their independent power, perhaps in collusion with management, to win something for themselves that was often detrimental to the best interests of the entire trade union movement. Yet the OGB with all its power was unable to cope with the problem, and could only recommend increased indoctrination of the Councils.

With this in mind it should not be difficult to understand the Communist's single-minded efforts to control the Works Councils. These Councils represented a force independent of the OGB, with the added attraction of being the organization closest to the lives of the workers. During the period from the summer of 1947 to the fall of 1950, the Socialists and Communists engaged in a heated struggle for control of the Works Councils. To the Communists the Works Councils were a springboard to the final control of the OGB; to the Socialists they were a constant threat to the coalition government's control of Austria. The Works Councils elections in the fall of 1947 were the first test of strength.

III

The Works Council law went into effect on August 2, 1947. The elections to replace the provisional councils were organized at the factories, the specific procedural instructions provided by the government. Firms with five to nine employees elected one representative (*Vertrauensmann*), those with 10 to 19, two.[41] Every firm or factory with 20 or more employees elected three or more representatives to the company's Works Council, depending on the number employed. For example, firms with 20 to 50 employees elected three representatives, those with 50 to 100 employees elected four representatives, and so forth. Where the firm consisted of two or more branches, there would be a Central Works Council (Zentralbetriebsrat) elected by the members of the branch Works Councils.

Just how seriously the Communists took this election is best illustrated by the staggering amount of election material and time the party was willing to expend during the campaign. The Works Council was described as "the most important basic unit of our party," and the party faithful were warned that "only when the right political direction of those massed in the concerns is assured will the battle for socialism be successfully pursued."[42]

In concert with the Communist tactics throughout Eastern Europe, the Austrian Communists decided to advance their candidates on a unity list, the so-called Einheitsliste. In this way they hoped not only to appeal to those non-Communists in the trade unions who sincerely desired unity in the working class movement, but to mislead others.

This maneuver put the Socialists in a very awkward and potentially dangerous position. They appreciated the advantages of a united trade union and prided themselves on the nonpartisan facade of the OGB. To have allowed to go unchallenged the Communists' claim that the workers would now have the opportunity of choosing representatives who were above party, although these "unity faction" candidates were in fact either Communists or crypto-Communists, would have resulted in a serious erosion of the Socialists' strength within the Works Council.

Under the circumstances, the Socialists had no real alternative to labeling the Einheitsliste a pure Communist front and entering a Socialist list rather than allowing the workers and salaried employees to submit names for the election without party labels. In an article in the *Arbeiter-Zeitung* entitled "Unity or Unity Lists?" the Socialists maintained that the Einheitsliste was a Communist creature and that Socialists within the factories were already being threatened if they refused to vote for the unity candidates.[43] Karl Maisel, a leader in the Socialist Party and a cabinet member in the Figl government, explained the decision of the Socialists to enter candidates this way:

The decision of the Socialist faction to enter separate lists is the result of Communist tactics in the past. We will never allow ourselves again to be bamboozled by the Communists, who through their maneuvers want to represent their small minority as a majority. Now we demand clarity and want to see who has what.[44]

In September the following instruction went out to all Austrian Socialists: "The party leadership therefore instructs all party organizations to support the Socialist trade unions in all firms through the nomination of Socialist lists for the Works Council activity and to offer them every support in the election campaign."[45] The Communists were equally unequivocal on the issue of the unity lists. On the very day the Socialists rallied their party members to the support of the Socialists' lists, the Central Committee of the KPO issued the following directive: "In those concerns where the order of the Socialist Party executive board to split the working class holds sway and the nomination of trade union unity lists becomes impossible, we Communists will enter the election campaign with a Communist list."[46] The preferred way, therefore, was the Einheitsliste; where the circumstances did not permit it, they would offer a list with an unabashed Communist label. The result of the 1947 Works Council elections must be evaluated against this background.

One would assume that the results of the Works Council elections, conducted as they are under Austrian law, would be a matter of public record. This is not the case. Presumably to obscure the fact that Socialist influence in the Works Council is not as extensive as advertised, both the OGB and the Vienna Chamber of Labor draw a dis-

creet but impenetrable veil over the election results. This is not to
say that the statistics issued are not accurate and reliable. They are,
but unfortunately they are so general that they become almost meaningless as a reflection of Communist strength in the Works Councils.

To illustrate this point it is only necessary to look at the statistics
furnished by the Austrian Trade Union Federation of Works Council
elections. The table below,[47] as given by the OGB, shows the number
from each party elected in 1947 and 1949 to the Works Councils, or,
alternately, as *Vertrauensmaenner* for firms with fewer than 20 employees. These figures are the same as those reported by the OGB in
its progress report. Here, however, the breakdown of mandates in
three of the provinces is also given (Lower Austria, Burgenland, and
Upper Austria). The highest percentage of Communist mandates was
13.8 per cent in Lower Austria, which was the center of the Soviet-
controlled industries, as Klenner has pointed out.[48]

	Socialist	Commu-nist	People's Party	Indepen-dent	Party Affiliation Unknown
1947: Mandates	17,948	1,976	1,044	—	7,998
Percentage	62.0%	6.8%	3.6%		27.6%
1949: Mandates	19,599	1,873	1,547	333	8,602
Percentage	61.5%	5.7%	4.9%	1.0%	26.9%

On the basis of these figures it appears that in 1947 through 1951
the Communists commanded the loyalties of roughly 6 per cent of the
members of the Works Councils and *Vertrauensmaenner,* a figure not
appreciably higher than the 5 per cent figure the Communists reached
in the general elections in 1945. The feverish Communist efforts to
win a substantial hold in the Works Councils seems to have been
wasted. Yet as early as June 1947 the Communists claimed that in 335
of the largest factories in the provisional Works Councils of Lower
Austria, they controlled 34 per cent of the Works Councilors.[49]

The discrepancy here, and between all the figures on the Works
Council elections as distributed by the Communists and by the Socialist OGB factions, was simply a variation on the "numbers game."
The press laws in Austria were very strict, with falsification punished
severely. In addition, the Allied Council kept a close watch on all the
publications. The Western powers were always anxious to catch the
Communist press in a misrepresentation, and the Soviets were equally
eager to accuse the Western press of misstatement or slander. Therefore, any statistics, whether they were in the *Volksstimme* or the *Arbeiter-Zeitung,* were accurate as far as they went.

The figures offered by Fritz Klenner and the OGB tell next to nothing about the success of the Communists in their efforts to win control of middle-sized and large industrial concerns. In the OGB figures we learn nothing of the relative proportion of *Vertrauensmaenner* (from concerns with five to 19 employees) to Works Councilors, nothing of what percentage of the total, including *Vertrauensmaenner,* were in the industrial sector, nothing of the relationship of these figures to the size of the concern, and, finally, nothing of what was done with those who voted for the Einheitsliste.

Fortunately, there is one source of reliable and fairly complete information on the outcome of the 1947 Works Council elections. This is the report of the Styrian Chamber of Labor.[50] Besides providing a detailed examination of the Communists' performance in an important geographical area, this report is interesting for other reasons: first, Styria was at this time in the British zone and, therefore, free of direct Communist pressures such as were applied in the Soviet zone; and second, Styria is a highly industrialized region, with a large percentage of its workers employed in industrial concerns of considerable size.

The elections in Styria were held over a six-month period, from September 1947 to March 1948, with each plant or firm having the local option on specifically when the election would take place. The Socialists in Styria were represented on the factory ballot by lists of candidates labeled Liste der SPO or Liste der sozialistischen Gewerkschafter; the People's Party was represented by the Liste der OVP or Liste der oesterreichischen Gewerkschafter; and the Communists, where they could not win approval for an Einheitsliste, used such labels as Einheitsliste der KPO, Liste der KPO, or, as in the 1949 Works Council election, the Liste der Linkssozialisten or Linksblock. The Communists preferred the Einheitsliste, where, according to the party, men were elected on the basis of ability, not party affiliation. In addition, with the 1949 elections, the workers could vote for the list of so-called Wahlpartei der Unabhaengigen, the supporters of an independent nationalistic group with pan-German ideas. For those workers who wished not to be associated with any politically oriented list, there was the Liste der Parteilosen, the list of the politically independent.

In the entire province of Styria during the 1947–48 elections, for both *Vertrauensmaenner* (representatives of firms with fewer than 20 employees) and members of the Works Councils, the respective groups received the following percentages of votes cast:

148   *The Struggle for the Trade Unions*

Socialists	68.0%
People's Party	4.1%
Communists	13.8%
Einheitsliste	6.3%
Nonpolitical	7.8%

This breakdown shows that the Communist faction—Communists and Einheitsliste—received 20.1 per cent of the votes cast in the important industrial province of Styria, a province entirely within the British zone of occupation.[51]

In Styria there are three cities of major industrial importance—Graz, Leoben, and Bruck.[52] In Graz, which is representative of the other two cities, the election and the later division of mandates showed this division:

	Percentage of Votes Cast	Percentage of Mandates
Socialists	58.5%	57.7%
People's Party	4.8%	4.1%
Communists	8.1%	3.8%
Einheitsliste	10.8%	—
Nonpolitical	17.8%	34.4%

How was it possible for the Communist bloc (Communists and Einheitsliste) to have won 18.9 per cent of the votes and received only 3.8 per cent of the mandates, while those described as nonpolitical received some 18 per cent of the votes cast but 34 per cent of the mandates? One answer is provided by the OGB itself. In its activity report covering the period from 1945 to 1947, the OGB admitted that its figures on the Styrian elections and those issued by the *Arbeiterkammer* in Graz were "essentially" different. The OGB offered the following explanation:

1. Many more of the results were reported to the *Arbeiterkammer* than were reported to us by the individual trade unions.
2. [The Graz results] followed a division of the votes and mandates into five groups. *We divided the mandates according to party affiliation.*[53]

Considering the well-advertised circumstances of the election, such a division was completely absurd. The Einheitsliste, by the Socialists' own admission, was a pure Communist front; to divide the mandates won by this list by "party affiliation" was a contradiction in terms. This method of assessing Communist strength in the Works Councils is open to serious question. The fact that the OGB of the Chambers of Labor gave a political label to the members of the councils had little to do with the actions of the individual council members. It will be recalled that the Works Councils were independent bodies not subject to the discipline of the OGB. Whether the OGB chose to call a man elected from the Einheitsliste a Socialist was quite beside the point when it came to the man's actions.

Until such time as all the individual factory figures become available, a complete, accurate assessment of the extent of the Communist success in the middle and larger concerns in the industrial sector will be impossible. However, from the reports of the Styrian Chamber of Labor and a thorough newspaper check of the results as they appeared, certain conclusions can be drawn. First of all, the Communists had the support of at least 20 per cent of all those who voted in the Works Council elections. Second, the larger the factory or firm, the greater the Communist strength; in the largest concerns this might in all probability amount to between 30 and 35 per cent, with the Socialists not controlling more than 40 to 45 per cent.

Demonstrations, riots, and general industrial unrest are best cultivated and organized in well-developed industrial areas made up of large factories. The Communists in Styria, as a result of the first Works Council elections, had made an excellent start in organizing an assault from below on the trade unions.

In the Russian-controlled plants in Eastern Austria, the problem of controlling the workers through the Works Councils was much easier than in Styria. All the pressures available by virtue of the Soviet administration of the plants—threat of firing, loss of seniority, suspension of welfare benefits—could be brought to bear on the workers in order to force them to vote for the Einheitsliste. *Volksstimme* reported with pride in November 1947 that a majority of the Soviet-operated plants had voted for the exclusive use of the Einheitsliste.[54]

The plant-by-plant results of the Works Council elections in the Soviet-controlled industrial complex reveal some interesting statistics. In those plants where a Socialist list appeared on the ballot, the Socialists did remarkably well, very often winning more mandates than the Communists.

The Communist grip on the Works Councils in the oil fields, however, was from the beginning particularly tight. In November 1947 the elections in the fields were completed, giving the Communists 65.7 per cent of the mandates, with 28.3 per cent going to the Socialists.[55] This figure apparently did not include the 28 Works Councilors (all Communists) representing the Werkschutz—plant guards —and the fire department who were assigned to the oil fields. There are two good explanations for the extent of Communist influence in the oil industry. The first is certainly the importance of the oil fields to the Soviet Union, particularly in the first few years after the war. To ensure continued oil deliveries, it was imperative to have stability, labor, and peace in the oil fields—Communist stability and Communist labor peace.

The second explanation may be extended to many concerns throughout Austria. Where the factory or industry concerned was developed after the Germans arrived in 1938 and a new source of labor was brought in, Communist influence after 1945 seems invariably to have been strong. This would apply both to the oil industry and to the heavy iron and steel plants. Here the Socialist trade unionists had no chance until 1945 to organize the workers, and these workers were prime targets for Communist propaganda after 1945. This fact alone says volumes for the successes and failures of the Communists in the Austrian trade unions.

Adding what we already know of the Communist successes in Styria to the success in the Soviet industries in Vienna and Lower Austria, it would be safe to say that Communist influence in the Works Councils of these three most important industrial areas after 1947 was very strong indeed. But to the Communist leaders this was but the first step.

The Communists were jubilant over the results of the elections. *Weg und Ziel,* the official journal of the party, saw the elections as proof of the political wisdom of anchoring the party to the *Betriebsorganisation.* Although the Communists admitted that there were still great weaknesses in the small and middle-sized concerns, the future was very bright. On the basis of the election returns, they concluded that they would substantially improve their position in the next national elections.*

Communist pleasure with the results of the campaign to gain control of the Works Councils and the steps to be taken in the future

---

* "Bilanz der Betriebsratswahlen," *Weg und Ziel,* VI, Nr. 1 (January 1948). The 1947 Communist lists for the Works Councils in the Donawitz plants in the Leoben area of Styria received a total of 2,261 votes, while in the November 1945 national elections the KPO had won only 2,424 in the entire Leoben area. Again in Eisenerz, the Communist list in 1947 won 953 in the Erzberg mines alone, in contrast to the 1945 national elections, when the Communists received only 982 votes in all of Eisenerz. From this the Communists assumed that they would make great strides in the 1949 general elections. In fact, however, in 1949 the KPO received only 3,623 votes in Leoben, and 1,041 in Eisenerz. Apparently many workers preferred the security of the national polls to local factory polls for expressing their real feelings. Austria, "Die Nationalratswahlen von 9. Oktober 1949," pp. 26, 49.

were highlighted in the 14th Communist Party Congress in the fall of 1948. The assembled Communists were told by a member of the Central Committee that there were many on the occasion of the 13th Party Congress who did not realize the value and meaning of the reorganization of the party on the basis of the concern (*Betriebsorganisation*). Since that time, the number of workers organized in the some 800 *Betriebsorganisationen* had risen from roughly 18,000 to 36,000, that is, to some 24 per cent of the entire membership of the party. In addition, in those 16 large concerns with more than 2,000 employees, the party now had 4,500 members.[56]

As if to underline the growing emphasis on the Works Councils, the 14th Party Congress approved a resolution of the Central Committee for the implementation of a new party statute which placed the *Betriebsorganisation* directly under the district (*Bezirk*) organization. Heretofore, it was under the *Ortsgruppe* (section), one step further down the chain of command. With this change the increasing importance of the *Betriebsorganisation* as an effective party instrument was brought home to the entire party. [57]

Aroused by their success in the 1947–48 Works Council elections, the Communists unleashed a bitter attack on the leadership of the OGB in the spring of 1948 and redoubled their efforts to win control at the factory level.[58] Two other forms of pressure were available to the Communist: the use of the so-called *Aktionskomitees* within the plants, to serve as counter groups to the Socialist-dominated Works Councils, and the threat of firing noncooperative Works Councilors in the Soviet-controlled (USIA) plants.

Most non-Communist Austrians found the use of *Aktionskomitees* by the Communists very disturbing. The increase in the number of *Aktionskomitees* reminded Austrians of the Communist techniques in Czechoslovakia, soon convincing the Austrian government and the OGB that the Austrian Communists intended to put their "action committees" to the same use. On March 8, the Executive Committee of the OGB forbade its members on the threat of expulsion to join the committees. Minister of the Interior Oskar Helmer followed this by declaring the *Aktionskomitees* illegal.[59]

In the firing of Works Councilors of the Soviet-controlled firms who refused to "cooperate," the Communists seem to have been remarkably unsuccessful. Although the Soviet Union had complete charge of the USIA/SMV complex, when the Communists resorted to the firing of uncooperative Works Councilors, the result was very often a strike against the Russian concern.[60]

Despite these setbacks the Communists anxiously awaited the next round of Works Council elections, scheduled for September–January, 1949–50. As the Communist leadership constantly reminded its members: "The first and strongest fighting party of the new type, the Bolshevik, grew and conquered because of its grounding in the *Betriebe*.[61]

IV

The results of the 1949–50 Works Council elections indicated that the Communists improved their position in Styria slightly. A comparison of the overall results of the Styrian elections of 1947–48 with those of 1949–50 reveals some interesting changes:

1947–48		1949–50	
Socialists	68.0%	Socialists	60.2%
People's Party	4.1%	People's Party	3.2%
Communists	13.0%	Communists	11.7%
Einheitsliste	6.3%	Einheitsliste	10.5%
Nonpolitical	7.8%	Nonpolitical	10.2%
		Independent	4.2%

The results of the elections in the highly industrialized city of Graz— the largest city in Styria—are particularly significant:[62]

	1947–48		1949–50	
	Votes	Mandates	Votes	Mandates
Socialists	58.5%	57.7%	46.6%	49.5%
People's Party	4.1%	4.1%	4.3%	3.9%
Communists	8.1%	3.8%	5.7%	3.7%
Einheitsliste	10.8%	—	18.0%	—
Nonpolitical	17.8%	34.4%	21.0%	41.0%
Independent	—	—	4.4%	1.9%

It seems clear, then, that in Styria the Communists had once again improved their position in the Works Councils, particularly in the most highly industrialized sectors. Equally important is the fact that the Socialists seem to have lost perhaps as much as 10 per cent of the support they had in 1948. Moreover, a new factor had been added— the VdU (Verband der Unabhaengigen)—a right-wing group of self-styled independents whose hatred of the Socialists was matched only by their hatred of the Communists. Events in the fall of 1950 were to demonstrate that Socialist fears of the VdU were not unwarranted.

In the absence of reports as comprehensive as those issued by the Styrian Chamber of Labor, it becomes considerably more difficult to estimate Communist strength in the Works Councils elsewhere in Austria after the 1949–50 elections. The results of many of the plant elections can be found in the Communist and Socialist newpapers, and, as mentioned, these figures are reliable as far as they go. But, understandably enough, the two parties were vitally interested in demonstrating how well they had done, and, therefore, the respective party papers recorded only clear-cut victories. In spite of this general lack of information, certain things are clear. There are few areas of industrial concentration in Austria, and most of these are located in the eastern part of the country. If the Communists controlled 25–30 per cent of the representatives on the Works Councils in Styria, an area occupied by the British, there is no reason to doubt that they did at least as well in the Soviet zone, where direct pressure could be applied. A sampling of the returns from some of the larger plants as reported in the press suggests this point.

In the USIA/SMV complex, which included 10 per cent of all those employed in the industrial sector of the Austrian economy, the Communists unquestionably made great strides in gaining unchallenged control of the Works Councils. A combination of cajolery, threats, bonus food rations (at least until 1950), and the presence of Soviet military authority gradually transformed a large number of the workers of the USIA and SMV concerns into a cadre of tough, well-disciplined men, ready at a moment's notice to stage hunger strikes and political protest strikes, and, at the proper moment, to spearhead an assault on the Austrian Trade Union Federation itself. Much to the chagrin of the Austrian Communists, however, the Russians, as we have seen, were very reluctant to allow "their" employees to participate in Communist street agitation except in a very perfunctory way. This was particularly true after the spring of 1948.

From 1945 to the beginning of 1950, the Austrian Communists had carefully pursued the tactical Communist doctrine that they hoped would transform the trade union movement into "an instrument of the class struggle"; champions of a centralized trade union movement, the Communists were unable to control the OGB and soon found themselves in opposition to its leadership—not the other way around, as it was supposed to have turned out.

The one hope of the Communists after 1946, it seems, was the Works Councils. Perhaps with the domination of this independent labor force, they could create a potent rival to the Socialist-controlled OGB. The stronger this rival became, the better chance the Communists would have to overthrow the Socialist leadership in the Trade Union Federation. Only time and a direct confrontation with the coalition government would tell whether the heavy investment in the Works Council would bring the anticipated dividends.

The Communist Putsch

The beginning of the year 1950 saw the Austrian Communist Party in a state of complete disarray. The national elections which took place on October 9, 1949, were a disaster of alarming consequences. Although the Communists had improved their vote by some 22 per cent—from 174,257 to 213,066—their share of the total votes cast remained a bleak 5 per cent; their share of the national parliament a mere five seats out of 165.[1]

The defeat was apparently as unexpected as it was decisive. The Communists had assumed that the impetus of their victories in the Works Council elections would carry them to similar gains on the national level. The *Volksstimme*, after reporting a whole series of successes in the factories, maintained that the Works Council elections had proved that the Communists had "at least doubled their membership" and that "on the basis of the Works Council elections one can reckon for all of Austria a vote of approximately 1,100,000."[2]

There were other signs that augured for a Communist gain in the election. First, the number of those eligible to vote rose some 942,000, or 27 per cent, owing to the reinstatement of some 400,000 "less implicated" Nazis, the return of prisoners of war, and a large number of foreign nationals who had acquired citizenship since 1945. While the Communists were not so foolish as to hope for the bulk of these new voters, they could have at least expected a number of the new voters to vote Communist if only out of sheer protest against the other parties. More important would be the possibility of splitting the vote of the People's Party. In 1949 the Allied Council, in permitting the organization of political parties beyond the original three, had authorized the activities of a group known as the Verband der Unabhaengigen (VdU), or Union of Independents. This group drew its strength from the pan-German, nationalist element in Austrian society, which has shown a variety of political faces over the last 45 years: Grossdeutsche Partei, National Wirtschaftsblock, VdU, and, most recently, the Freiheitliche Partei Oesterreichs (FPO). In 1945 the supporters of this political faction had no choice but to vote for the People's Party in the absence of a party better tailored to their political philosophy. The Communists in 1949 had good reason to hope that the emergence of the VdU would split the People's Party and thus increase the Communists' own chances.

Moreover, the Communists in 1949 endeavored to create a new public image of the party. In April 1949 the defrocked Socialist, Erwin Scharf, formed a group called the Union of Progressive Socialists. In the fall of 1949, Scharf's group signed a pact with the Communist Party whereby the two factions would merge for the October elections. The resulting coalition appeared on the ballot as the Linksblock (Left Bloc). Although the other parties, with some justification, accused the Communists of attempting to deceive the electorate by flying false colors, the fact was that the Linksblock had obvious appeal for dissident or extreme left-wing Socialists.

The election was very clearly a test of the coalition government's hold on the Austrian people, including the decision of the coalition partners to cast their lot with the Western powers through participation in the Marshall Plan. The results justified the efforts of the coalition partners, who between them drew 82.7 per cent of the valid votes cast—44.0 per cent for the People's Party and 38.7 per cent for the Socialists. Nevertheless, this percentage was less than their combined 94.4 per cent in 1945. This loss was caused, not by any particular Communist gain, but by the remarkable success of the VdU, which polled some 489,000 votes, or 11.6 per cent of the total. The fact that some half-million people, exclusive of the Communists, were dissatisfied with the coalition government posed a potential threat to its continuation. The seriousness of this threat became all too clear in September and October of 1950, when the coalition government was forced to meet its last and most serious challenge.[3]

The success of the VdU was of little comfort to the Communists. Four years of constant effort to exploit the hunger, confusion, and uncertainty that was Austria's lot, particularly from 1945 to 1949, had failed to better their political position. The Communists' hope that their success in the Works Council elections was indicative of a general upswing in the party's fortunes proved groundless. Communist influence there was certainly powerful and growing, but it represented no significant gains in terms of national strength.

It would seem that the Communists drew a proper and sound conclusion from the national elections of 1949—that Communist ambitions in Austria would never be satisfied by appealing to the dissatisfied elements in the country. This dissatisfaction had been fed by the economic chaos and privation that came as a result of the war, and now the growing effect of the Marshall Plan aid was slowly removing many of the causes of unrest. Under these circumstances, the Communists had no real choice if they were to win control of the government, or at least obtain more influence in it, than to rally their remaining strength in Austria for one last and, this time, violent attempt to reverse the tide.

Besides the obvious advantage of choosing the time and the circumstance, the Communists had a number of important assets in any showdown. First, they had considerable and well-placed power in the Works Councils, particularly in the critical areas of Graz, Leoben, Linz, and Vienna. Second, although deprived of the position of power that Dr. Duermayer had held in his two-year control of the state police, the Communists were in complete control of the police districts in the Russian sector of Vienna. Third, they could be confident that the police (security forces) in the Russian zone would either actively participate in any show of force or would be effectively neutralized by the Soviet occupation forces. And finally, the Russians had successfully prevented the rearming of the police in Vienna, with the result that the police loyal to the coalition would be at a great disadvantage if forced to deal with the well-armed Werkschutz from the oil fields.[4]

To these points could be added the strength of the workers in the USIA concerns and those employed by the SMV. Here the Communists had at their disposal large groups of well-disciplined workers who could be turned out in any strike or demonstration by their Soviet directors on request of the Communist Party. On the other hand, however, there was the problem of keeping them out on strike. The Austrian Communists had learned in 1948 that Soviet support did not include sacrificing production.

Beyond all this, however, was the most critical question of what the attitude of the Soviet military authorities would be in any Communist adventure involving the use of force against the coalition government. The simplest answer would be that since a Communist success would be to the advantage of the Soviet Union and a failure would be a severe blow to its prestige, the Russians would go to whatever lengths were necessary to ensure success. The two major Austrian accounts of the September–October "Putsch," in their understandable pride in the role played by the Austrian workers and security forces in the suppression of the Communist power play, tend to ignore the fact that the attitude of the Soviet Union toward the Communist general strike was probably the most crucial factor of the entire affair.[5]

What the Communists needed was a moment of intense dissatisfaction on the part of the Austrian people with the coalition government. The cause of this dissatisfaction would have to be dramatic enough to create a broad base of general discontent capable of breaking down party lines. For only with the support of large numbers of dissatisfied Socialist workers could the Communists hope to succeed in an attempt to shake or unseat the coalition government.

The summer of 1950 provided that opportunity, when the Austrian government reluctantly and belatedly came to terms with the economic adjustments necessitated by the impending termination of Marshall Plan aid. The adjustment itself would have been difficult enough had it been handled with confidence and good sense. But this was not to be the case, and the Communists were quick to exploit both the developing crisis and the initial incompetence of the coalition government in coping with it. Because five years of Austrian postwar economic development form the immediate background to the events of September–October, 1950, a brief résumé of this period—during which Austria sought the basis of a viable peacetime economy—is useful.

I

In 1945, when Austria was severed from Germany, the problems of economic reconstruction were at first compounded by the legacies of the total integration of the Austrian economy into that of Germany. With Austria's prewar Eastern markets nothing more than a memory after seven years of German economic assimilation, the industrial complexities created by the Germans to serve a larger economic area were so badly damaged that they seemed more of an economic liability than an asset. To this must be added Austria's war damages and losses: war deaths amounting to almost 5 per cent of the prewar population, severe material damage, particularly in the eastern provinces, the legacy of looting and demolition, extensive dismantling of factories by the Russians, and total disintegration of the German administrative machinery. In the spring of 1945, the situation in Austria could only be described as chaotic, with the prospects for economic recovery very bleak.

With the arrival of the Allies it was soon apparent that the most urgent problem was food. In Vienna, during the month of May 1945, daily calories available to the average citizen had fallen to 600—well below the necessary minimal human requirement.[6] The depletion of livestock, the lack of artificial fertilizers, the shortage of labor, the general exhaustion of the soil during the war, all combined to make large-scale food deliveries from abroad an absolute necessity. In the fall of 1945, the United Nations Relief and Rehabilitation Administration was invited to participate in a program of supplying Austria with basic foodstuffs, a responsibility that had heretofore been undertaken by the occupying powers.

The UNRRA aid was clearly intended to be a stopgap measure, a relief program of limited duration which would sustain the Austrian economy until the process of general reconstruction was well rooted. In the autumn of 1946, as the UNRRA program was coming to an end, both the Austrian government and the occupation authorities were acutely aware that, without the continuation of large-scale aid, the Austrian economy would quickly revert to the complete privation of 1945. Furthermore, by 1946 it was generally acknowledged that foreign aid could not be limited to relief measures but must be extended to include basic economic rehabilitation if Austria was to become economically viable.

The Austrian government found an answer to its economic problems in the European Recovery Program, better known as the Marshall Plan. The decision of the coalition government to join the ERP was one of decisive importance for Austria's economic and political future.

When the Austrian coalition government chose to participate in ERP despite strong Soviet pressures—pressures similar to those that had caused Austria's closest counterpart in the postwar period, Finland, to drop out—the choice had far-reaching political and economic consequences. The decision meant the renunciation, at least for the foreseeable future, of Austria's coveted Eastern markets. There was no longer an economic middle ground in Europe. Austria's economic choice had laid the groundwork for the political decision, taken only in 1948 after the Czechoslovakian coup, to seek a *de facto* alliance with the West. Austria officially joined the ERP section of the Marshall Plan on April 3, 1948, and with the signing of the Austro-American agreement of July 2, 1948, the machinery for distribution of aid was organized.

In assessing Austria's economic problems and possibilities, ERP officials quickly decided that the most immediate requirements were those of food, the acquisition of materials to rebuild the industrial foundation of the economy, and the revitalization of Austria's almost nonexistent export trade. Certain conditions strongly influenced the choice of how this objective should be reached. First, both the ERP authorities and the United States Congress were interested in immediate and dramatic results. Second, the ERP authorities were naturally anxious to keep most of the aid out of the Russian sector and, ideally, within the American zone, where administrative control could be best exercised, not to mention the incentive of creating a "show window" within the United States zone.

The legacy of the German industries built during the war mainly in western Austria around Linz well served these purposes. The iron and steel works, the nitrogen works, the Ranshofen aluminum works, built mainly by the Germans, employed thousands of men in the American zone and possessed great potential as producers of the capital goods that Western Europe in 1948 so badly neeeded. In addition, the traditional iron and steel centers of Styria were in the British zone. Although on the surface it might appear that the reconstruction of two major iron and steel centers in a country the size of Austria was ill-advised, the immediate postwar needs of Europe and Austria for the basic goods was immense; therefore the Marshall Plan administrators chose to develop both areas.

This decision to depart from Austria's long-standing dependence on high-quality consumer goods production, and to emphasize development of heavy industry instead, brought immediate and remarkably successful results. One encouraging and dramatic result of this emphasis on investment in heavy industry was the increase in industrial production. Using 1937 as a base (1937 = 100), industrial production rose under the stimulus of the Marshall Plan from 74.7 in the first quarter of 1948 to 150.7 in the first quarter of 1951.[7]

The immediate and tangible effects on industrial production levels brought about by this strong concentration on industrial investment on the part of both the ERP administration and the Austrian private money market had significant drawbacks as well. Almost overlooked in the passion for developing heavy industry were the building trades and the so-called *Gewerbe* (crafts or small businesses). This was true despite the fact that almost half of those employed in Austrian industry in 1948 were in these two categories.[8] Moreover, with the tendency toward increasing modernization of the means of production, the traditional high quality, low production level of consumer goods would have suffered in any event after the war. What the ERP and

Austrian private investment did was to accelerate this process and temporarily increase unemployment in some fields.

There were other weak points in the Austrian economic reconstruction. The two most important were a depressing failure to revitalize the agriculture of the country and a mounting inflation that periodically threatened to get out of control entirely.

Considering the depletion of livestock and the abuse of the soil which took place during the war, it was only natural that agricultural production, by its very nature relatively insensitive to "crash programs," had a difficult road to recovery in Austria. However, despite the introduction of new machinery, the increased use of fertilizers, better seeds, and the like, by the end of 1949 agricultural production had reached only 78 per cent of the prewar level.[9]

Considering the fact that Austria, in the best of prewar circumstances, had never been agriculturally self-sufficient, this failure to raise domestic production made it necessary to rely on a high percentage of food imports; food imports for example, from April 1948 to December 1949, represented some 65 per cent of imports under direct Marshall Plan assistance. The problem of agricultural production was heightened by a system of artificially maintained low prices of grain products within Austria. This system forced the ERP authorities to allow the Austrian government to buy grain abroad at an exchange rate for the schilling that was substantially higher than the international rate. In essence, it amounted to a price-gap subsidy from the ERP, permitting the Austrian government to distribute grain products at an artificially low price. ERP resistance to this form of subsidy, which was tying up so much of ERP funds in Austria, grew stronger as the program approached its projected termination point in 1952. This issue reached a crisis in 1950, when the reluctant adjustment of the Austrian government to the realities of world grain prices precipitated the September–October disturbances.[10]

Austrian currency problems were among the most serious faced by the country in 1945. Austria was initially faced with a flood of virtually worthless German currency, which was further swollen by more from the Eastern European states. This factor, plus the deficit spending necessitated by occupation expenses, and an overevaluation of the schilling, created major price and wage movements, which in turn produced strong inflationary pressures. One result was the necessity for a currency devaluation in 1949; another was that the cost-of-living index rose from a base of 100 in April 1945 to 577.9 in October 1950, while wages rose during the same period only to 436.5.[11]

A high degree of capital formation, a high rate of reinvestment, and a low level of private consumption are among the more familiar signs of a society striving to industrialize and modernize its means of production and thus accelerate the production of capital goods. Such a policy, if carried out systematically and efficiently, with the necessary restrictions on prices to protect the workers, who may be living on a bare subsistence level, can be very successful. Austria's problem was that the economic policy of reconstruction was often badly managed: the manner of reinvestment was very often determined by private interests rather than by the government; too few controls were imposed on farmers in order to ensure delivery of farm products; restrictions on the importation of luxury goods were rarely enforced; inflation often destroyed incentive for the accumulation of private savings; competition was stifled by "market regulating" on the part of producers.

In order to deal with the problem of inflation, the Austrian government in concert with the powerful Chambers of Labor, Industry, and Agriculture would negotiate a so-called "price-wage" agreement. Essentially, the object of these agreements was to control inflation by adjusting the whole price structure upward, while simultaneously redressing major discrepancies in the wage structure. These agreements had the approval of all the major political and economic factions in the country and were extremely broad in scope, affecting utilities, transportation costs, wages, and all major food prices.

The first of these agreements, signed in August 1947, was successful in temporarily stabilizing wages and prices. When prices began to rise again, the experiment was repeated in 1948. Since this approach was little more than a means of adjusting to inflationary pressures at intervals, the technique became less and less successful and the time between major price movements increasingly shorter. The third price-wage agreement, in 1949, had demonstrated to many that basic reforms, not gimmicks, were necessary.[12]

II

It is clear that in the spring of 1950, Austria was facing its severest test in the transition from economic privation to a unified and viable economy. The abolition of subsidies was a crucial step which would serve to adjust the Austrian price structure to world prices and thus allow a relatively larger portion of ERP aid to be used for the reconstruction of the economy. The sobering fact was that Austria in 1950 faced a $100 million cut in foreign aid (259.3 to 158.8). Since in 1949 some 28 per cent of Austria's investment capital was provided by the ERP, an ERP cutback was bound to increase unemployment.[13] The new investment program for 1950–51 devised by the ERP and approved in May 1950 stressed the necessity of achieving an equilibrium in the balance of payments, an increase in exports, a stabilization of the currency, and a gradual lifting of agricultural subsidies.[14]

As has been noted, agriculture was recognized as a major stumbling block in Austria's path to economic recovery. Moreover, any adjustment in agricultural prices that would increase the burden on the working class was bound to create major political difficulties. The urban population of Austria, with some justification, had long felt that the farmers had suffered little during the war or during the grim days of 1945–48; that they had in fact profited from the misery of the townspeople. Inevitably, a move to raise agricultural prices would cause serious strains.

This key issue was first raised in the spring of 1950, when the *Bauernbund*, which represented the agricultural interests within the People's Party, served notice that new and higher agricultural prices were necessary.[15] At first there was hope that the transition to agricultural prices more in line with the world market could be managed smoothly. In fact, until June 1950, there were hopeful signs of price stabilization. Then came the Korean crisis.

The most immediate effect in Austria of the Korean crisis was a rising demand for scarce consumer goods, which caused severe inflationary pressures. In addition, world market prices of raw materials rose sharply. Since Austria was dependent on the importation of raw materials, there was mounting pressure on domestic prices throughout the summer of 1950. As a result, from mid-June to mid-September the overall index of wholesale prices rose by almost 9 per cent, while the wage index rose only 3 per cent during the same period.[16]

The task of the negotiators, representing the government and the Chambers of Labor, Industry, and Agriculture, as well as the Trade Union Federation, was not an easy one. The hard bargaining began in late June. The representatives of labor, although prepared to concede that food prices must go up, were in no mood or position to grant sweeping concessions. After extended negotiations the talks were broken off at the end of July, and not resumed until late in August.[17]

The longer this prolonged debate continued the more dangerous the situation became. As the summer wore on, more and more crops came to harvest. The farmers, anticipating the upward movement of prices, were hesitant to place their goods on the market. The result-

ing scarcity of food made the official price indexes only a pale reflection of the exorbitant prices many consumers had to pay. When
no goods were available at the official prices, the consumer was forced
to turn to the black market, where supplies were available at considerably higher prices.

What was required of the coalition government and the Trade Union Federation during those difficult days was a sober and tough-
minded public approach to the problem. Given the circumstances, it
was imperative that the public be prepared for the adjustment, stressing why it was necessary and what was being considered, if serious
unrest was to be avoided. Instead, the negotiators chose to conduct
the bargaining in complete secrecy. Perhaps they hoped that the ERP
authorities would suddenly drop their demand for removal of agricultural subsidies. Or perhaps they felt, as did Chancellor Figl, who
later defended the secrecy of the negotiations, that public knowledge
of the controversy would have caused confusion and would have been
used against the government.[18] Whatever the motivation for the secrecy, the results were nearly disastrous.

It was only during the first week of September, with the negotiations still deadlocked and the situation daily growing more desperate,
as the farmers refused to make deliveries until the new prices had been
fixed, that the first cracks appeared in the Socialist–People's Party
coalition. First, Karl Boehm, president of the OGB, complained that
the negotiations had not been completed "because the representatives
of agriculture have gone too far in their demands. If met, these demands would cause an exorbitant increase in the price of bread and
flour."[19] This was followed on September 17 by a blast from Julius
Raab, at the time representing the Austrian industrial interests, who
contended that, since the price-wage agreement, prices had gone
down and wages up some 5 per cent.[20] Karl Mantler, president of
the Arbeiterkammer, answered by attacking Raab's figures, charging
that wages were at least 17 per cent behind prices.[21]

The coalition government had lost its gamble. The smoldering
mutual suspicion between the interest groups, aggravated by weeks
of fruitless discussion, had now erupted into a public quarrel. To the
astonishment and dismay of the public, the air was now alive with
mutual recrimination. The coalition partners had panicked; and in
this atmosphere the Communists were given a priceless opportunity.

The role of champion of the working class was ready-made. The
tangle of misinformation and rumors, and the growing suspicion on
the part of the average workman that he had been betrayed, quickly

formed the broad base of discontent that the Communists knew was necessary if any action on their part was to have a chance of success.

The Communist press attacked the pact that was being concluded "behind the backs of the workers" and demanded—not a fourth price-wage agreement—but straight wage increases with prices frozen.[22] Bombarding the population with such slogans as "an end to rising prices," the Communists called for a minimum raise of 15 per cent in wages and salaries.

The fact was that the workers had a genuine grievance. To raise the price of farm products to international levels was bound to cause an outcry in any event, because the workers knew that their wages were below the world standard. More important, however, was the air of uncertainty that clouded the whole issue. Deprived of information from the government on the impending price-wage pact, the population was naturally vulnerable to the Communist propaganda barrage.

Compounding the confusion surrounding the secret negotiations, the coalition newspapers simply announced on September 23 that, on the day before, at a meeting of the cabinet with representatives of the chambers, a price-wage agreement had been reached, the results of which would be announced on Tuesday the 26th. That was all; nothing was included about the reasons behind the impending change or what it might entail.[23]

This was all the invitation the Communists needed. Charging that "the betrayal is complete," the Communist press warned the workers that although the results of the negotiations had not been officially released, the pact included a drastic increase of prices, of which the proposed wage boost would cover only a third. Citing Karl Mantler's contention that even before any price-wage agreement was concluded the real wages of the workers had declined some 17 per cent since the first agreement, the Communists maintained that after the new pact this 17 per cent would be 25 per cent. On September 24 the Communists threatened: "Now it is the workers' turn!" On the 26th, the day the government was to announce for the first time the price and wage changes, and the day that the Executive Committee of the Trade Union Federation was called to discuss the pact, the *Volksstimme* announced that the workers throughout Austria had begun to strike.[24]

The developing strike was the most dangerous since the end of the war. The Communists had successfully capitalized on the inept-ness of the coalition government in handling the price-wage negotiations, and as a result the loyalties of the workers in such a strike were uncertain because of the widespread discontent over the new agreement. That was not all. The United States was at this moment engaged in the most uncertain stage of the Korean war, with the fate of the Pusan perimeter still in doubt. U.S. military resources would thus have been sorely strained if the West had been faced with a military confrontation in Austria. Moreover, pressure for price adjustment of farm products was known to have come from the United States, and as a result the United States was held indirectly responsible for the problem. In addition, September was the month that the U.S. High Commissioner was chairman of the Allied Council, and he would naturally be reluctant to interfere in a crisis with which the United States was so intimately connected.

But the most disturbing question was the intention of the Soviet military authorities. On the day before the first demonstrations—September 25—the Soviet military commander in Vienna ordered all police in the Russian districts to remain in their own zones in case of disturbances.[25] This action meant, first of all, that the government would be prevented from making most effective use of its police force, a disadvantage heightened by the fact that, owing primarily to Soviet obstruction, the security forces under Helmer were poorly armed and equipped. A more critical threat than the action itself was the realization that for the first time the Russians had coupled interference with the police system with a particular action of the Austrian Communist Party.

The Austrian Socialists have long contended that the objective of the Communist Party in the fall of 1950 was the overthrow of the coalition government and the establishment of a "people's democracy" in Austria.[26] This is certainly true to the extent that such a takeover was the ultimate objective of the Communist Party. It would seem, however, that in September 1950 the Austrian Communists were hardly so unrealistic as to believe that even the most successful strike would topple the government and lead to a coup along Czechoslovakian lines. True, the Communists had several important assets in any showdown with the coalition government. Nevertheless, the weaknesses of the Communist position were equally manifest. The number of active, reliable party members was pathetically small; the Communist Party of Austria had never excited the imagination of the people as a whole, nor was it fortunate enough to have capable leadership. Although Communist support in the Works Councils was strong, control of the Austrian Trade Union Federation was firmly in the hands of the Socialists. Deprived of any influence in the Ministry of the Interior, the Communists had to rely on hold-overs from Honner's short-lived ministry. In the communication field, Communist influence was mainly limited to their own newspapers and press. Much has been made of the fact that there was Commu-nist influence within RAVAG, the official Austrian radio corpora-tion.* Yet in comparison with the output of the American station, this propaganda effort was unimpressive.

Despite the favorable moment, then, Communist success was de-pendent on holding the support of the dissident Socialist workers. The longer they could hold this support and that of some members of the Union of Independents (VdU) in the factories, who despised the coalition government more than the Communists, the more suc-cess they would have. The two key questions, then, were: how long could the Austrian Communists hold the backing of those Socialists who were initially sympathetic to the strike; and would the Soviet military broaden its tacit support of the Communists into open mili-tary assistance? On the first question hinged the success or failure of the Communists to achieve what was probably their primary objec-tive in the September–October strikes—to gain control of the trade unions and to regain some of the positions they once held in the gov-ernment. The answer to the second question seems to have rested partially on how well the Austrian Communists were able to ac-complish their primary objective and partially on the limits the Soviet Union applied to the use of its power in Austria.

The test was not long in coming. On the morning of September 26 the Communist offensive began, when work was stopped simul-taneously in the USIA factories in Vienna and masses of working-men began to move toward the center of the city.

III

The centers of Communist strength in Vienna lay in the Tenth (Favoriten), Twentieth (Brigittenau) and Twenty-first (Floridsdorf) districts of Vienna. All of these districts were within the Russian sector of the city and contained some of the largest factories con-trolled by the USIA system. Sparked by the closing of the USIA con-

* Unlike the Western Allies, who built their own radio stations in Austria, the Russians chose to demand time from RAVAG. The result was such programs as "the Russian Hour." In the beginning of September 1950, the Russians raised their demands on RAVAG, bringing the amount of time devoted to Soviet-inspired programs to an average of two and a quarter hours a day, all at prime hours. *Arbeiter-Zeitung*, September 13, 1950; see also *ibid.*, July 28, 1950.

cerns, Communist workers went from factory to factory encouraging mass participation in the march to the center of the city. Reflecting the deep-seated resentment of the workers in general, whether Socialist or Communist, by 10:00 A.M. some 15,000 demonstrators were in motion. Streaming over the Danube bridges, the crowds marched to the center of the city to protest the price-wage pact in front of the Federal Chancellery.

It was a credit to Communist timing and organization that the demonstrators pressed their way through police lines and barricades just before 11:00 A.M. It was well known in Austria that the weekly meeting of the cabinet began on Tuesday of each week at 10:00 A.M.—and September 26 was a Tuesday. However, at the suggestion of Vice-Chancellor Schaerf, the cabinet meeting had been moved up two hours. Chancellor Figl chose to remain in the building as the crowd, urged on by Communists Fischer and Honner, surrounded it. Figl refused to receive a delegation, and, after a series of clashes with the police that resulted in 23 police injuries, the crowd drifted away by 1:00 P.M.[27]

During the first phase of the strike the police had trouble keeping control. Soviet orders had prevented the use of police force from the Soviet sector. Moreover, on the orders of the Minister of the Interior the police were unarmed, in order to avoid bloodshed, which might be all the provocation the Soviets required to intervene.[28] Equally disturbing was the news that a plea for aid had been refused by the American High Commission.[29] Furthermore, when the U.S. City Commander, acting under the provisions of the Vienna Inter-Allied Command Agreement, called for an emergency meeting of the Four Powers to consider the situation in the First District, the Soviet Commander failed to send a representative.[30]

While the demonstration went on in the Ballhausplatz, other strikers were concentrating on disrupting transportation throughout the city. Streetcar barns were stormed and cement was poured into tracks, barricades were thrown up in key traffic areas and windows on city buses were broken.[31]

More serious, perhaps, were the activities of the strikers throughout Lower Austria. Since the province of Lower Austria (Soviet zone) completely surrounds Vienna, any major disruption of communication and transportation would have effectively sealed off the city. Beginning on September 26, strikers attempted to occupy the important railway stations along rail lines to Vienna, such as the St. Poelten and Wiener Neustadt, and to block the tracks. Post offices in Gaenserndorf, Suessenbrunn, Deutsch Wagram, and Wiener Neustadt were taken. In Austria this was particularly serious, since post offices serve as telephone and telegraph centers. Once in control of the post offices, the strikers were able to force officials to allow only the transmission of messages of the central strike committee (*Streikleitung*), while instructions from the government could be suppressed.[32]

Roads were blocked with trucks, automobiles, and boulders. Tracks were covered with stones. At one point, a Soviet tank was, as the U.S. representative acidly put it, "fortuitously and conveniently" stalled on the railroad tracks at Langenzerdorf.[33] Again, when employees of the USIA plants rioted and took over railroad yards, the local Soviet military commanders prevented the police from interfering.

The disturbances in chief industrial centers of Upper Austria, primarily in the cities of Linz and Steyr and in Styria, were of particular importance. For in the pattern and sequence of the strikes, the techniques and the apparent objectives of the Communists were well defined.

Linz is of course one of the most highly industrialized and important cities in Austria. With the huge iron and steel works of VOEST and numerous other large concerns, the city had a high proportion of industrial workers. For a number of reasons Linz and the nearby city of Steyr were potentially extremely dangerous centers of labor unrest. Most of the industries in this area had been developed since the German takeover, and therefore the roots of Socialist trade unionism did not go as deep as in the older firms. In addition, after the war there was a high influx of refugee labor in the plants. These new workers, many of them dissatisfied with their condition, joined the ranks of the Union of Independents (VdU). As a result, the Works Council of VOEST, the major concern in Linz, was made up of 12 Socialists, two Communists, and 14 Independents.[34] In the five other important factories of Linz the proportion was roughly the same but with the Socialists normally having the plurality.

At about 3:00 P.M. on September 26, the workers of the VOEST plants led the other major concerns in Linz into a general strike. It is important to realize that at this stage in the strike the Socialist rank and file were solidly behind the general strike movement. The committee selected to represent the workers in a formal protest to the provincial government was led by a Socialist. In the absence of a coherent explanation from Vienna, the Socialist workers were only aware that a wave of price increases was in motion and that food prices, because of the refusal of farmers to make deliveries, were climbing.

Throughout the afternoon of the 26th the crowds in the streets grew in size, so that by late afternoon there were over 15,000 men and women demonstrating. The police were virtually powerless to handle the crowds at this point. The situation in Steyr was much the same.[35]

Considering that Linz was in the American zone and VOEST was a nationalized industry, the worsening situation became extremely embarrassing to both the U.S. military authorities and the coalition government. Although Linz is on the Danube, which marked the boundary between the Soviet and American zones, and presumably much of the direction of the strike came from the Soviet side, the extensive unrest was a sign of widespread disapproval of the pact as well as testimony to the Communist claim that the demonstrations were spontaneous.

The course of events in Linz and Steyr was closely paralleled in the British-occupied province of Styria. In the major industrial areas of Graz, Leoben, and Donawitz, however, the Communists were not dependent on the VdU for support; this was an area where the Communists could claim a majority in many Works Councils. Again the Socialist trade union leaders found themselves forced to take the lead in protesting the pact. As in Linz, the only information they had on the wage-price agreement was from the newspapers. Aware only that prices were going up as the merchants drew their own conclusions from impending price adjustments, the Socialist leaders knew that the disturbances would become increasingly serious as rumors of "exorbitant" price increases spread throughout the province.

On the evening of September 26 the Communist Party called a Vienna conference of the shop stewards representing the so-called unity list—Einheitsliste. Here both the Communist Party leader, Koplenig, and the top Communist in the Austrian Trade Union Federation, Gottlieb Fiala, spoke. Their remarks clearly reflect how pleased the party was with the first day of the general strike. This satisfaction certainly seemed justified. Admittedly an insignificant minority in Austria, the Communist Party, capitalizing on a promising situation, had rallied thousands of nominally loyal Socialists to a strike movement that was growing not only in size but in its capacity to disrupt communications and to paralyze the economic life of the country. As the resolution adopted at the end of the Communist conference pointedly warned: "Today's battle has demonstrated our strength; that of tomorrow will bring us complete success."[36]

Central to this resolution was a demand that seemed to anticipate, or perhaps set in motion, the events of September 27. It read in part:

The events of today have shown that Boehm and Company [the leadership of the OGB] no longer have the right to speak for the working class and negotiate agreements. . . . The working class and the white-collar workers must insist that they be removed from leading positions in the trade unions, which they no longer have a right to.[37]

A key question was the reaction of the Socialist Party to this growing crisis, which threatened their leadership of the working class. Moreover, what action would the coalition government take to contain the wave of strikes?

Initially both the Socialists and their conservative partners within the coalition government were caught completely off balance. They had assumed that, after confirmation of the pact by the OGB at the meeting called for September 26, there would be time enough to educate the public on what the negotiators had agreed to. The release of the provisions of the agreement on the 26th was preceded by the comforting headline: "After October 1 wage increases from 10 to 18 per cent." The fact that the OGB formally approved the agreement the same day did little to improve the situation. Fritz Klenner, the official historian of the Austrian Trade Union Federation, has admitted that on the morning of the 26th, although the *Arbeiter-Zeitung* in Vienna carried the contents of the pact and some explanation by Boehm, there was not a word in the Linz or Graz newspapers concerning the true content of the agreement.[38] Under these circumstances there is little wonder that Socialist participation in the strikes was so heavy.

Then, too, the response of the government at first was purely defensive. In its initial confusion and panic, the coalition government publicly called upon the Allied Council for assistance, an action that might well have led to a situation in which the two power blocs openly supported one or the other side. Fortunately, the U.S. High Commissioner, who chaired the September meetings, refused to involve occupation troops.

It was only on Wednesday, September 27, that the Socialist Party and the Austrian Trade Union Federation began to stem the Communist propaganda tide by bringing to bear their immense powers of member discipline and efficient organization. In the meantime, however, the Communists had proceeded to what might be called Step 2 in their plan—gaining control of the local OGB headquarters and the regional Arbeiterkammern.

On the morning of the 27th some 3,000 demonstrators from the VOEST works converged on the Lower Austria Arbeiterkammer building in Linz, which also housed the regional headquarters of the OGB. While the president of the Upper Austria Arbeiterkammer, Heinrich Kandl, a man of 76, was reporting on the results of the meeting of the Executive Committee of the Trade Union Federation in Vienna, which approved the pact, a demonstration broke out in the hall. In the ensuing battle, Kandl was badly mauled, and when the strikers threatened to thrown him from a balcony to the crowd below, he very wisely resigned. The strikers then occupied the entire building, organized a "Provisional Trade Union Committee," and, in the name of the workers of Upper Austria, demanded the resignation of the entire leadership of the OGB. Seizing the telephone facilities in the building, the provisional committee proceeded to telephone strike orders to all the factories in the name of the OGB.[39] Simultaneously, other strikers occupied the railroad stations and blockaded the tracks, while other groups of strikers went from factory to factory threatening those who would not participate in the strike.

In Graz the police had anticipated an attempt on the Trade Union Federation headquarters, and on the 27th they surrounded the building. When police protection was removed at the request of the provincial government of Styria, the strikers infiltrated the building, taking over offices and telephoning instructions to the plants in the name of the OGB.[40]

However, the next day, September 28, some 70 Communists from the oil fields made a halfhearted attempt to break into the national headquarters of the OGB in Vienna. Finding the building locked, they attempted to force their way in, only to be routed by the police. The complete futility of this effort, when compared with the all-out and dangerous assault on the Arbeiterkammer in Linz just 24 hours before, graphically illustrates how far Communist fortunes had declined in those few hours.

The reason was simple enough. The Communists had lost control of those Socialist workers whose support was essential to the successful prosecution of the strike. Working frantically throughout September 26 and 27, the Socialist Party and the Trade Union Federation called meetings, issued pamphlets, and used the extensive facilities of both the British and American radio networks to counteract Communist propaganda—all in a massive effort to regain the ear and, hopefully, the confidence of the working class. Both the Socialists and the OGB attacked the Communists with the charge that the strikes and demonstrations were an attempt to distract the public from what was in reality an effort to overthrow the government and establish a *Volksdemokratie* in Austria. This was no economic strike, but a dangerous assault on the elected government by an alliance of the Fascist (VdU) and Communist conspirators.[41]

One story perhaps best illustrates the attitude of a majority of the Austrian workers to the call for a general strike. On the morning of the second day of the strike, a Russian officer appeared at the construction site and demanded to know why the men were not on strike. A representative of the men said they had no such instructions from the Trade Union Federation. The officer demanded that they strike anyway. In reply, the workers asked if the Soviet military authorities would be willing to make up the loss of pay that would result from striking. When the officer was forced to admit that they could not do this, the men said they would remain on the job.

Such skepticism and general unwillingness to disobey the orders of the Trade Union Federation, once the OGB had made its position clear, gradually convinced the workers that wage-price agreement, no matter how unpleasant, was better than what the Communists were offering. When the issue was finally drawn clearly—that to support the strike was to support the ambitions of the Communist Party—the Communist cause, despite Soviet support, was hopelessly lost.

Throughout the day on the 27th, it was becoming increasingly apparent that the strike had lost its momentum. Under the direct orders of the OGB, work was gradually resumed in most concerns. By Thursday morning, September 28, the strike that had initially pulled 120,000 workers off their jobs had been reduced to a few pockets of resistance in Upper Austria and Styria—most notably the VOEST works in Linz and the Donawitz plant of the Alphine-Montan Company in Styria.

Equally discouraging, probably, to the Communists was the effective use to which the government put the police and gendarmerie in the Allied zones. The group of strikers that had occupied the Arbeiterkammer in Linz soon discovered that the building was surrounded by gendarmerie elements in steel helmets armed with fixed bayonets. The American-trained *Alarmbataillon* of Colonel Mayr easily routed the demonstrators from the building. The gendarmerie in Graz and Leoben were equally efficient in containing the strike.[42]

In the late afternoon of Wednesday, the 27th, although there was still some doubt of the outcome of the seizure of the Arbeiterkammer in Linz, the strike committee that met in Vienna could only conclude that the strike was a failure.*

About 7:00 P.M. the workers were instructed via radio during the "Russian Hour" to take up their work again and await instructions from an "all-Austrian shop stewards conference" (Works Council) that would be held starting September 30. The next day the Communist papers announced that this conference had been called on the initiative of a number of Socialist, Communist, and Independent shop stewards from Vienna.[43] It is logical to assume that this "all-Austrian shop stewards conference" had been planned well in advance and was not a desperate last-minute maneuver. Concentration of all the strikers on capturing positions in the local trade unions would have been a natural buildup to such a conference. Moreover, there was the Czechoslovakian precedent of the effective use of an emergency shop stewards conference amid the general strike of February 1948. In like manner, if the Austrian Communists had been able to sustain the planned general strike, the "all-Austrian shop stewards conference" could have played an important role in bringing pressure on the government.

That the Austrian Communists were forced to hold the conference without the backdrop of a general strike was presumably born of a desperate attempt to rescue something from the ashes of their grand design. Austrians have often referred to the September–October disturbances as a two-act affair. From the Communist point of view, this was certainly not a matter of choice. But by this time they were too deeply involved. Police officials had already directly disobeyed orders from the Minister of the Interior. Communist trade unionists had fostered a strike against the explicit directives of the OGB—a violation of a basic tenet of the statutes of the Trade Union Federation. The Communists could, therefore, be certain that as a result of their defiance they would be expelled from the trade unions and thus lose the influence they had painstakingly built up. The Socialists in the late September days had rallied their supporters with the cry "Es geht uns Ganze." Once the Communists had com-

* It was widely held in Vienna that this meeting revealed a deep split in the Communist Party leadership on what action to take next. Altmann, Ernst Fischer, and Koplenig took the position that any further strike action should center on the use of the general strike. On the other side were Gottlieb Fiala, leading Communist in the OGB, and Friedl Fuernberg, party theorist, who wanted to storm the headquarters of the OGB in Vienna and set Fiala up as provisional president. *Wiener Kurier*, September 28, October 5, 1950.

mitted themselves so completely, that expression was better applied to them.

The Gesamtoesterreichische Betriebsraetekonferenz met on September 30 in the assembly hall of the Floridsdorfer locomotive factory. Assembled were 2,417 "shop stewards and delegates of the strike committees." The conference very quickly drew up an ultimatum to the government, which included withdrawal of the pact or doubling of the wage increases called for in the agreement, a general freeze of prices, and payment out of the OGB fund of wages lost by the strikers. Significantly, the ultimatum did not repeat earlier demands that the leaders of the Trade Union Federation be removed. The resolution maintained that the attack was not against the trade unions; quite the contrary, "we desire only that they become once again the representatives of the true interests of the worker and the salaried employee."[44]

The government had until October 3 to consider the ultimatum. If it was not accepted by this time, the Executive Committee of the conference would call a general strike, to begin on October 4.

Both the conciliatory tone and the actual content of this ultimatum seem to indicate that the Communists by September 30 were simply looking for a way of minimizing their losses. Had the OGB agreed to pay the strike wages, this would have tacitly legitimized the strike and freed the leaders from the threat of expulsion. The Communists were perfectly aware that no general strike could succeed without Socialist participation in large numbers. By September 30 this hope was all but gone. If the government refused to consider the ultimatum, or even to negotiate, the Communists had one remaining hope. If they could launch an assault on the government, concentrating on Vienna and Lower Austria, which was so intense as to disrupt public order completely, then the Soviet forces could justifiably intervene. At best, such intervention could provoke a division of Austria, with Vienna falling to the Communists. At worst, the Communist trade unionists could claim Soviet protection. It all depended on the Soviet Union. The possibility of such intervention was likewise the coalition government's only fear.

Any hopes the Communists might have had that the coalition government and the OGB would welcome a chance to negotiate a settlement were put to rest on October 2, when the ultimatum was rejected *in toto*. As if to underline the government position, the same day seven Communist and VdU members who participated in the seizure of the Linz Arbeiterkammer were arrested by the state police.[45] The preparations made by the coalition government, the Socialist Party, and the OGB for the impending strike action were thorough and well conceived, and they subsequently proved to be remarkably successful in containing the strike. A conference of the Socialist shop stewards was called for October 3. Here, before an audience of 1,500 Socialist trade unionists, Karl Boehm and other high officials of the OGB explained the price-wage agreement and how to combat the strike at the factory level. At the same time, there were meetings throughout the city of Socialist Party functionaries.[46] Thousands of pamphlets, posters, and special editions of trade union publications were distributed. The propaganda counteroffensive centered on what was described as the "real" intentions of the strikers. According to the Socialists, the choice was very clear: "Those who support the Communists in their actions place in jeopardy not only the freedom of Austria but their personal freedom and that of their families."[47]

The government for its part issued a dramatic appeal to the people on October 3, urging the workers to stay at their posts and if necessary to defend by force their right to work.[48]

Considering the elaborate preparations taken by the government and the apparent success of the Socialist Party and the OGB in controlling their members, there is little doubt that the second wave of Communist-directed strikes without direct assistance from the Soviet forces had little chance of success. The question yet to be answered on the evening before the general strike was what role the Soviet military would play once the strike began. Considering the disastrous results of the first strike wave, it was possible that the Russians would stay completely clear of the affair, not wishing to engage Soviet prestige in such an uncertain venture. Or were they already completely committed? Would a humiliating Communist defeat reflect so unfavorably on the Soviet Union that they would feel compelled to take action even though such action would necessarily involve open use of force—something the Russians had heretofore shied away from in Austria?

A partial answer to the question came on October 3, when Colonel Pankratov, the deputy Soviet commander of Vienna, called the President of the Viennese police system, Josef Holaubek. Holaubek received the following orders for the succeeding day, the day the general strike was to begin: All police forces assigned to the Soviet area must be immediately recalled; police forces within the Soviet sector must not be used elsewhere; transfers or dismissals of police officials in the Soviet sector or zone must not be ordered without Soviet permission.[49]

Moreover, Oskar Helmer's plan to transfer gendarmerie forces to Vienna was thwarted when the Soviet commander in Moedling refused to permit the transfer of men from the central gendarmerie school located there.[50] There were numerous other such incidents throughout Lower Austria, where the local Soviet military commanders issued orders on October 3 that the gendarmerie were to stay off the streets on the following day.

Added to this was a flood of rumors telling of Czechoslovakian troops poised at the border or of large numbers of Russian tanks and aircraft in motion. The Viennese were obviously uneasy about what the next day would bring. John MacCormac, reporter for the *New York Times,* wrote that, as the Viennese went home on the night of October 3—many after buying a few extra provisions and a candle—they were asking themselves whether the Russians would actually aid the Communists in an attempt to seal off Vienna.[51]

IV

When the Communists first struck, in the early morning hours of Wednesday, October 4, it was with great force, highly concentrated. Unlike the first wave of strikes, the action was centered almost entirely in Vienna and Lower Austria. The rest of Austria, including the previous trouble spots of Linz, Graz, and Leoben, was remarkably quiet. This was certainly due in part to efforts of the OGB and the Socialist Party to prevent the strike. The arrest of many of the strike leaders in the Western zones by the Austrian police also helped. Nevertheless, the very contrast of the extensive violence in the Soviet zone and Vienna with the rest of Austria says a good deal about the intentions of the Communists in the second-wave strikes.

No sooner had the general strike begun than the Communists found that the efforts of the Socialists and the OGB had been extremely successful even in Lower Austria in preventing widespread walkouts. As an indication of how shallow the Communist base of support had become, we know that of the 86 factories in Lower Austria that voted to strike, 69, or 80 per cent, were USIA plants. Other plants were forcibly closed, however, by Communist workers, although they were in a minority. All in all, some 19 per cent of those industrially employed in Lower Austria finally participated in the strike.[52]

Deprived of a broad base of popular support, the Communists

ignored mass demonstrations and concentrated on disrupting communications and transportation. An account of the strike as it affected rail transportation provides a good example of the pattern. Some excerpts:

Wednesday, October 4, 1950

8:18. The railroad station at Stadlau surrounded—attack beaten off.

9:00. From Krems a report that the railroad station is threatened. St. Poelten reports that the Voith Works [USIA iron and steel plants] have blockaded the railroad station.

9:03. The railroad station at St. Valentin taken.

9:20. The Stadlau railroad station occupied, barricades erected.

9:50. The St. Valentin railroad station retaken.

10:10. Stadlau station free again.

10:30. 500 strikers march on Stadlau. Unable to gain entrance to the station, they blockade the tracks.

18:00. Rail traffic rolling without obstacle.

Thursday, October 5, 1950

5:10. Stretches of track near Stadlau, Deutsch-Wagram, and Suessenbrunn blockaded.

9:05. The north railroad [*Nordbahnhof*] in Vienna taken by strikers.

10:20. The main railroad station in St. Poelten occupied.

14:00. Strikers threaten the south railroad station [*Suedbahnhof*]. . . . After midnight the traffic is completely normal.[53]

The same timetable could be repeated with variations for the clash over control of the streetcar and bus transportation facilities in Vienna, the gas and electric works, and the main highways and bridges leading into Vienna.[54] As the strike developed throughout October 4 and 5 in Vienna and Lower Austria, the high level of coordination became more evident. The objective was apparently to seize all major railroad stations, to block tracks, and to control bridges around Vienna. Simultaneously, local transportation was attacked in order to paralyze Vienna internally. While groups of strikers, often transported in Russian vehicles, disrupted transportation, others went from factory to factory spreading rumors and threatening those who on the order of the Socialists and the OGB would not strike. Where persuasion failed, physical force was used to close down the plants. In addition to railroad stations, post offices with their important telephone systems were seized for the use of the strikers.

In combating the strikers in Vienna and Lower Austria, the Austrian internal security forces were at a hopeless disadvantage. Unable to move police and gendarmerie into trouble areas, cautioned not

to fire on the strikers because of the threat of immediate Soviet interference, and burdened, particularly in Vienna, with a large number of disobedient police officials, the police were incapable of handling the strike alone. And yet the strike was a complete failure, and
by the morning of October 6 all had returned to normal. Two compelling reasons for this total defeat within the Russian zone and
Vienna stem from the actions of the majority of Austrian workers
and from the attitude of the Soviet military forces. During the last
hours before the strike, the Austrian government realized that its
outcome in Vienna and Lower Austria depended ultimately on the
attitude of the workers. There was no doubt that the vast majority
of them were opposed to the strike and would heed the orders of the
OGB and the Socialist Party not to participate. But the government
also knew that if the majority stood passively aside during the strike,
an aggressive minority could create such chaos that the Soviet Union
might be tempted to split Austria apart. For this reason the government proclamation issued on the day before the strike made the
obligation of every worker quite clear: "Each man should remain at
his post and courageously repel every act of terror; no factory dare
close under pressure of agents. Destroy illegal roadblocks; drive the
presumptuous intruders out of the factories!"[55]

What cost the Communists any chance of success in the October
strike was the response of the workers to this appeal. The personal
courage shown by many Austrian workers during these two critical
days drew all too little comment in the Western press. In Wiener
Neustadt, Ternitz, Neunkirchen, and many other cities in the Russian zone, workers armed with scraps of wood, hand tools, or often
only their fists, fought pitched battles with gangs of men from striking plants who sought to drive the nonstriking workers from their
machines. In Ternitz, for example, during one of these struggles, 17
nonstriking workers were injured badly enough to require hospitali-
zation.[56] During the seesaw battles over possession of the railroad
stations in Lower Austria, it was the railroad employees rather than
the police who fought the strikers. In Vienna, Franz Olah, until recently Austria's Minister of the Interior, first made a national reputation when, as leader of the construction workers union, he organized these tough workers into what the Communists were later to
call the "Olah Bataillone." Divided into groups roughly the size of
the Communist bands which were disrupting transportation, blockading streets, and the like, Olah's men, armed with clubs, engaged
the Communists in hard-fought battles all over the city.[57]

That nonstriking workers beat the Communist strikers at their own game must certainly have influenced the Russians in their decision not to intervene. Soviet actions during those critical days, although the battlefield was mainly in their own zone, were limited to indirect assistance to the Communist strikers. The Russians restricted the use of the police and gendarmerie, sent the gendarmerie in one case into the woods to look for bandits while the Communists seized the railroad station and key bridges, ordered the arrest by Austrian police of nonstrikers battling the strikers. But there was no coordinated, direct assistance to the strikers and no direct Soviet intervention. Indeed, after the first day of the strike the Soviet factory managers allowed only very small cadres of workers from USIA and SMV to participate in the action.

Much had been made of Soviet action in Wiener Neustadt during the strike. On October 4, strikers forcibly occupied the important post office building in Wiener Neustadt containing the central telephone exchange. That afternoon, the Austrian cabinet meeting in the Ministry of the Interior decided to send a detachment of 100 gendarmerie under the command of Colonel Kaes from the gendarmerie school in Vienna to restore order. After a number of delays the detachment reached Wiener Neustadt in the early morning hours of October 5. After a sharp struggle with the strikers, during which some 20 of the gendarmerie and police were injured, Colonel Kaes's detachment succeeded in clearing the building. No sooner had the gendarmerie taken up their positions when a representative of the Soviet commandant arrived and ordered the detachment out within ten minutes or the Soviet military would force them out.[58]

This action on the part of the Soviet military commandant was at odds with the Allied Control Agreement, which called for the Allied powers to assist the Austrian government in assuming full control of internal security affairs (Article 3(d)) and permitted interference with matters of internal security only when the Austrian government was unable to handle the situation. Nevertheless, Major General Tsinev, in his defense of Soviet actions made at the Allied Council meeting of October 6, raised a telling point when he asked what the Western powers would have done had a detachment from the Soviet zone arrived in their area of authority.[59] The Wiener Neustadt incident remains, however, the only significant case of open Soviet interference that occurred during the entire strike.

Nevertheless Foreign Minister Gruber took advantage of the incident to address a letter of protest to the foreign ministers of the four occupying powers. During the course of the same day, October 5, the three Western powers answered the note. Failing to receive an answer from the Soviets, Gruber requested that a Soviet representative come to the Federal Chancellery. Upon his arrival Gruber asked what was meant by the action of the Soviet commandant in Wiener Neustadt. Gruber writes that the Russian diplomat professed to know nothing of the incident in question and assured the Austrian government that the Soviet Union intended to live up to the terms of the Control Agreement.[60]

A few hours later the Communist strike committee called off the strike. This decision was a quick reversal for the Austrian Communist leaders, for in banner headlines just a few hours before the *Volksstimme* had proclaimed: "One last effort and the strike is complete."[61] On the following day the Communists could only report that the strike was over. Charges that the coalition government had resorted to bloodshed to subdue the strike could not cover the fact that the Austrian Communists had suffered their most crushing defeat since the elections of 1945. They had gambled everything in one massive effort to recapture the initiative in Austria and had lost.

Quite apart from the immediate outcome of the strike, the larger question remains: Why did the Soviet Union allow the Communist Party in Austria to suffer such a calamitous setback when direct intervention on their part could have assured the success of the strike in the Soviet zone and provided a pretext to split Eastern Austria away from the Western-controlled zones? The answer involves something much more fundamental than Soviet actions with respect to a particular event and touches on a basic truth of Soviet policy in occupied Austria. The Soviet Union was simply not prepared to go the limit. Confronted with the dilemma of either allowing the Communist Party to suffer a crushing defeat or committing the Soviet troops necessary to stave off such a setback, the Russians backed off.

The Russians had done everything possible to indirectly aid the Communists. But when the nonstrikers in the Soviet zone actively resisted the strikers and fought to stay at their workbenches, all pretense of widespread support for the strike was stripped away. When the nonstrikers successfully defended themselves and broke the Communist strike, the Russians refused to intervene directly. Soviet troops had never been used directly in creation of "people's democracies" throughout Eastern Europe, and the Soviet Union did not break the pattern in Austria.

With the collapse of the strike the Austrian Communists were not long in discovering the consequences of risking so much and then losing. On October 19, the Central Council of the Austrian Trade Union Federation removed Gottlieb Fiala from his position as a vice-president of the OGB. This was the highest position held by a Communist in the OGB, and Fiala's removal symbolized the collapse of three-party control of the trade unions—an equality that had been, in fact, a myth since the time the workers first had a chance to express their choice. Fiala's removal was only one of many purges that went on throughout the entire trade union movement. Dr. Fels-Margulies, once head of the economic police, lost his influential and important position as chief of the education section and executive committee member of the Union of Public Employees. Many lesser lights in the trade union leadership were also expelled.[62]

Disciplinary action was also taken against police officials and gendarmerie in Lower Austria and Vienna who had participated in the demonstrations or refused to heed orders from the Ministry of Interior. On October 20, the police commissioners in the Second, Fourth, Twentieth, and Twenty-first and Twenty-fifth districts of Vienna were dismissed by Police President Josef Holaubek. These men were all well-known Communists, including Max Goldberger and Peter Hofer, two former officers in the Honner Brigade. At the same time, one of the most important Communists in the Vienna police system, Police Commissioner Armand Frisch, of the international district, was transferred to Innsbruck.[63]

Nevertheless, ordering the dismissal of these men and carrying out the orders turned out to be two very different things. The Communist officials in question refused to obey the orders, and they were backed up by the Soviet military authorities. Chancellor Figl wrote two letters of protest to the Allied Council, and the United States sent an official letter of protest, but to no affect.[64] For the next five years, until the end of the occupation, the Austrian government was in the incongruous situation of appointing police commissioners who were unable to assume office, while the Communist officials continued to occupy the positions in complete defiance of the government. Only after the occupation came to an end in 1955 was Police President Holaubek able to enforce the changes.[65]

The mantle of Soviet protection was not so effective on the lower levels of the security system however. In November 1950 it was reported that some 300 policemen and gendarmerie were being investigated in connection with their activities during the strike.[66] Although Austrian officials are still reluctant to discuss the subject, there is every reason to accept the figures used by Lieutenant General V. P. Sviridov, when he raised the issue of the dismissal of Austrian police and gendarmerie at the Allied Council. Sviridov contended that on April 1, 1951, as a result of the September–October strikes, 249 "democratically minded" persons were dismissed by the President of the Vienna Police.[67]

Wholly accurate or not, the Soviet complaint pointed up one important result of the September–October riots. Communist power in the internal security system, which had been on the wane since the dismissal of Dr. Duermayer in 1947, was now completely broken. To this must be added the effect of the purges in the trade union movements. Many Communists were removed, but still more devastating was the extent to which they were discredited in the eyes of the working class. By the time the strike had come to an end, it was apparent to all that the Communist stake in the demonstrations was more than economic: disruption of the country by a small minority, acting in direct violation of the orders of the Trade Union Federation.

The Austrian Communists had staked their position on this one last attempt in the fall of 1950. Their defeat marked the end of any significant Communist strength in Austria apart from the Red Army. Five long years of intense effort had ended in complete failure.

The Road to Neutrality

To the intense disappointment of the Austrian government the obvious inability of the Austrian Communist Party to develop a genuine revolutionary situation in Austria, so conclusively demonstrated in 1950, failed to weaken Soviet determination to hold on to East Austria indefinitely. The Austrian treaty negotiations—a virtual marathon of discussions which had gone on sporadically since 1946 —were actually suspended in December 1950 for over two years, when the Soviets insisted that the abandonment of the Anglo-American base in Trieste was somehow related to further progress on the Austrian treaty. When one excuse evaporated, another was quickly mustered, and so it went on for four more years.

American frustration with this continuing chain of Soviet obstructive tactics reached a boiling point during the Council of Foreign Ministers meeting in Berlin in February 1954. Exasperated with the latest Soviet success in blocking a settlement, Secretary of State Dulles complained:

Can we sit here as the Foreign Ministers of our four countries solemnly and seriously addressing ourselves to agenda item no. 3 [the conclusion of an Austrian state treaty] and dare admit that the 374 previous discussions on this one item over a seven-year period have not explored every conceivable nook and cranny of the Austrian State Treaty?[1]

Despite the willingness of the Austrian delegation to accept Molotov's demand that an independent Austria must be a neutral Austria, the negotiations collapsed.[2] Moreover, Molotov's further insistence that the military occupation of Austria continue even after independence, "pending the conclusion of a peace treaty with Germany," meant in Dulles' view nothing more than the "indefinite occupation" of Austria.[3] Thus the Austrian treaty negotiations met the same unhappy fate at Berlin as those over the future of Germany. Dulles' concluding remarks at the last session of the conference, that "we have failed to satisfy the hopes which many throughout the world placed in us," were hardly promising for the future of the Austrian Treaty negotiations.

Seen against this one brief glimpse of what by 1954 was to the West an all too familiar story of Western frustration and Soviet temporizing, it is little wonder that the Western world was baffled when V. M. Molotov in a speech before the Supreme Soviet on February 8, 1955, announced Moscow's decision to uncouple the Austrian from the German peace treaty, thereby removing what had become the major obstacle to a settlement.[4] Even more startling than this announcement, which came less than a year after the Berlin impasse, was the pace at which this sudden reversal of Soviet policy was translated into action. On March 25 Austrian Chancellor Julius Raab, who had succeeded Leopold Figl in 1953, was invited to Moscow. The Austrian delegation duly arrived on April 12, and on April 15, 1955, the so-called "Moscow Memorandum" was signed.

In contrast to all the tortuous negotiations that had gone before, the two parties, in the space of a few days and fewer pages of text, had settled the remaining details of the German assets and reparations questions, and then went on to agree that Austria would assume the following political obligation: "In the sense of the declaration already given by Austria at the conference in Berlin in 1954 to join no military alliances and to permit no military bases on its territory, the Austrian federal government will make a declaration in a form which will obligate Austria internationally to practice in perpetuity a neutrality of the type maintained by Switzerland."[5] For its part, the Soviet Union promised to sign "without delay" the Austrian State Treaty, as amended by the Moscow agreements, leading to the complete withdrawal of occupation forces no later than December 31, 1955, and to participate with the other major powers in guaranteeing Austrian neutrality.

Following the Moscow agreements, events moved at an even more bewildering pace. A conference of the ambassadors of the four occupying powers was convened on May 2; and on May 15, 1955, the Austrian State Treaty was signed.[6] Partially in deference to American sensitivity on the point, the declaration of neutrality called for in the Soviet-Austrian memorandum was not mentioned in the treaty and was instead given legal effect by an amendment of the Austrian con-

stitution adopted on October 26, 1955.[7] Thus, after ten years of occupation and frustration, Austria was suddenly cast into the free world
—now neutralized and virtually demilitarized by virtue of the stringent military clauses in the treaty—but free. Obviously a bit non-
plussed by the sudden turn of events, the United States Senate Committee on Foreign Relations noted in its report of the draft treaty:
"In the space of seven weeks, between the Soviet invitation and the
signing, every obstacle thrown up during the previous seven years
was withdrawn or compromised by the Soviet Union and a treaty
acceptable to the Western Powers and Austria was signed."[8]

Uncertainty as to Soviet motives did not, however, slow the pace
of ratification; and by July 27 the process was finished, with the de-
posit of the French ratification of the State Treaty in Moscow. The
same day the Allied Council met for the 249th, and last, time. For
most Austrians, however, the end of the occupation did not come
until September 19, 1955, when, more than ten years after the Red
Army had appeared on the heights of the Kahlenberg, the last Russian soldier left Austria.

It is now over ten years since V. M. Molotov signed the Austrian
State Treaty for the Soviet Union, an event that marked the first—
and thus far the only—time the Soviet Union has consented to a
major readjustment of the rough line of demarcation established in
Europe by World War II. Thus, not only was the event unprece-
dented, but the precipitous, almost bizarre manner in which it was
carried out has prompted continuing speculation on the "lingering
enigma" of the Soviet withdrawal.[9]

The most prevalent view of the Soviet move emphasizes the net
gains for the West accruing from the Soviet decision, or uses the
eventual success of the negotiations as an example of what can happen
if we persist in negotiating with the Russians.[10] This general satisfaction of the West with the 1955 solution to the "Austrian problem"
was most exuberantly expressed by Secretary of State John Foster
Dulles in his report to the American people on May 17, 1955, after
his return from Vienna. Dulles recalled the sense of frustration that
had marked the long struggle to achieve an Austrian treaty, a struggle
that had gone on without success throughout 379 separate meetings
by the end of 1954. Then, as he put it:

And all of a sudden, a few weeks ago, out of the blue, came this announcement that the Russians were willing to take their troops out of Austria. I
don't think anyone yet knows fully the significance—the full significance—of
that. It is just one of those breaks that come if you keep on steadily, steadily,

keeping the pressure on. And all of a sudden you get a break—and this break came—

This is the first time a segment of the Red Army will have turned around and started to go back. Now that is going to have a tremendous impact in the other countries where the Red Armies are in occupation. It is going to create a desire—a mounting desire—on the part of those people to get the same freedom from that type of occupation that the Austrians have got. . . .

Why they are doing it, we are not quite sure. Except that we can be quite certain the policies of strength and firmness that we are adopting, in partnership with the other free countries of Europe, are beginning to pay off. And the people of Austria are the first to say—and all of them did say to me— this is the first dividend from the creation of Western European unity and the bringing of Germany into NATO.[11]

Those with a picture of the delightfully cynical Viennese may be excused for doubting that the Austrians did say any such thing, but the remarks do underline the questions surrounding the Russian move: why did the Russians abandon Eastern Austria when they did, and what are the practical consequences of that action for both East and West? The issues raised here go beyond the "Austrian problem" and touch on the forces and perceptions that shaped, and continue to shape, Soviet foreign policy.

I

There have been few exercises in diplomacy that have levied more stringent demands on patience and endurance than the Austrian treaty negotiations.* During the 1954 Berlin Conference, after the conclusion of the treaty had somehow again eluded the foreign ministers, John Foster Dulles, in a rare moment of humor, offered the following characterization of the tortured negotiations:

Mr. Chairman, for about two thousand years now there has been a figure in mythology who symbolizes tragic futility. That was Sisyphus, who, according to the Greek story, was given the task of rolling a great stone up to the top of a hill. Each time when, after great struggle and sweating, the stone was just at the brow of the hill, some evil force manifested itself and pushed the stone down. So poor Sisyphus had to start his task over again.

I suspect that for the next two thousand years that story will be forgotten, when generation after generation is told the story, the tragic story, of the Austrian State Treaty.[12]

---

* The material for this summary of the Austrian State Treaty comes mainly from the Dulles Papers, Category VIII, Council of Foreign Ministers (Moscow, 1947, 4 vols.; London, 1947, 2 vols.; Paris, 1949, 4 vols.), and Category IX, Statements— CFM [Council of Foreign Ministers]—Berlin. Dulles attended these meetings first as a Republican Party representative and later as Secretary of State. See also U.S. Dept. of State, *The Austrian State Treaty;* and Byrnes, *Speaking Frankly.*

Clearly, in Dulles' view no profound intelligence was required to determine who was "Sisyphus" and who the "evil force." Nevertheless, although this characterization fairly defines the roles most often played by the United States and the Soviet Union, it fails to draw attention to what appears to be a distinct evolution of both Soviet and Western attitudes toward the evacuation of Austria throughout the 1945-55 period. In looking back at the negotiations now, we can perceive several distinct phases. The first began in 1945 with a strenuous but fruitless effort by the West to give Austria its promised freedom, and ended in late 1947 with both sides equally unwilling to withdraw.

Secretary of State James F. Byrnes made the first attempt to launch Allied consideration of an Austrian treaty when he tried in the spring of 1946 to place the subject on the agenda of the Paris meeting of the Council of Foreign Ministers. Soviet Foreign Minister Molotov, however, refused to allow the question on the agenda, giving as one of his reasons that it was first necessary to conclude treaties with Germany's former allies (Bulgaria, Finland, Rumania, Hungary, and Italy). Therefore, once these treaties were signed (the Hungarian and Rumanian treaties, significantly enough, included clauses that permitted the Soviet Union to keep troops in those countries in order to maintain lines of communication as long as there was a Soviet occupation force in Austria), the Soviets did agree to an American plan, offered at the New York foreign ministers meeting in December 1946, to establish a special committee of deputies to work on the Austrian treaty. After meeting in London in January and February of 1947, this committee, the so-called Deputies for Austria, was able to prepare a draft treaty with approximately half the articles agreed to. This draft was presented to the foreign ministers at their Moscow meeting in March and April of 1947.

At Moscow the principal Austrian issue that divided the foreign ministers centered around the question of the disposition of the former German properties (Article 35 of the draft treaty), particularly the matter of the future of the oil fields. The greatest controversy was waged not over whether the Russians had a right to the "German assets" but how to define the term; Western carelessness at Potsdam was exacting its toll. Since the Russians had by this time seized what they considered to be "German assets," they were obviously anxious to arrive at a definition of what constituted an illegal transfer to the Germans (for this was the real issue) that agreed with their working interpretation. Consequently, Molotov proposed at the Moscow meeting that the deputies for Austria be instructed to "prepare a definition of German assets in Austria excluding property seized by the Germans as a result of directly violent action or as measures of Aryanization and without compensation."[13]

On another persistently controversial point, that of Yugoslavian territorial claims on southern Austria and demands for reparations, it was difficult to tell just how determined the Soviets were to back their fellow Communists. At one point Molotov remarked that since the ministers were considering the claims of Western nationals in Austria for compensation for property destroyed or seized, there was no reason to deny the Yugoslav claims.[14] But this seems to be as far as Molotov wished to push the issue. The Soviet position on the Yugoslavian claims was one of support in principle, with the recommendation that the question be referred back to the deputies for study. Indeed, the Soviets were so ambiguous on this issue that the U.S. delegation in one of its status reports could only say: "It is uncertain whether the Soviet action represents more than a gesture of support for a loyal ally, or whether the Soviet position will finally be abandoned in favor of agreement with the other delegations."[15]

The negotiations became critical when further progress hung on a decision of the Western Allies whether to accept the Soviet definition of "German assets" and a Soviet demand that Austria should place no restrictions on the export of profits from the confiscated German properties in the form of either products or currency. Moreover, the Russians wanted Austria's tiny post-occupation army (53,000 men) to be armed only with weapons of "national manufacture" and for the border fortifications to be left destroyed.[16] Western, and particularly American, resistance to these proposals was so intense and total that at one point the Austrian delegation in what was certainly one of the more classic ironies of these long negotiations pleaded with the Western Allies not to defend Austrian interests with such tenacity. In a secret memorandum to the Western delegations, Austrian Foreign Minister Gruber asked, in view of the overwhelming importance to the Austrian population of a speedy conclusion to the Treaty of Austria, that "the Delegations of the Western powers will not reject, *out of pure considerations of principle*, proposals which the Soviet delegation might put forward in answer to such an attempt —always under the condition that the practical gist of those proposals should be considered bearable by the Austrian government."[17]

John Foster Dulles, who was at the time serving as a Republican adviser to Secretary of State Marshall, was somewhat dismayed at the

Austrian attitude. In a letter to Senator Arthur H. Vandenberg, dated March 29, 1947, Dulles remarked: "Gruber, the Austrian Minister of Foreign Affairs, is here. I saw him a minute or two yesterday. He is so eager to get out the Soviet troops that I think he would accept almost any economic terms."[18] A week or so later, when the conference was beginning to bog down on the Austrian issue, Dulles was to include in a letter to Vandenberg what, by the spring of 1947, had become the American position on the treaty.

There is growing doubt that an Austrian treaty will be possible unless we let the Soviet Union pretty much write [its] own ticket, which will make Austria into a Soviet colony. It is going to be a hard decision, as the Austrian government, which is very able and quite anti-Soviet, is so eager to get the Soviet troops out that they would want almost any economic solution.[19]

Thus, in the American view, Soviet control of 10–15 per cent of Austria's industrial sector—this was the figure used by Gruber at Moscow—combined with the unrestricted export of profits and products, would make Austria, as Secretary of State Marshall put it, a "puppet" of the Soviet Union.[20] American resolve on this point thus made it clear that in the spring of 1947 both the Soviet Union and the Western powers took a very uncompromising line on the conditions under which Austria would be set adrift. All this contributed to the general despair of the Austrian delegation, particularly Gruber, who later complained of the tactical clumsiness of the West in handling the Austrian question.[21] With the positions of East and West so frozen on economic provisions of the treaty, the Austrian negotiations added to the general failure of the Moscow conference. The only positive result of the Moscow conference on the Austrian issue was the appointment of a special Austria Treaty Commission, which met in Vienna from May to October of 1947 in an attempt to make further progress with the treaty.

An explanation for Soviet behavior at the conference table during the period from 1945 to the spring of 1947 can best be found by considering the changing pattern of internal Austrian political circumstances, and the relationship of this pattern to broader East-West problems. The Soviets certainly wanted political control of all Austria, but once this was quite out of the question, they saw no advantage or necessity, as they did in Germany, to construct a rump state. Eastern Austria would have been a parody of a "sovereign" nation, even by Soviet standards. To have forced the division of the country would have deprived Eastern Austria of the industrial raw materials and electrical power of Western Austria. Without these materials and power, Eastern Austria's industries would have been paralyzed unless the necessary resources were taken from the already hard-pressed satellite economies. It was apparently easier to allow the Marshall Plan to revitalize the suppliers of raw materials in the Western zone. Since there was already an all-Austrian national government established in Vienna's international zone as a result of the Soviet Union's initiative, the creation of an East Austrian government would have been for the Russians a propaganda nightmare as well as an economic liability.

Confronted with such an unpleasant alternative to living with the consequences of the November elections, the Russians adopted a wait-and-see attitude. Austria was on the brink of starvation and economic chaos during the winter of 1945–46, the classic ingredients of social disintegration— obviously a situation that would make serious inroads into the popular support of the coalition government. Moreover, even after the November debacle, the Austrian Communists retained powerful political assets in the security forces and in the trade unions. It is little wonder, then, that Western efforts to get the Austrian question on the agenda of the Council of Foreign Ministers in 1946 proved fruitless. Soviet hopes for the peaceful political integration of all Austria into the Communist bloc were as yet not fully dispelled.

Beginning in 1947, the future of Austria became inexorably bound up with shifting East-West power relationships. By 1947 Soviet expansionist probes had provoked American efforts to stabilize the deteriorating security situation in Greece with the Truman Doctrine and to shore up Western European governments with the economic aid of the Marshall Plan. These efforts were met "in kind" with even more hostility and militancy in Soviet foreign policy, a hostility expressed most notably in A. A. Zhdanov's violently anti-Western direction of the newly organized Cominform.

The clouds of this storm period of East-West relations were just beginning to form when the Foreign Ministers Council meeting in Moscow took up the Austrian question, in the spring of 1947. The brutally hard, uncompromising line taken by both East and West on the Austrian treaty bitterly disappointed the Austrians and contributed to one of the Austrian government's most difficult moments.

The winter of 1946–47 in Vienna had been one of the worst in memory, far grimmer than the preceding year. A depressing shortage of food, heat, and electricity made the failure of the Moscow conference a particularly hard blow. Moreover, UNRRA shipments of food had ceased in May, and the Marshall Plan aid, still but an idea in Washington, would take another year to reach Austria. Events in

Hungary added to the general unrest. In May 1947 Hungary was in the last stages of a Communist take-over, and the proceedings soon had an ominous echo in Vienna.

On May 5, 1947, the Austrian Communists staged an impressive food riot, which culminated in an attack on the Federal Chancellery. Shortly thereafter, Communist leader Ernst Fischer suggested to Chancellor Figl that Soviet concessions might be forthcoming if the Austrian government were reorganized to include more Communists. Fischer also proposed that Dr. Josef Dobretsberger, a Communist fellow traveler, be chosen Chancellor.[22] The offer was less than politely refused, but the attempt showed that Communist militancy in Austria had not as yet reached its highwater mark.

After the failure at Moscow to break the deadlock over Austria, prospects for a negotiated settlement grew still dimmer despite the existence of the special committee in Vienna. During the Council of Foreign Ministers meeting in London in November and December of 1947, Molotov revealed the extent of Soviet interest in moving on with the Austrian treaty by insisting that the issue, although first on the agenda, be discussed after the German question. Later, in response to a French plan, which proposed that the German assets problem be handled by drawing up a percentage scheme for the control of oil production and making a lump-sum payment to the Soviet Union for the other German assets, Molotov said simply that the plan was not "an appropriate basis for settlement."[23] And then, just two days before the conference ended, Molotov indicated that, although the French proposals were unacceptable, he did think that some Soviet concessions were possible.[24] On the last day of the London conference, December 17, the Deputies for the Austrian Treaty decided to reconvene no later than five days after the receipt of a promised Soviet counterproposal to the French scheme.

When the Soviet proposals, dated January 24, 1948, arrived, the American deputy, Samuel Reber, in his capacity as acting chairman of the Deputies for Austria, called for a meeting of the group in February.[25] With the convening of the deputies in London, the stage was set for one of the most curious episodes in the entire tangled tale of the Austrian State Treaty.

It is the official American view of the London discussions, which took place in the spring of 1948, that while some progress was made on the German assets question, the negotiations faltered on the matter of the Soviet Union's uncompromising support of the Yugoslavian claims to parts of Southern Austria.[26] The controversy was so serious, and apparently so insoluble, that when Reber informed the Council of Foreign Ministers of the suspension of the talks, he stated that the deputies were unable to set a date for the resumption of negotiations.[27] All this, it will be remembered, happened some three weeks before the break-up of the Berlin Four-Power Committee and the beginnings of the Berlin crisis. Thus the high hopes of January resulted in a complete break by May, and all because of the Yugoslavian issue. Yet a careful reading of the available material on the proceedings suggests a slightly different story, a story more in keeping with the events outside the London meeting.[28]

A comparison of the French and Soviet proposals for the economic sections of the draft treaty submitted at the opening of the London meetings is testimony to the ever-narrowing area of disagreement. The French proposal would have given the Soviets one-half of Austria's oil production and one-third of oil exploration rights for a period to be agreed on; the Soviet plan was for two-thirds of both for a period of 50 years. For the other assets the French suggested a sum of $100 million to be paid to the Soviets over ten years; the Soviet proposal was $200 million over a two-year period.[29]

As the weeks of negotiation wore on, and particularly after the Soviet delegation returned from Moscow after the Easter recess bearing new concessions, it appeared that the economic clauses of the treaty were close to final agreement. First of all, the Soviets consented to reduce the lump-sum payment from $200 million to $150 million and to extend the repayment period from two to six years. Second, in a Four-Power agreement of April 6, 1948—an agreement that has never been officially mentioned by the United States—it was agreed that the Soviet Union would have the following rights to Austrian oil properties confiscated as German assets: (1) for the extraction of oil from areas already under exploration—30 years; (2) for oil exploration—eight years, with a further period of 25 years for extraction, to run from the time when oil has been discovered in the explored areas.[30]

With the economic sections of the treaty all but resolved and the discussions on the rest of the treaty proceeding smoothly, the Austrians began to hope that success was at hand.[31] But as was to happen with depressing frequency over the years, the negotiations suddenly faltered and were broken off abruptly, this time with no promise of renewal. The Western position on the reason for the breakdown was that the Soviets were uncompromising on the Yugoslavian territorial claims. Austrian Foreign Minister Gruber, on the other hand, alleges that he was told by a British diplomat that the British delegation had instructions to force the Russians to give an unequivocal answer on

Yugoslavian claims or move to end the conference. Gruber also contends that the Russians were not unbending on the issue and were prepared to discuss any counterproposal.[32]

Whatever the relative merits of these interpretations, and additional evidence will be necessary to finally resolve the question, certain things are clear about the 1948 negotiations: (1) the Soviet delegates made a strenuous effort to reach agreement on the economic clauses, to the point of offering important concessions after a trip back to Moscow; (2) the Yugoslavian issue, which had been played down the year before, brought the discussion to a sudden end, with the Western powers demanding Russian assurances on the maintenance of Austria's 1937 borders before the West would resume negotiations (a pre-condition which the West would ignore in 1949).

Why the Soviets would be so amenable on the economic clauses of the treaty and so obstinate on the Yugoslavian issue is unclear. They must have realized that there was no give on the Western and Austrian position on the integrity of the Austrian border. Moreover, from what we now know of the nature of Yugoslavian-Soviet relations after the war, and particularly during the first months of 1948, it could be argued that if Stalin thought it was in the interest of the Soviet Union to conclude an Austrian treaty, Yugoslavia's interests would have been quickly sacrificed.[33] The counterargument that Stalin was actually defending Yugoslavian interests to the point of wrecking the London conference in order to head off the developing Yugoslavian-Soviet split has merit; but it fails to explain why the Soviets were so anxious to reach agreement on the economic clauses. In any event, it is clear that the West was not anxious to stay in London to debate the border issue; and it would not be until spring of 1949 that discussion on the Austrian treaty was once more reactivated.

The best explanation for what appears to have been a reversal of roles during the first few months of 1948—that is, Soviet interest and Western disinterest in an Austrian treaty—can be found in events outside the conference halls.

First of all, February 1948 saw the Prague putsch, a Communist take-over without the use of Soviet troops. With the Communists successful in Czechoslovakia, the Russians had an additional reason to believe that the Italian elections set for April 18 would result in a Communist victory. In Austria itself, an end to the occupation would remove the Western troops, a proven obstacle to the extension of Communist influence, before the Marshall Plan had a chance to show results. Indeed, since Austria was not to join the European Recovery Program until April 16, 1948, an agreement on an Austrian treaty might have forestalled—even prevented—participation by Austria in the Marshall Plan. Moreover, assurance of the continued economic presence of the Soviet Union in Austria after the signing of the treaty would have given the Russians considerable leverage to harass the coalition government and to force the return of the Austrian Communists to the government. With Italy on the threshold of communism, a demilitarized and economically vulnerable Austria would have little chance to avoid becoming part of a Communist chain extending from the Soviet zone of Germany through Czechoslovakia and Austria to Italy. As a bonus effect, the unruly Yugoslavia would be completely isolated, and more vulnerable to Soviet discipline.

For their part, the Western powers had every reason to remain in Austria during these critical and uncertain months. The Czechoslovakian coup had been a great shock to the West. Given the total military vacuum that would have been left in the wake of a withdrawal of Western military forces and the certainty that the Soviets would retain an economic foothold in Austria, there was good reason to suspect that Austria was a likely candidate to follow Czechoslovakia. It would seem, therefore, that in the spring of 1948 the United States had come to the conclusion that there could be no Austrian settlement until a Western-trained military force could take over and the country had been brought to its economic feet by liberal doses of Marshall Plan aid.

If this reasoning is correct, then the sudden breakoff of the treaty negotiations, when it appeared that the Soviets actually may have wanted a settlement, and the beginning of the organization of a Western-trained paramilitary group in Austria as the cadre for an Austrian army (see Chapter 5) fit together nicely. In any event, by June 1948 whatever plans East or West had for Austria were caught up in the swirl of crisis, beginning with the collapse of Four-Power control in Germany, the Berlin blockade, and the emergence of a West Germany sponsored by the United States and Britain. But for a brief moment it appears that the roles Secretary of State Dulles assigned in his story of Sisyphus had become slightly confused.

II

Broadly speaking, after the spring of 1948 the major policy initiatives within Austria were taken by the Western powers. The Marshall Plan, the development of a powerful mobile gendarme force, preparations for a post-occupation Austrian army are all in ready contrast to the official passiveness of the Soviet Union. The Soviets seemed content to protect their assets in the security forces and the trade unions in hopes that the Austrian Communist Party would be able to regain the political initiative. The most pressing task for the Soviet Union after 1948 was to short-circuit the formation of a Western-sponsored West German government. Austria, with the continuing failure of Communist militancy to make inroads into the strength of the coalition government, was decidedly a secondary issue.

The passiveness of the Soviet military forces in Austria was a blow to the hopes of the Austrian Communists. Throughout the occupation period, Soviet support of the KPO always stopped short of direct military involvement. This was as true in 1947, when failure meant the near destruction of Communist influence in the internal security forces outside the Soviet zone, as it was in 1950, when Soviet refusal to become directly involved meant the final failure of Communist militancy in Austria. Particularly painful for the Austrian Communists, and particularly revealing of Soviet intentions in Austria after the spring of 1948, was the refusal of the Soviet managers of the USIA plants to allow the workers to do more than make a first-day appearance during the "general strike" of September 1948.

Politically embarrassed by the Soviet Union's economic exploitation of Austria, the KPO was to find during the period of Communist militancy (1947–50) no compensating support from the Soviet military in the party's efforts to harass and unseat the coalition government. By 1949 the Austrian Communists might well have questioned the advantage of having Soviet troops in Austria, since the elections of 1945 had cost the KPO its decisive positions in the government— positions that, incidentally, the Austrian Communists owed to the Red Army. More significant than the misgivings the Austrian Communist Party might have had were signs that Moscow was also beginning to question the advantage of a Soviet military presence in Austria.

If there was one thing that kept monotonous pace with the Austrian treaty negotiations, it was the Council of Foreign Ministers meetings. At the sixth session of the meetings, held in Paris from May 23 to June 16, 1949, the United States was represented by Dean Acheson, France by Robert Schuman, the Soviet Union by A. Y. Vyshinsky, and Britain by Ernest Bevin.

In a letter to Arthur H. Vandenberg written at about the halfway point of the 1949 Paris Foreign Ministers meeting, John Foster Dulles summed up what he thought the Soviets were after in Paris:

It now seems apparent that what the Soviet[s] want most is a resumption of the regular Four Power talks—about Berlin, about Germany, about a German Peace Treaty, about East-West trade—which will create the appearance of ending the "cold war." I think they want that in order to reassure their own people, the satellite people, and perhaps most of all the American people, in order to remove the stimulus to such U.S. effort as is exemplified in the E.R.P., Atlantic Pact, M.A.P. [Military Assistance Program], our own military establishment, etc.

Of course most of us would like to see the tension relaxed—*if* there is real reason for it. But I think that there is need of some actual *acts* on the Soviet side, such as the conclusion of the Austrian Treaty, recognition of more adequate right of access to Berlin, etc.[34]

Dulles' impression that the spring of 1949 had brought with it a change in Soviet tactics, due primarily to a need for a breathing spell while an unfavorable power relationship could be corrected, has been elaborated recently into a provocative thesis about the evolution of Soviet foreign policy. Marshall Shulman argues that 1949, rather than Stalin's death in 1953, marks the beginnings of "a marked evolution in the Soviet strategic outlook toward Western Europe, of a groping toward a more effective adaptation to the new political and technological facts of life." The reasons for this shift were as follows: "With the failure of the Berlin blockade, it became clear that a provisional stabilization had been established in Europe and that the aggressive militancy of the first postwar period of Soviet policy had resulted in an interacting spiral of international tension and a growth of Western military power. The prime need in Soviet policy, therefore, was to check the adverse trend by relaxing international tension and playing up Western divergencies."[35]

Mr. Shulman's point is well taken when it comes to Austria. At the Paris meeting, the Soviet Union was apparently genuinely interested in Austrian settlement and made the necessary concessions on the Yugoslavian and reparations issues to get such a settlement. During a restricted meeting of the four foreign ministers on June 12, Vyshinsky agreed that the borders should remain those of prewar Austria and that Yugoslavia would receive its reparations from Austrian property in Yugoslavia. In agreeing to this compromise Vyshinsky made it clear that while the Yugoslavs' other claims were just, "we cannot, however, postpone the Austrian treaty indefinitely, and problems which present difficulties cannot be a permanent obstacle to a settlement."[36] Two days later, at a formal meeting of the foreign ministers, Vyshinsky announced that because the Western delegates were now prepared to accept the Soviet proposal of January 24, 1948, as

amended (which was essentially true), there was no reason that the
final draft of the treaty could not be ready by September 1. He also
repeated the terms of the Yugoslavian deal as agreed to on June 12.[37]

Thus, Dulles was undoubtedly correct in suggesting that the conclusion of the Austrian treaty was a gesture the Soviets were willing
to make in order to induce a period of *détente* and coexistence. What
is unique about the Paris meeting, in comparison with all the other
moments when an Austrian treaty seemed at hand, is that for the first
time both sides apparently wanted a settlement. For its part, the
United States probably felt that Austria had recovered sufficiently to
stand the strains of Communist internal and external pressure.

Given the degree of consensus and the apparent determination of
all Four Powers when they left Paris to conclude a treaty, the subsequent collapse of the negotiations, in the fall of 1949, was particularly
baffling to many observers, although "collapse" had long since become the hallmark of the Austrian discussions. Moreover, the Soviets
soon made it clear that they had no intention of going on with the
treaty negotiations. Consequently, after 1949 they began to employ
a series of obstructive tactics—the future of Trieste, the disposition
of such important items as dried peas, an alleged resurgence of
Nazism, etc.—which have been described as "implausible, irrelevant
side issues."[38] This brand of Soviet obstructionism was to last right
through the Berlin conference in 1954.

The cause of the abrupt change in Soviet policy toward an Austrian
settlement after Paris is rooted in a change of Soviet tactics which
occurred in the fall of 1949. Vyshinsky had failed at Paris to secure a
return to Four-Power control in Germany, a maneuver designed to
prevent the onrushing establishment of West Germany. When the
Federal Republic of Germany was formally baptized with the convening of the Bundestag on September 7, 1949, the Soviet Union was
quick to follow with the formation in October of the German Democratic Republic.

With the freezing of the German situation, there was little immediate hope for an Austrian settlement. Conciliatory gestures in the interest of *détente* were hardly appropriate in such a moment of high
European tension. Moreover, the explosion of the first Soviet atomic
device in September 1949 and the final victory of the Chinese Communists gave renewed confidence to the Soviet Union, restoring the
power balance obviously tipped in favor of the West in the spring of
1949. Then, too, the summer of 1949 ushered in a period of witch-
hunting throughout the Soviet bloc while all traces of the Tito heresy

were ruthlessly rooted out. The process of intense Stalinization and economic integration, which began in Eastern Europe in 1950, was obviously preoccupying and required privacy. In such circumstances, negotiations that might have led to a Western-advanced position adjacent to Czechoslovakia were completely out of the question. Eastern Austria thus once again assumed the role of an insulating zone, while Stalin, this time, put his house in order.

Given these circumstances, it is no wonder that beginning in November 1949 the Soviet Union, in spite of substantial treaty concessions on the part of the West, appeared less and less interested. By 1950, it was clear that the Russians had no intention of moving on with the treaty negotiations. In 1951, for example, not a single meeting of deputies was held. In 1952, the West presented a revised and much shorter draft treaty, but Soviet resistance to even discussing a new approach was total. Thus, six years after the negotiations began, Austrian independence seemed further away than ever.

III

After the death of Stalin in 1953, the style of the Soviet Union's holding action in Austria changed noticeably. The appointment in June 1953 of a civilian Soviet High Commissioner (the Western powers had made the shift in 1950), the relaxation of zonal controls, the abolition of censorship in 1953—these were the most notable signs of the shift.

To the disappointment of the Austrians, however, these gestures were relevant to Austria's future only in the sense that they underlined the Soviet Union's acceptance of the fact that Austria could not be "peacefully" brought into the Communist fold. The last doubts about this were removed with the 1953 national elections, when the Communists were again unable to pull above 5 per cent. Perhaps more important than the national totals, however, was the remarkable fact that after almost ten years of occupation the Communists could command only 5 per cent of the votes in Lower Austria and Burgenland—both in the Soviet zone. As a result, in 1953 not one Communist delegate went to parliament from Burgenland, and only by the grace of the proportional representation system did one arrive from Lower Austria.[39]

Nevertheless, although Austria seemed a hopelessly barren ground for communism—and after 1953 a safe place in which the Soviet Union could make gestures of good will—this did not mean that in 1953 Russia was willing to withdraw. That Austria had become a

;aining counter in a larger game was made apparent at the Berlin
:ting of foreign ministers in early 1954. Dulles' frustration at this
eting was index enough that the Soviet position, as championed by
ɔlotov, of coupling the German and Austrian settlements admitted
﹍ no negotiation. Not a year later, however, came the *volte-face* of
February 8, 1955, and the door was opened to an Austrian settlement
—ironically enough, by Molotov himself.

Although John Foster Dulles saw the Soviet decision to leave Austria as "just one of those breaks that come if you keep on steadily,
steadily, keeping the pressure on," he was forced to concede to President Eisenhower that "the cause of this change of policy can only be
conjectured."[40]

What follows is also conjecture, but conjecture formed against a
backdrop of what we now know about the course of those events
inside and outside Austria that shaped, and possibly also explain, the
Soviet decision. The essence of the argument is that, in "giving up"
Austria, the Soviets were in fact giving up very little, and in making
the decision, the Soviets saw the Austrian move as an integral part of
a long-term effort to turn the concept of "neutralism" to the Soviet
Union's advantage.

As the year 1955 began, the Russian government could hardly
have been pleased with the events of the preceding 12 months. The
military advantage the Soviets had attained in 1953 in exploding a
usable hydrogen weapon (the United States had tested an admittedly undeliverable hydrogen device some months before) had been lost
with the successful testing of a U.S. hydrogen bomb in early 1954.
On the economic front, the Soviet Union was faced with a serious
grain crisis at a moment when Malenkov's emphasis on the consumer
economy was detracting from military expenditures.[41] Perhaps even
more adverse to Soviet interests than a momentary imbalance of military power and a faltering economy was Moscow's lack of success
in preventing the military integration of West Germany into the
Western alliance. Molotov's insistence at the Berlin conference that
there would be no Austrian settlement until a solution of the German problem acceptable to Moscow had been worked out was just
one more way of raising the price for bringing West Germany into
the Western alliance.

Nevertheless, despite Soviet pressure, the Paris agreements of October 1954 created the machinery for the admission of West Germany
into NATO. Shortly thereafter, at the December ministerial meeting
of the North Atlantic Council in Paris, Secretary of State Dulles, in

pressing for the adoption of the so-called "forward strategy," which envisioned the defense of Europe to begin on the eastern border of the Federal Republic, declared that "atomic weapons were increasingly becoming the equivalent of conventional weapons."[42] For the Soviet Union this meant that the entry of West Germany into NATO could mean the implacement of tactical nuclear weapons on the East German border. In response, the Soviet Union unleashed a blistering, if badly belated, campaign designed to prevent ratification of the Paris agreements. During this campaign, the Russians played their Austrian card in curiously hesitant fashion.

At one point in the campaign Moscow made it painfully clear to the West Germans what ratification of the Paris agreements would mean.

The Paris agreements run counter to the interests of the German people particularly and especially because they would prolong the division of Germany for many years and would be an obstacle to her peaceful reunification. Union of the peaceful German Democratic Republic with a German Federal Republic which had been militarized and made a party to military alliances would obviously be impossible. . . . [On the other hand] There still exist unexplored possibilities of achieving agreement on the reunification of Germany with due regard to the legitimate interests of her people, and on the holding of free all-German elections for this purpose in 1955.[43]

This statement was made on January 15, 1955, when the Soviet Union could not have reasonably expected to head off the ratification process in West Germany. But there was at least a chance, particularly because of the resistance of the West German Social Democrats, who were apparently persuaded that ratification meant the end of hopes for reunification. The decision of the West German government to postpone twice the second reading of the ratification bill must also have encouraged Moscow. Nevertheless, the measure was finally approved on February 27 by the Bundestag after much uproar and one of the most bitter debates in West German parliamentary history.

One of the more interesting sidelights of this intensive and ultimately unsuccessful Soviet campaign was that the Russians had made little use of its hostage, Eastern Austria, in attempting to frustrate the entry of West Germany into the Western alliance. Molotov's speech on February 8 came far too late to have any real effect on the West German decision. Had the Soviets made the offer of exchanging Austrian neutralization for reunification in, say, the spring of 1954 and held out the possibility of a similar deal in Germany, the gesture could have been very helpful in keeping West Germany out of

NATO. Why the Soviet Union waited so long to bring forth the Austrian offer, and then for reasons that seem only partially related to Germany, remains somewhat of a mystery. The best explanation probably lies in the nature of the power struggle that was then going on within the Kremlin.

Although details of the struggle between Khrushchev and the Malenkov-Molotov government remain obscure, it now appears that one of the controversies between Khrushchev and Molotov was what the Soviet Union should do with its obviously indigestible slice of Austria. Molotov, who was also opposed to Khrushchev's desire for a *rapprochement* with Yugoslavia, was convinced that Austria could never be a genuine neutral. Moreover, to abandon permanently a territorial prize of World War II would establish a bad precedent.[44] Khrushchev of course prevailed, and Molotov himself announced the new Austrian course on the very day the Khrushchev era began, with the resignation of G. M. Malenkov and the launching of the policy of "relaxation."

The 1955 decision was prompted not by Soviet objectives in Austria itself but by Khrushchev's view of the dangers and opportunities on the international horizon. Responding to an internal need for new policies to overcome economic deficiencies, and to an external need for relaxation of tension while Soviet military technology coped with the Western advantage in aircraft-delivered hydrogen weapons, Khrushchev sought a period of East-West *détente*, as Stalin had in 1949. The economic effort led to a reemphasis on heavy industry and the only partially successful virgin lands program; the military effort led to Sputnik in 1957 and the initial Soviet advantage in space technology.

In the meantime, while the Warsaw Pact consolidated security arrangements within Eastern Europe, the Soviet Union sought to lessen Western military pressures by initiating a campaign against military alliances and for "disarmament" and "neutralism." The pilgrimage to Belgrade to make peace with Tito, the public relations junkets of Khrushchev and Bulganin, Soviet enthusiasm for the 1955 Bandung Conference of Afro-Asians, the disarmament proposals of May 10, 1955, the invitation to Adenauer to visit Moscow, the offer to conclude a peace treaty with Japan, were all part of the same diplomatic offensive. But most of all, Khrushchev wanted a "summit" meeting. And here the Austrian hostage played a major role.

We have it on the authority of former President Eisenhower what role the Austrian settlement played in bringing a reluctant Secretary Dulles to the "summit." Eisenhower recalls that he always gave the

same "stock answer" to all suggestions that the United States respond
to Churchill's call for a summit meeting: "I would not go to a summit meeting merely because of friendly words and plausible promises
by the men in the Kremlin; actual deeds giving some indication of
a Communist readiness to negotiate constructively will have to be
produced before I would agree to such a meeting." But Khrushchev
was soon to take away this prop.

Almost simultaneously the Soviets took a step that at least gave a glimmer
of hope that they, under their new leadership, might be genuinely seeking
mutually acceptable answers. This act involved Austria. . . .
    Because of the Soviets' action, and not wishing to appear senselessly stub-
born in my attitude toward a summit meeting—so hopefully desired by so
many—I instructed Secretary Dulles to let it be known through diplomatic
channels that if the other powers were genuinely interested in such a meeting we were ready to listen to their reasoning.[45]

Even after the meeting was arranged, Secretary Dulles had nothing
but the gravest misgivings. In a secret memorandum to the President,
he listed among the "Soviet goals at Geneva":

An appearance that the West concede the Soviet rulers a moral and social
equality which will help the Soviets maintain their satellite rule by disheart-
ening potential resistance, *and help increase neutralism by spreading the
impression that only "power" rivalries, and not basic principles, create present tensions.*[46]

As to the possibility of preventing Soviet success in achieving these
goals, Dulles was gloomy. On the matter of achieving "moral and
social equality," Dulles wrote: "The Soviets will probably make considerable gains in this respect. These gains can be minimized by the
President avoiding social meeting where he will be photographed
with Bulganin, Khrushchev, etc., and by maintaining an austere
countenance on occasions where photographing together is inevi-
table." On neutralism and demilitarization, he wrote: "It will probably be impossible to prevent some slight increase within Germany
of neutralism and demilitarization, and within France, of the public
nostalgia for a resumption of special relations between France and
Russia to contain Germany."[47]
    However unrealistic Dulles may have been about President Eisen-
hower's "maintaining an austere countenance," his worries about an
increase in "neutralism" were apparently matched by Soviet expecta-
tions. It is at this point that the role of Austria in Soviet calculations
comes back into focus, and we can begin to draw up a balance sheet
on why the Soviet Union let Austria go and what the decision tells
us about Soviet foreign policy behavior.

In letting Austria go, Khrushchev probably reasoned that since the country could not be peacefully assimilated into the "Socialist camp," signing the State Treaty would not be too expensive, for the following reasons.

1. By 1955 the strategic and political necessity for maintaining a forward and insulating zone in Austria had largely disappeared. Until 1948 Austria could have been considered a military and political staging area for probes against Western Europe. With the military unification and political pacification of Western Europe, Eastern Austria had become an exposed position for the Soviet Union. The Czechoslovakia border provided a more defensible military line. Then, too, Khrushchev probably thought that his Eastern European political house was in order by 1955 and an insulating zone such as Stalin used in 1949–50 was unnecessary. (A year later he would not have been so sure.) Moreover, until 1955 the continuance of the Austrian occupation had given the Soviets the treaty right to keep troops in Rumania and Hungary. The Warsaw Pact now gave the Soviets the same rights, this time in Czechoslovakia as well.

2. The military and political restrictions imposed on Austria by the treaty are such that not only is Anschluss with Germany forbidden, but Austria is now virtually a military vacuum in the center of Europe. Because Czechoslovakia and Hungary can fortify their Austrian borders and West Germany and Italy cannot (this is not a treaty provision but simply a political reality), Austria forms a convenient gateway to attack on Western Europe.

3. With the neutralization of Austria, the lines of communication and supply between two of the most important NATO countries—West Germany and Italy—must now pass through France (the Austrian prohibition of military overflights during the 1958 Lebanon crisis is one example of the problems the West has with Austria's strategic position). If France's withdrawal of its military forces from NATO is eventually followed with a denial of French territory to NATO activities, the North Atlantic Treaty area would be split by a neutral belt, a situation that would have serious military implications for the West. Even now, however, the difficulties of moving men and supplies from the Elbe to Verona illustrates the logistic problems caused by the neutralization of Austria.

4. Austria had become by 1955 an economic liability, thereby removing one of the major reasons for continued Soviet occupation. Austrian oil was no longer a useful commodity for the Russians, who by this time had enough domestic oil to threaten the world markets of the West. Moreover, the USIA industries had been on the verge of

bankruptcy for a number of years, utterly unable to compete on the Austrian market (the massive rehabilitation job necessary after 1955 is evidence of this).

5. For the Soviets there was no particular ideological problem involved in the release of Austria. The Austrians, even in the Soviet zone, had never embraced Communist dogma; consequently, they remained in Soviet eyes ideological infidels—a condition certainly more acceptable to the Soviets than if the Austrians had first embraced and then attempted to renounce communism. In 1956 the Hungarians were to learn how the Russians deal with converts who consider apostasy. Furthermore, as long as the Soviet Union had control of an area where political dissent was openly expressed, and apparently tolerated by the Russians, there was always the possibility that this pocket of discontent could begin to affect the rest of Eastern Europe.

The most compelling justification for Khrushchev's action, however, was not a short-range tally sheet of practical dividends vs. costs, but a long-term calculation that the Austrian settlement would serve as a model—an inducement for some to accept demilitarization, for others to point up the advantages of staying out of military alliances. Part of this calculation may have been based on what seemed in 1955 to be the United States' inability to cope with the idea of "neutralism."

In the Austrian case the United States only grudgingly came to accept the idea of neutrality. At the Berlin meeting of foreign ministers in 1954, Dulles responded to the Soviet demand for, and the Austrian acceptance of, neutralization with the following remarks:

A neutral status is an honorable status if it is voluntarily chosen by a nation. ... Under the Austrian State Treaty as heretofore drafted, Austria would be free to choose for itself to be a neutral state like Switzerland. Certainly the United States would fully respect its choice in this respect, as it fully respects the comparable choice of the Swiss nation.

However, it is one thing for a nation to choose to be neutral. It is another for a nation to have neutrality forcibly imposed on it by other nations as a perpetual servitude.*

Although Austrians may argue that their acceptance of neutrality was indeed "voluntary," the record indicates that there was at least a compelling *sine qua non* on the Soviet side. As to the idea of neutral-

* Dulles Papers, Category IX, Council of Foreign Ministers, Berlin, FPM (54)60, February 13, 1954. Dulles would later contend that the roles at Berlin were reversed. He told reporters at an off-the-record briefing that there was nothing new about neutralization: "The Austrians proposed that in Berlin a year ago last February, and at that time that proposal was looked upon with favor by the

ity on the "Swiss model," the treaty restrictions, not to mention the Austrians' own inclinations, make the armed neutrality of Switzerland an utterly unrealistic model.

A few days before the Austrian State Treaty was signed in Vienna, N. A. Bulganin gave the Warsaw Conference, then in the process of constructing the Warsaw Pact, the first indication of how the Soviet Union planned to use the Austrian model:

It must be admitted that the full restoration of the political and economic independence of a neutral Austria will be a significant contribution to the strengthening of European peace. That there proved to be public forces in Austria who determinedly took this course testifies to the great potentialities for promoting cooperation among states, regardless of their social systems. *It would be wrong to assume that this attitude is held by the Austrian government alone. There are quite a number of states, both in Europe and in Asia, which are adverse to joining aggressive military blocs.*[48]

In Europe the most immediate objective was to use the Austrian example as a temptation to those in Italy or West Germany who for ideological or practical reasons were hesitant about NATO. Here is one example of what the Italians were hearing from Moscow in 1955:

The proponents of [Italy's] "Atlantic" policy realize only too well what a defeat they sustained with the signing of the Austria State Treaty. The fact is that Italy's northern neighbour by adopting a status of perpetual neutrality conclusively exposes the false argument that participation in pro-American blocs is the only possible course open to Italy.[49]

As for the West Germans, a *Pravda* editorial had the following to say about the Austrian example:

It is no accident that people in Western Germany are beginning to ponder this example more and more. There the following question is being asked more and more often: If little Austria with its 7,000,000 inhabitants not only did not lose its independence but on the contrary strengthened it, why must the German Federal Republic reject such a policy? Why must it contribute vast sums to the arms race and restrict its sovereignty for the benefit of the military bloc of the Western powers?[50]

Among the diverse reasons why the Soviet Union released Austria, an important one may have been the use of Austria as an example of the advantages of neutralism. With Austria and Finland as showpieces, it is likely that the Soviet Union envisioned in 1955 a band or corridor of neutral states running from Sweden and Finland in the

---

Western powers, and the Soviet Union rejected it at that time. Now they are having to change their position" (*ibid.*). Verbatim transcript of Dulles' background briefing at Ambassador Dillon's residence, Paris, May 7, 1955.

north through West Germany and Austria in the center, to Yugo-slavia and Italy in the south. The advantages to the Soviet Union of such a corridor would have been enormous, particularly for strategic considerations, in pushing the West's military forces back from the Warsaw Pact frontier. The effort failed, since Italy and West Germany chose to bind themselves tightly to NATO. But in the days when Adenauer's trip to Moscow raised troubled memories of Rapallo in the West and Pietro Nenni's Socialists had not as yet made their peace with NATO, the effort surely must have seemed worth making.

IV

One characteristic of Soviet foreign policy behavior that emerges strongly throughout the occupation period is that of intelligent and continual adaptation of Moscow's Austrian policy to the changing international situation. The recurrent periods of Soviet interest in an Austrian settlement bear this out: first in 1948, when the Four-Power evacuation of Austria would have left the country militarily exposed and economically vulnerable at a moment when the Kremlin was pressing hard for Communist control in Italy and France; then again for a brief moment in 1949, when the concluding of an Austrian treaty was offered by the Soviet Union as proof of Soviet interest in a lull in international tension born of a Soviet sense of military inequality with the West; and finally, in 1955, when the Russians, anxious for time to cope with their domestic problems and to press on into the missile age, launched a "peaceful coexistence" campaign designed to turn members, or potential members, of the Western alliance into neutrals, and neutrals into dependent states.

How successful the Soviets will be in this long-term effort remains to be seen. John Foster Dulles, for one, was not optimistic about the United States' chance of countering the Geneva line. In an assessment of the Geneva meeting written for President Eisenhower in August 1955, Dulles wrote:

Geneva has certainly created problems for the free nations. For eight years they have been held together largely by a cement compounded of fear and a sense of moral superiority. Now the fear is diminished and the moral demarcation is somewhat blurred. There is some bewilderment among leaders and peoples of the free nations as to what happened, and as to how to adjust to the new situation.[51]

Austria's role in this broad Soviet diplomatic offensive was of course minor; but it was the occasion that launched the offensive and it has remained for the Soviets, as Khrushchev put it in 1958, "an object lesson in the principles of coexistence."[52] More recently Moscow has portrayed Austria as the model of the policy of "atomic neutrality," one that should be emulated by such countries as Japan, Italy, and Norway.[53]

The Austrian example has also found a place in the writings of Western observers on contemporary problems. Now that the Austrian episode is behind us, it is only natural that attempts will be made to apply the "lessons" of this experience in East-West negotiations to other situations. Henry Kissinger, for example, has suggested that one possible way out of the German reunification deadlock is to apply an "Austrian solution" to the East German problem: begin by making East Germany "independent, neutral, and demilitarized." According to Kissinger's plan, East Germany in a loose confederation with West Germany would have this Austrian status for ten years. After this time a plebiscite supervised by neutrals (including Austria) would determine whether East Germany would remain in confederation with West Germany or unify on a federal basis.[54]

Whatever the merits of the rest of the plan, the use of the Austrian case is decidedly not helpful in that it suggests that the Soviet Union, having accepted an "independent, neutral, and demilitarized" Austria, would accept a similar status for East Germany. The fact is that there is nothing really comparable about the two situations, except perhaps the incompatibility of the population and communism. Eastern Austria was never more than a territorial enclave—moreover, an enclave that could not be organized into an economic and political entity. Austria was also of scant strategic value to the Soviet Union, particularly after 1948. Thus, the Soviet Union—and the Western powers, for that matter—could afford to disengage in Austria. East Germany, on the other hand, is a viable political and economic unit and remains an area of the highest strategic concern to the Soviet Union—not only because of East Germany's size and position, but because a united Germany, unlike a unified Austria, could become an acute threat to Soviet security.

The Austrian experience holds many lessons for the West, but there is nothing ready-made about the "Austrian solution" that can be applied elsewhere. The independence of Austria is no monument to the virtues of marathon bargaining, Western negotiating finesse, or Soviet cleverness, but is an example of how divergent East-West objectives can sometimes evolve to a point where, for a brief moment, both parties are best served by "half a loaf."

To emphasize the evolution of the political objectives and tactics of the Soviet Union in Austria may contribute to our understanding of the forces that shaped Soviet policy after 1945, but to stop there would be to miss one of the major points of the Austrian story. The success of the Soviet Union in managing its Austrian policy after 1948 should not be allowed to obscure the fact that political communism failed in Austria. Although the country had most of the theoretical prerequisites for a Communist political victory—a large urban proletariat burdened with the legacy of seven years of Nazism and war, a well-schooled Communist Party cadre, the core of a Communist paramilitary force—Austria, despite the presence of the Red Army, traveled a different path from Czechoslovakia and Hungary.

The Austrian Communists' lack of success was in part the consequence of the disaster of the first election, in part the result of skillful counteractions of a Socialist Party that capitalized on its experience and reputation, in part the product of the nature of the Four-Power occupation, and in part the result of the creation of a resilient and tough-minded Socialist-Conservative coalition, which for all its faults successfully bridged the gulf between one-time congenital ideological enemies.

There was a further obstacle to Communist success in Austria. Throughout the occupation, there seemed to be something innately hostile in the makeup of the slightly cynical, traditionally negative, often hypercivilized Austrian toward the tough, ideologically minded Russian. If the long years of Socialist-Conservative warfare and Nazi occupation have had any effect on the individual Austrian, they have convinced him that ideological commitment is sheer folly. The two caricatures—the herculean Ivan and the ultracynical Herr Karl in most Austrians—mixed badly. Karl Renner once remarked that Stalin had made only two mistakes in Austria—he showed the Russians Austria, and the Austrians the Russians.

Notes

INTRODUCTION

1. Adam Wandruszka, "Oesterreichs politische Struktur," in Heinrich Benedikt, ed., *Geschichte der Republik Oesterreich* (Munich: Oldenbourg Verlag, 1954), pp. 291f. For the most complete description of the interwar period, see Gulick, *Austria from Habsburg to Hitler,* and Shepherd, *The Austrian Odyssey.*

2. For a thorough and sympathetic description of the programs, see Gulick, *Austria from Habsburg to Hitler,* I, 354–504.

3. Shell, p. 86. For an excellent description of the workings of the party, see his chap. 3.

4. The following account is based primarily on Buttinger, *passim.* See also Shell, pp. 21–28; Gulick, *Austria from Habsburg to Hitler,* II, chap. 30; and Bauer, *Die Illegale Partei.*

5. Buttinger, p. 263.

6. *Ibid.,* p. 139.

7. For an account of the process of conversion, see Erwin Scharf, "Auf dem Weg zur KPOe," in *Aus der Vergangenheit der KPOe.*

8. Helmer, *50 Jahre erlebte Geschichte,* pp. 176–77. Helmer, a right-wing Socialist and later Minister of the Interior in the Second Republic, was involved in the negotiations.

9. See in particular *Die Kommunisten im Kampf fuer die Unabhaengigkeit Oesterreichs,* pp. 121–41.

10. *Ibid.,* p. 125.

11. For a description of the Austrian resistance movement, see Austria, Red-White-Red Book. For an excellent summary, including Allied reactions, see John Mair, "Four-Power Control in Austria, 1945–1946," in Balfour and Mair, pp. 290–95.

CHAPTER 1

1. Austria, Red-White-Red Book, p. 201. For the principal sources of material on the liberation of Vienna, see Adolf Schaerf, *Oesterreichs Wiederaufrichtung im Jahre 1945,* pp. 11–12; Balfour and Mair, pp. 295–300; Molden, pp. 218–57; Helmer, *50 Jahre erlebte Geschichte,* pp. 179–98.

2. Molden, pp. 227–29, 257.

3. For details on the formation of the provisional administration before the return of Karl Renner, see Adolf Schaerf, *Oesterreichs Wiederaufrichtung im Jahre 1945*, pp. 22–51.

4. For a discussion of the Austrians in exile, see Balfour and Mair, pp. 275–76; and Pollak, pp. 146–51.

5. See Adolf Schaerf, *Oesterreichs Erneuerung, 1945–1955*, pp. 9–23; Austria, *Die Zweite Oesterreichische Republik und ihre Repraesentanten* (Vienna: Herausgegeben vom oesterreichischen Pressebuero, 1960), p. vii.

6. Shell, p. 4.

7. Adolf Schaerf, *Oesterreichs Wiederaufrichtung im Jahre 1945*, pp. 52–53.

8. *Ibid.*, p. 54; Helmer, pp. 211–13.

9. For Erwin Scharf's apologia on the course of events that led to his removal from the Socialist Party, see his *Ich darf nicht Schweigen*. See also Adolf Schaerf, *Oesterreichs Wiederaufrichtung im Jahre 1945*, pp. 146–52; Helmer, p. 213; Shell, pp. 120–22.

10. Erwin Scharf, pp. 10–12.

11. Hurdes, pp. 11–14; conversation with Leopold Figl, 1961.

12. Vodopivec, pp. 106–7.

13. See Adolf Schaerf, *Oesterreichs Wiederaufrichtung im Jahre 1945*, pp. 62–63, 66–67.

14. Hiscocks, p. 30.

15. See in particular Renner's own account, *Denkschrift ueber die Geschichte der Unabhaengigkeitserklaerung Oesterreichs*, pp. 9–19; or Renner, *Oesterreich von der Ersten zur Zweiten Republik*, pp. 232–33.

16. Vodopivec, p. 73.

17. Renner, *Denkschrift*, p. 20.

18. Best accounts of these negotiations are Adolf Schaerf, *Oesterreichs Wiederaufrichtung im Jahre 1945*, pp. 69–72, and his *Oesterreichs Erneuerung, 1945–1955*, pp. 28–40; as well as Renner, *Oesterreich von der Ersten zur Zweiten Republik*, pp. 234–35. Particularly interesting is the only Communist account of the proceedings, in Honner, "Die Kommunisten in der Provisorischen Regierung," pp. 11–16.

19. Adolf Schaerf, *Oesterreichs Wiederaufrichtung im Jahre 1945*, pp. 70–71.

20. Adolf Schaerf, *Oesterreichs Erneuerung 1945–1955*, pp. 103–4.

21. Text in Renner, *Denkschrift*, pp. 71–74.

22. For details on the revitalization of the 1920 constitution as well as the legislative efforts of the provisional government, see Adolf Schaerf, *Oesterreichs Erneuerung 1945–1955*, pp. 25, 31–35; and Renner, *Denkschrift*, pp. 33–39.

23. Adolf Schaerf, *Oesterreichs Wiederaufrichtung im Jahre 1945*, p. 102.

24. For details see the *Neues Oesterreich*, April 30, 1945.

CHAPTER 2

1. Material for this section on Austria at Potsdam was drawn largely from a collection of documents dealing with the Potsdam Conference: U.S. Dept. of State, *Foreign Relations of the United States, the Conference of Berlin*

(*The Potsdam Conference*), *1945* (referred to hereafter as the *Potsdam Conference*). The release of these important documents followed the publication of Herbert Feis's excellent book on the conference based on this material, *Between War and Peace—The Potsdam Conference*. See also Bader, "Oesterreich in Potsdam."

2. For an analysis of the formation of Allied policy on Austria, see Balfour and Mair, pp. 273–79, or Grayson, pp. 53–65. See also Fellner, pp. 581–95.

3. Text in U.S. Senate Foreign Relations Committee, *A Decade of American Foreign Policy*, p. 11.

4. Balfour and Mair, pp. 282–90; Grayson, pp. 69–81; see also Erickson, "The Zoning of Austria."

5. Feis, *Churchill–Roosevelt–Stalin*, pp. 623–24.

6. *Ibid.*, p. 625. See also Grew, II, 1453–54. Mr. Grew, at that time American acting Secretary of State, includes here a report of a meeting on April 30 with President Truman on the subject of Churchill's message. Grew told the President that the Renner government was obviously set up "under Russian instigation," and that the U.S. should join the British in protesting the Soviet action.

7. *Potsdam Conference*, I, Doc. 279, pp. 348–49. See also Feis, *Churchill–Roosevelt–Stalin*, p. 626; Truman, pp. 303–4; Churchill, pp. 603–6.

8. *Potsdam Conference*, I, Doc. 145, pp. 158–59.

9. *Ibid.*, Doc. 152, p. 164.

10. *Ibid.*, Doc. 152, p. 168.

11. *Ibid.*, Doc. 268, dated June 23, 1945, pp. 334–35.

12. *Ibid.*, II, Doc. 761, pp. 659–61.

13. *Ibid.*, I, Doc. 272, pp. 341–42. The text of the directive was given to the Department of State by the British Embassy in Washington.

14. *Potsdam Conference*, II, Fourth Plenary Meeting, July 20, 1945, Llewellyn E. Thompson Minutes, pp. 175–77. On July 16 representatives of the Western Allies held two meetings with the Soviets in Vienna. The Soviet representatives at this meeting maintained that since no final arrangements had been made at the EAC level, they could not discuss any details. Extremely disgruntled, the Allied representatives complained bitterly of Soviet "obstructionism." *Ibid.*, Docs. 773 and 774, pp. 669–71.

15. *Potsdam Conference*, II, Sixth Plenary Meeting, July 22, 1945, Thompson Minutes, p. 244; see also Doc. 780, pp. 674–75, and Doc. 787, p. 680.

16. *Ibid.*, Seventh Plenary Meeting, July 23, 1945, Dept. of State Minutes, p. 311.

17. *Ibid.*, Eighth Plenary Meeting, July 24, 1945, Thompson Minutes, p. 368.

18. *Ibid.*, "Protocol of the Proceedings of the Berlin Conference," August 1, 1945, Doc. 1383, p. 1490.

19. See Birke and Neumann for a recent study of the process stressing the all-encompassing nature of the Soviet efforts. For an excellent study of Soviet economic policy in Eastern Europe see Spulber, *The Economics of Communist Eastern Europe*.

20. U.S. Senate Foreign Relations Committee, *A Decade of American Foreign Policy*, p. 11. The Moscow Conference took place October 19–30, 1943. The communiqué containing the declaration was released on November 1. The best account of these events is given by Philip E. Mosely, a par-

ticipant at the conference, including all sessions of the drafting committee, in "The Treaty with Austria," p. 227. See also Hull, II, 1274–1307.

21. *Potsdam Conference,* I, Doc. 273, pp. 342–43.

22. *Ibid.* Quite the opposite from possible reparations demands, Acting Secretary of State Joseph C. Grew on June 18 submitted a memorandum to President Truman suggesting that "plans for the extension of assistance to Austria should be considered as a necessary means of implementing the Moscow Declaration" (Doc. 160, p. 179).

23. *Ibid.,* Doc. 276, pp. 346–47. For the text of the "Agreement on Control Machinery in Austria," signed on July 4, 1945, see Doc. 282, pp. 351–55.

24. *Ibid.,* II, Third Meeting of the Foreign Ministers, July 20, 1945, Dept. of State Minutes, pp. 147–49.

25. *Ibid.,* Doc. 769, p. 666. See also Seventh Meeting of the Foreign Ministers, July 24, p. 323.

26. *Ibid.,* Doc. 770, July 30, 1945.

27. *Ibid.,* Ninth Meeting of the Foreign Ministers, Dept. of State Minutes, pp. 432–34.

28. *Ibid.,* Doc. 1104, dated July 30, 1945, pp. 1095–96.

29. *Ibid.,* Byrnes-Molotov Meeting, July 30, 1945, Charles E. Bohlen Minutes, pp. 482–83.

30. For a thorough discussion of the German reparations question, see Feis, *Between War and Peace,* esp. pp. 259–71. See also *Potsdam Conference,* II, esp. Doc. 953, pp. 913–14, and the Tenth Meeting of the Foreign Ministers, July 30, 1945, Dept. of State Minutes, pp. 484–92. For the text of the final agreement on German reparations, *ibid.,* "Protocol of the Proceedings of the Berlin Conference," August 1, 1945, Sec. III, Doc. 1383, pp. 1485–87.

31. On July 31, the heads of government, who had normally left the establishment of committees to the foreign ministers, appointed this committee directly. The U.S. representatives were William L. Clayton, Assistant Secretary of State (for Economic Affairs) and Edwin W. Pauley. Whatever shortcomings the U.S. delegation showed while on this committee, they did not stem from any lack of background on the problems involved.

32. *Potsdam Conference,* II, Doc. 972, August 1, 1945, pp. 931–33. This report of the Drafting Committee was presented to the Twelfth Plenary Meeting on August 1.

33. *Ibid.* Italics in original. The phrase "and from German external assets" was not accepted by the Soviet representative and was so footnoted in the original.

34. At the Eleventh Plenary Meeting of July 1, when the German reparation percentage issue was hammered out, Stalin advanced the Soviet claims to German gold abroad, as specified in a proposal that gave the Russians 30 per cent of German external investments and 30 per cent of German gold that had come into the hands of Western Allies. When questioned on this, Stalin said that he had in mind the foreign assets frozen in other countries. *Ibid.,* Doc. 1425, undated, pp. 1593–94, and the Eleventh Plenary Meeting, July 31, 1945, pp. 515–16.

35. *Ibid.,* Doc. 988, July 22, 1945, p. 954. The U.S. Delegation advanced the same solution to the problem on July 30 (*ibid.,* Doc. 1000, July 30, 1945, pp. 961–62).

36. *Ibid.*, Eleventh Meeting of the Foreign Ministers, August 1, 1945, Dept. of State Minutes, p. 562.

37. *Ibid.*, Twelfth Plenary Meeting, August 1, 1945, 4:00 P.M., Thompson Minutes, pp. 566–67.

38. *Ibid.*, Twelfth Plenary Meeting, Cohen Notes, p. 579.

39. *Ibid.*, Twelfth Plenary Meeting, Thompson Minutes, pp. 566–69; Cohen Notes, pp. 579–80.

40. The decision to spare Austria reparations payments consisted of a two-sentence exchange between Attlee and Stalin. *Potsdam Conference*, II, Thompson Minutes, p. 571.

41. President Truman writes in his memoirs (p. 409) that the meeting was originally set to convene at 9:00 that evening. But it was delayed until 10:40 P.M. to give the protocol committee more time. This delay is an excellent example of the terrible pressure under which the delegates must have worked.

42. *Potsdam Conference*, II, "Protocol of the Proceedings of the Berlin Conference," Sec. III, pp. 1485–87. Paragraph three, the original point of disagreement, read in the draft: "The reparation claims of the United States . . . shall be met from the Western Zones and from German external assets." As a result of the decision on August 1, this was changed to read "and from *appropriate* German external assets." (Italics mine.) *Ibid.*, Thirteenth Plenary Meeting, August 1, 1945, 10:40 P.M., Dept. of State Minutes, pp. 586–87.

43. *Ibid.*, "Communiqué," August 2, 1945, Doc. 1384, pp. 1507–8.

44. *Ibid.*, "Protocol of the Proceedings," August 1, 1945, Doc. 1384, p. 1490. Grayson mistakenly says the decision was *not* written into the Protocol (Grayson, p. 79). This error is also repeated in Balfour and Mair (p. 310).

45. *Potsdam Conference*, II, Thirteenth Plenary Meeting, August 1, 1945, Dept. of State Minutes, pp. 591–92; Cohen Notes, p. 599. Considering President Truman's desire to accommodate the last-minute suggestions of the Soviet Union on what was to go into the communiqué, his memoirs give a particularly erroneous impression of the happenings. Truman relates that at the Twelfth Meeting, after it was finally agreed to divide the German assets along the demarcation line, Stalin pressed that this decision should be put in the Protocol but not in the communiqué. To this, Truman writes (p. 407): "I objected at once. I could see no reason for this secrecy, and I said so. Stalin thereupon withdrew his suggestion." More serious than the factual mistakes is the impression conveyed that Truman stood up to Stalin in such matters.

46. *Potsdam Conference*, II, Doc. 1003, pp. 964–68.

47. *Ibid.*, "Protocol of the Proceedings," Doc. 1383, p. 1485.

48. Clay, pp. 334–35. For the text of the decree actually adopted by the Allied Control Council in Germany (Allied Control Law No. 5, October 30, 1945), see *United States Economic Policy Toward Germany* (Washington, D.C.: Government Printing Office, 1946), p. 88.

49. *Neues Oesterreich*, April 30, 1945.

50. *Neues Oesterreich*, the coalition paper of the three parties, announced after Potsdam (August 4, 1945) that "it further emerges from the communiqué that the Russians at the Potsdam Conference were the guardians of Austria's interest." At the 14th Party Day of the Austrian Communist Party, Friedl Fuernberg contended that it was not Renner, but the Soviet Union,

that had resisted the attempts of America to make Austria part of Germany (*Der 14. Parteitag der Kommunistischen Partei Oesterreichs,* pp. 120–21). From the side of Austrian political leaders, both Karl Renner and Adolf Schaerf write of their dismay at the suspicious attitude of the Western Allies. See Schaerf, *Oesterreichs Erneuerung, 1945–1955,* pp. 62–63; and Renner, *Oesterreich von der Ersten zur Zweiten Republik,* pp. 232–38.

51. Allied Commission for Austria, *Protocol of the First Meeting of the Four Commanders in Chief,* August 23, 1945. The first meeting of the Allied Council proper was not until September 11.

52. *Proceedings of the Allied Commission,* Minutes of the Meeting of September 20, 1945, ALCO/M(45)3, pp. 7–10.

53. For a description of this conference, see Gruber, pp. 34–37.

54. *Proceedings of the Allied Commission,* Minutes of the Meeting of October 1, 1945, ALCO/M(45)4. Text of the resolution may be found as Annex 3.

55. *Ibid.,* Minutes of the Meeting of October 20, 1945, ALCO/M(45)7. The Soviet Union continued to curry favor with the Renner government by informing the Austrian government the very same day that it was willing to exchange diplomatic representatives—a point not discussed by the Allied Council.

CHAPTER 3

1. See the *Proceedings of the Allied Commission,* Minutes of the Allied Council, ALCO/M(45)1, September 11, 1945, Annex III.

2. *Neues Oesterreich,* October 10, 11, 1945; Adolf Schaerf, *Oesterreichs Wiederaufrichtung im Jahre 1945,* p. 129.

3. See *Oesterreichische Volksstimme,* September 11, 12, 18, 1945; *Neues Oesterreich,* October 1, 1945.

4. *Volksstimme,* November 22, 1945.

5. *Ibid.,* August 5, 1945.

6. *Ibid.,* October 30, 1945.

7. Matejka, pp. 26–28.

8. See *Volksstimme,* November 13, 1945, and *Neues Oesterreich,* June 5, 1945, article by Genner.

9. For examples see *Wiener Polizei oder Polizei gegen die Wiener?* and *Neues Oesterreich,* October 4 and October 13, 1945.

10. See *Volksstimme,* October 23, 24, and November 1, 1945. Naturally enough, the Communist triumph in France made the greatest impression.

11. *Arbeiter-Zeitung,* September 30, 1945.

12. Vodopivec, pp. 232–33.

13. *Volksstimme,* October 27, November 9, 1945. There was no comment at all on the November 4 elections until the 9th.

14. The Internal Affairs Committee of the Allied Commission had informed a subcommittee for the purpose of observing the elections. The report of this committee and subsequent motions by the Allied Council clearly indicate that the elections were fairly conducted. See *Proceedings of the Allied Commission,* Meeting of December 10, 1945, ALCO/P(45)30 and ALCO/M(45)11.

15. Austria, "Die Nationalratswahlen vom 25. November 1945," p. 12. The Demokratische Partei Oesterreichs, a conservative party, although un-

recognized by the Allied Commission, actually appeared on the ballot in some areas.

16. *Ibid.*, p. 15.

17. *Ibid.*, p. 9.

18. *Ibid.*, p. 13.

19. *Proceedings of the Allied Commission,* "Special Report No. 4—The Proposed Cabinet of Chancellor-Designate Figl (an analysis of the composition, party representation, and personnel of the proposed cabinet of Chancellor Figl, to be considered by the Executive Committee of the Allied Council, Austria, on December 14, 1945)," Intelligence coordination, G-2 Sec., Headquarters, USFA, December 11, 1945. This document, along with "Supplement to Special Report No. 4—the Proposed Cabinet of Chancellor-Designate Figl, dated December 18, 1945," was submitted to the American authorities by the same G-2 source following sections on the Figl government. See also *Proceedings of the Allied Commission,* EXCO/P(45)72, for the first letter of nomination. See Schaerf, *Oesterreichs Wiederaufrichtung,* pp. 213–15, for the Austrian version of the struggle over the cabinet selection.

20. *Proceedings of the Allied Commission,* EXCO/P(45)72; Special Report No. 4.

21. Curiously enough, most knowledgeable Austrians, particularly Schaerf and Figl, have never admitted that Boehm was even nominated. See Adolf Schaerf, *Osterreichs Wiederaufrichtung,* pp. 213–15. Johann Boehm's own autobiography, *Erinnerungen aus meinen Leben,* makes no mention of it.

22. *Proceedings of the Allied Commission,* Annex I to ALCO/P(46)35. Seventeenth Meeting, February 25, 1946.

23. Leonhard, p. 425.

24. Leonhard, pp. 446–48.

25. Simon, pp. 343–47.

26. For details see *Die Presse,* February 11, 1956, and July 29, 1955.

27. Freidl Fuernberg, pp. 183, 188.

28. The first description is that of Otto Kirchheimer in "The Waning of the Opposition in Parliamentary Regimes," p. 136; the second is from John MacCormac, "The Improbable Coalition that Governs Austria," p. 34. For an excellent description of the process of drawing up a coalition agreement, see Frederick C. Engelmann, "Haggling for the Equilibrium: The Renegotiation of the Austrian Coalition, 1959," pp. 651–62. For the best Austrian analysis, see Alexander Vodopivec, *Wer regiert in Oesterreich, passim.* See also Herbert P. Secher, "Coalition Government: The Case of the Second Austrian Republic," pp. 791–808.

29. Text in *Wiener-Zeitung,* June 27, 1956; for an excerpt in English, see Kirchheimer, p. 137n.

30. For criticisms of the system, see Kirchheimer, pp. 136–42; MacCormac, pp. 33–36; and Vodopivec, particularly pp. 9–19 and 337–41.

31. MacCormac, p. 36.

32. *Ibid.*

CHAPTER 4

1. *Potsdam Conference,* I, Doc. 286, dated July 5, 1945, p. 363; see also Doc. 287, pp. 366–70; Doc. 288, pp. 370–74.

2. *Ibid.*, I, Doc. 464, pp. 683–84.

3. Text in U.S. Senate Foreign Relations Committee, *A Decade of American Foreign Policy, 1941–1949,* p. 11.

4. *Potsdam Conference,* I, Doc. 270, pp. 338–39.

5. U.S. Dept. of State, *Germany, 1947–1949: The Story in Documents* (Publication 3556, JCS 1067, April 1945; Washington, D.C.: U.S. Government Printing Office, 1950), pp. 22–23.

6. For a description of the negotiations see Erickson, pp. 106–13, and Mosely. For much of the background on the zonal agreement, I must acknowledge my indebtedness to Professor Mosely, who gave me the benefit of his personal experience as the chief American negotiator at the EAC on Austrian questions.

7. Erickson, p. 111.

8. The part of Styria bordering on Hungary referred to here was actually part of pre-1938 Burgenland. The Germans changed the boundary line, and, as in the case of the larger Vienna, the Western Allies wanted to keep it that way.

9. For the text of the agreements see Great Britain, Foreign Office, *Agreements,* Cmd. 6958. This is a particularly useful source, since it contains all the pertinent agreements affecting the occupation of Austria.

10. Great Britain, Cmd. 6958, p. 3; *Potsdam Conference,* I, Doc. 282, p. 352.

11. Balfour and Mair, pp. 308–11.

12. See *Proceedings of the Allied Commission,* Minutes of the Meeting of the Allied Council, September 11, 1945, ALCO/M(45)1.

13. Konev, in 1946, would replace Zhukov as Commander in Chief, USSR Ground Forces, and Deputy Minister of Defense; in 1955 he became Commander in Chief of the armed forces of the Warsaw Pact states. After Stalin's death, Zheltov became chief of the Main Political Administration, USSR Ministry of Defense.

14. Minutes of the Meeting of the Allied Council, September 11, 1945, Annex I.

15. *Ibid.,* Annex V.

16. Great Britain, Cmd. 6958, p. 6.

17. *Proceedings of the Allied Commission,* ALCO/M(45)9, p. 4.

18. ALCO/M(46)19, p. 6.

19. For the original text dated February 9, see EXCO/P(46)45, Appendix A, and Annex I, pp. 1–5.

20. For text see Great Britain, Cmd. 6958.

21. Adolf Schaerf, *Oesterreichs Erneuerung, 1945–1955,* p. 111. Schaerf at the same time advanced the claim that his visit with Dr. Bruno Pittermann, present Chairman of the Socialist Party, to England in April 1946 was instrumental in gaining the new Control Agreement for Austria. Considering the fact that the draft agreement had already been submitted in March, it is doubtful whether the presence of Schaerf and Pittermann had any real effect on the course of the negotiations.

22. Great Britain, Cmd. 6958, p. 23. Italics mine.

23. For example, see Balfour and Mair, p. 328.

24. Text of February 9, 1946, *Proceedings of the Allied Commission,* EXCO/P(46)45, Annex I, p. 1.

25. ALCO/P(46)76, p. 1; for discussion of the article at the Executive Committee level see EXCO/M(46)42, pp. 1–3. The original British draft is included as EXCO/P(46)45. The phrasing in italics was that in dispute and was so marked.

26. ALCO/P(46)76, p. 1.

27. *Ibid.*, Annex I, p. 3.

28. *Ibid.*, p. 3. Again any phrasing or word choice that was not agreed upon was given in italics.

29. *Ibid.*

30. ALCO/P(46)23, Meeting of May 24, 1946, pp. 4–5.

31. EXCO/P(46)160; EXCO/M(46)43, p. 4.

32. EXCO/M(46)43, p. 5.

33. ALCO/M(46)24, Meeting of June 14, 1946, pp. 1–2.

34. *Ibid.*

35. ALCO/M(46)25, pp. 2–3; ALCO/M(46)26, p. 6.

36. See below, Chapter 7.

37. See a letter of General Kurasov to General Clark dated June 13, 1946, in *USFA to Soviet Element/Soviet Element to USFA,* 1946, No. 162.

38. ALCO/M(46)28, pp. 1–2.

39. *Ibid.*

40. EXCO/M(46)53; for text see ALCO/P(46)115.

41. ALCO/M(46)30, pp. 6–7.

42. ALCO/M(46)30, pp. 14–15.

43. ALCO/P(46)118, Annex A.

44. EXCO/UM(46)58, p. 6.

45. For a discussion of the Soviet Union's record in honoring international agreements, see Jan F. Triska and Robert M. Slusser, *The Theory, Law, and Policy of Soviet Treaties* (Stanford, Calif.: Stanford University Press, 1962), see esp. pp. 389–406.

CHAPTER 5

1. For the best general history of the Viennese police in the postwar period, see Austria, *80 Jahre Wiener Sicherheitswache,* pp. 95ff.

2. *Ibid.*, p. 131; conversation with Oberstleutnant Ferdinand Kaes, Commandant of the Gendarmerieschule des Bundesministeriums fuer Inneres, July 6, 1961.

3. Conversation on February 22, 1961, with Oskar Helmer, former Undersecretary in the Ministry of the Interior under Honner and Minister of the Interior from December 1945 to July 1959.

4. Austria, *80 Jahre Wiener Sicherheitswache,* pp. 134–38.

5. *Neues Oesterreich,* May 16 and 17, 1945.

6. *Proceedings of the Allied Commission,* EXCO/P(46)40, Annex V, February 7, 1946.

7. For a description of the Polizeilicher Hilfsdienst see the article by the present President of the Vienna Police, Josef Holaubek, "Der Schwierige Personalaufbau in der Wiener Polizei," pp. 1–3; Austria, *80 Jahre Wiener Sicherheitswache,* pp. 145–46. The fact that armed robberies and other outrages were committed by men with such arm bands did not help the reputa-

tion of either the Russians or the Communist Party. In one case a gang of 31 men were sentenced to jail for armed robbery, robberies committed while they were wearing the arm bands of the "P-H" although they had no connection with the auxiliary police. *Wiener Kurier,* August 18, 1947.

8. Adolf Schaerf, *Oesterreichs Wiederaufrichtung im Jahre 1945,* p. 137.

9. See Adolf Schaerf, *Oesterreichs Erneuerung, 1945–1955,* p. 147, and *Oesterreichs Wiederaufrichtung im Jahre 1945,* p. 137. The first organizational and personal register for the Viennese police was published in 1949. See Austria, *Provisorisches Personal-Standesverzeichnis fuer das Jahr 1949.* It is extremely difficult to obtain information on who ran what departments before 1949, although much information can be gained from this register, using dates of appointments. Most of the information on the appointment of Pamer was given to me by Oskar Helmer (conversation on February 22, 1961).

10. For text see the *Neues Oesterreich,* June 13, 1945, or Austria, *Amtsblatt der Polizeidirektion Wien,* Jahrgang 1945, Nr. 1, August 21, 1945.

11. For the original "Geschaeftsplan der Polizeidirektion Wien," see Austrian, *Amtsblatt der Polizeidirektion Wien,* P. 60/c of July 31, 1945, Jahrgang 1945, Nr. 1, August 21, 1945; see also Austria, *80 Jahre Wiener Sicherheitswache,* p. 153, for a diagram of the organization of the Viennese police system.

12. Austria, *Tages Befehl,* Nr. 1, August 28, 1945; see also Austria, *80 Jahre Wiener Sicherheitswache,* p. 138. Linhart assumed office on July 19, 1945.

13. Austria, *Amtsblatt der Polizeidirektion Wien,* P. 1/c of July 13, 1945, Jahrgang 1945, Nr. 1, August 21, 1945.

14. *Volksstimme,* August 23, 1946; see also Austria, *Beiblatt zur Parlamentskorrespondenz,* 79/A.B. to 13J of December 28, 1953.

15. *Wiener Polizei oder Polizei gegen die Wiener,* p. 5.

16. *Volksstimme,* October 28, 1945.

17. *Proceedings of the Allied Commission,* EXCO/P(45)11, Annex I and Appendix A; EXCO/M(45)10, pp. 11–13.

18. For Helmer's background see his autobiography, *50 Jahre erlebte Geschichte.* My impressions of Minister Helmer were derived in part from a series of interviews in the winter of 1961.

19. Adolf Schaerf, *Oesterreichs Erneuerung, 1945–1955,* p. 147.

20. The circumstances of this maneuver were related to me by Minister Helmer on February 22, 1961.

21. Holaubek, p. 2.

22. See in particular *Volksstimme,* July 19, 1946, and October 16, 1946.

23. *Volksstimme,* March 3, 1947.

24. Allied Commission for Austria, *Report of the U.S. High Commissioner,* III, January 1946, p. 25; *ibid.,* IV, February 1946, p. 165; *ibid.,* V, March 1946, p. 203; *Wiener-Zeitung,* January 19, 1946.

25. Austria, *Tages Befehl,* Nr. 3, January 10, 1946; Austria, Amtsdruckerei der Bundespolizeidirektion Wien, *Chronik der Sicherheitswache fuer das Jahr 1947* (Vienna, 1948), pp. 5–9.

26. The Communists complained of this in parliament, mentioning several officials who had been similarly removed. Austria, *Stenographisches*

Protokoll des Nationalrates, V.G.P., 62. Sitzung, October 22, 1947, p. 1672.

27. Helmer, *50 Jahre erlebte Geschichte,* p. 229.

28. *Proceedings of the Allied Commission,* EXCO/P(46)40, February 7, 1946. The Heeresamt, under Allied Council orders, was abolished.

29. Helmer, *50 Jahre erlebte Geschichte,* pp. 231–32.

30. Austria, *Provisorisches Personal-Standesverzeichnis fuer das Jahr 1949,* p. 5; *Wiener-Zeitung,* July 18, 1946.

31. Interview with Duermayer, April 17, 1961; *Volksstimme,* March 28, 1947.

32. Hiscocks, p. 211.

33. Austria, Akt zu 1603/57, p. 36. Testimony of Dr. Oswald Peterlunger, chief of the Staatspolizei in 1957, who, significantly enough, would reduce the force to 270 men after the removal of Duermayer.

34. Conversation with Duermayer, April 17, 1961. See also the testimony of Peterlunger, Akt zu 1603/57, p. 35.

35. Marsalek, *Mauthausen mahnt!* See also the article by Sobek, p. 15.

36. Akt zu 1603/57, pp. 2–3; Austria, *Beiblatt zur Parlamentskorrespondenz,* 365/A.B. zu 395/J, December 12, 1955. These detention areas were in and around Vienna. There was also one in the vicinity of Wiener Neustadt and another in Semmering.

37. *Wiener-Zeitung,* March 12, 1946.

38. Akt zu 1603/57, pp. 11–15.

39. *Ibid.,* p. 4.

40. Letter of Lebedenko and subsequent letter of Koerner to the Viennese police president, in which Koerner stressed the seriousness of the situation, may be found in Akt zu 1603/57, pp. 34–35.

41. Sensitivity of the Soviets on this point was demonstrated in 1955, when they insisted that preservation and care of the statue by the Austrians be included in the State Treaty.

42. Akt zu 1603/57, Abschriften des Aktes Zl.102.717–3/47, "Beschwerde des Hofrates Dr. Heinrich Duermayer gegen Sektionsrat Dr. Franz Mayer," Einlageblatt Nr. 4, p. 28. This is a certified copy of the full-scale investigation of the entire Russian memorial affair as conducted for the Federal Ministry of the Interior in August–September, 1947. See also the testimony of Minister Helmer, Akt zu 1603/57, p. 16.

43. Testimony of Franz Mayer, Akt zu 1603/57, pp. 18–25.

44. For examples see *Volksstimme,* January 22, March 8 and 29, and April 19, 1947.

45. Staatspolizei Exekutive I/24851/d/46, dated June 24, 1947, included as supporting evidence at the trial of Kocanda, Schwab, and Sauter, Akt zu HV 1573/47-VglVr 4492/47, p. 6. Hereafter the page references will be those of the court record (Akt) rather than page numbers of the individual documents.

46. Akt zu HV 1573/47-VglVr 4492/47, p. 6.

47. *Ibid.,* p. 13.

48. *Ibid.,* p. 8.

49. Akt zu 1603/57, p. 4. See also the testimony of Dr. Oswald Peterlunger in Akt zu 1159/59, pp. 9–10.

50. Mayer claimed during the first libel trial that he only heard of the case through the newspaper disclosure on the afternoon of July 7 (Akt zu 1603/57, p. 18). Helmer contradicted this the same day in saying he was well aware of what was going on before the 7th *(ibid., p. 14).* Peterlunger, who as director of Abteilung II was appointed by Helmer to participate in the initial investigation, said in 1960, "I knew of it long before the newspaper article" (Akt zu 1159/59, p. 10). Mayer was apparently overdramatizing the conspiracy of silence within the Staatspolizei.

51. Akt zu 1603/, p. 16.

52. *Die Welt am Montag,* July 7, 1947.

53. Akt zu HV 1573/47-VglVr 4492/47, pp. 126–27. Mayer's entire report, included here, has the reference Zl.24851/d/46, dated July 9, 1947. It consisted of a series of reports, the first dated July 7, 1947; included are interrogations of the principals in the case.

54. Akt zu 1603/57, Abschriften des Aktes Zl.102.717-3/47, "Beschwerde des Hofrates Dr. Heinrich Duermayer gegen Sektionsrat Dr. Franz Mayer," Einlageblatt Nr. 4.

55. Akt zu 1603/57, testimony of Dr. Heinrich Duermayer, December 30, 1958; letter of Duermayer to the Viennese police president, Dr. Klausner, I/RES.149.47, dated August 13, 1947, marked "Streng Vertraulich." His contention that he knew nothing of the Kocanda case in its initial stages won both libel cases for Duermayer against Helmer. Helmer charged in his memoirs, *50 Jahre erlebte Geschichte,* that Duermayer was aware of the existence of a plot to destroy the memorial. Such things are hard to prove, and the publisher lost the first case after Helmer pleaded parliamentary immunity. Helmer himself lost the second case after he was out of office. It seems unlikely that Duermayer was unaware of what his organization was doing in such an important case, particularly since the Russians were aware of it from the very first, but Helmer could produce no documentary proof that Duermayer was involved until the beginning of the Mayer investigation.

56. Akt zu 1603/57, I/RES.149.47, Duermayer to Klausner, letter dated August 13, 1947.

57. *Ibid.,* letter dated August 28, 1947.

58. Akt zu 1603/57, p. 16.

59. Testimony of Dr. Oswald Peterlunger, Akt zu 1159/59, p. 10.

60. *Arbeiter-Zeitung,* September 3, 1947.

61. *Ibid.,* September 3, 1947.

62. Testimony of Dr. Maximilian Pamer, Akt zu 1159/59, p. 5.

63. For the Communist press reaction, see *Volksstimme,* September 4, 8, 12, 1947; the reaction of the Allied press is typified by the *Wiener Kurier,* the American paper, on September 3, 1947, which briefly reported the basic details, avoiding any reference to the fact that Duermayer was a Communist or that this had anything to do with his removal.

64. Austria, *Amtsblatt der Bundespolizeidirektion Wien,* Nr. 4, March 12, 1948.

65. *Ibid.,* Nr. 2, January 28, 1948.

66. *New York Times,* May 27, 1948; *Arbeiter-Zeitung,* May 27, 1948. The change in leadership was explained in terms of recognizing the growing importance of the economic police, necessitating the creation of an indepen-

dent department. Formerly the economic police had been under the criminal section.

67. Adolf Schaerf, *Oesterreichs Wiederaufrichtung im Jahre 1945*, p. 137.

68. Austria, *Tages Befehl*, I, Nr. 17, August 19, 1946, p. 70.

69. Austria, *Beiblatt zur Parlamentskorrespondenz*, 79/A.B. zu 13/J, December 28, 1953, 1–2 Beiblaetter.

70. *Proceedings of the Allied Commission*, EXCO/P(46)90; *ibid.*, ALCO/M(46)20, pp. 4–5, and ALCO/P(46)51.

71. *Ibid.*, EXCO/M(47)68, U.S. Minutes, p. 9.

72. *Proceedings of the Allied Commission*, Meeting of June 13, 1947, ALCO/M(47)51, pp. 5–6; Meeting of August 29, 1947, ALCO/M(47)56, pp. 9–12. ALCO/P(47)99, submitted at the latter meeting, was a proposal of the Russians that the combined strength of both the police and the gendarmerie be fixed at 19,500. At the June 13 meeting the figure was 26,300. The Duermayer case had broken in the intervening period, and perhaps the added evidence of the deteriorating Communist strength in the police system caused the change.

73. *Ibid.*, ALCO/P(47)99 and ALCO/M(47)56, pp. 9–12.

74. *Ibid.*, EXCO/P(47)121, letter is marked Zl.106.952-POL/47.

75. *Ibid.*, EXCO/P(47)5, Annex A. letter is marked as Zl.2752-Pr/46.

76. *Ibid.*, EXCO/M(48)123, Annex A.

77. Austria, *Stenographisches Protokoll des Nationalrates*, V.G.P., 62. Sitzung, October 22, 1947, p. 1669; for debate on the dismissals see pp. 1658, 1675; see also *Arbeiter-Zeitung*, October 14, 15, 23, 1948.

78. For examples see *Proceedings of the Allied Commission*, EXCO/P(49)-204 and Helmer, *50 Jahre erlebte Geschichte*, pp. 251–52. Two well-known cases of kidnapping police officials were of a policeman named Franz Kiridus, who was never returned, and Inspector Anton Marek, a senior official in the Ministry of the Interior, who was returned to Austria only in June 1955. The Marek kidnapping was probably in retaliation for his part in the Duermayer affair.

79. *New York Times*, May 24, 1948.

80. Conversation with Oskar Helmer, April 14, 1961.

81. *Proceedings of the Allied Commission*, EXCO/P(48)223, letter of Minister Helmer to the Allied Council, Zl.190.673-Gd.5/48.

82. *Ibid.*, ALCO/M(48)72, Annex A.

83. *Ibid.*, ALCO/P(48)98; EXCO/P(48)98, Annex A.

84. *Ibid.*, ALCO/M(48)73, pp. 3–5.

85. *Ibid.*, ALCO/P(48)40.

86. *Ibid.*, ALCO/M(48)76, p. 507, Meeting of June 11, 1948.

87. John MacCormac of the *New York Times* reported in the issue of April 17, 1948, that the British were sure this proposal, together with the interference with Western Traffic to the city, "smelled of a coup plot."

88. In addition to the material cited below, see the short but very enlightening article by Oberstleutnant d.G. Gustav Habermann, pp. 474–79. Habermann leaves no doubt that the Austrian gendarmerie held the cadre for the new Austrian army. See also Jedlicka, pp. 231–56, esp. pp. 245–51.

89. Letter of Chancellor Figl to Lieutenant General Goeffrey Keyes, dated

June 24, 1948. *Proceedings of the Allied Commission, Austrian Chancellor to USFA HQS/USFA/HQS to Austrian Chancellor, 1948.*

90. See U.S. Dept. of State, *Correspondence between the Austrian Chancellor and the USFA Headquarters,* 1949. Included here are informal routing slips, a memorandum from the Office of the Ordnance Officer dated August 23, 1949, and a letter from Chancellor Figl to General Keyes dated October 7, 1949, all relating to the transfer of U.S. Army supplies and equipment to the Austrians.

91. Austria, *Bundesgesetzblatt fuer die Republik Oesterreich,* Jahrgang 1949, 8. Stueck, Nr. 44, p. 82.

92. Austria, *Stenographisches Protokoll des Nationalrates,* V.G.P., 94. Sitzung, December 10, 1948, p. 2641.

93. *Proceedings of the Allied Commission,* EXCO/P(49)86; EXCO/M-(49)140, pp. 3–4; ALCO/M(50)121, pp. 2–4.

94. *Ibid.,* EXCO/P(50)50; EXCO/M(50)161, pp. 6–10; ALCO/M(50)121, pp. 2–4.

95. Letter from Vice-Chancellor Adolf Schaerf to Brigadier General Jesmond D. Balmer, U.S. Deputy High Commissioner, dated July 13, 1949, included in U.S. Dept. of State, *Correspondence between Various Ministries and the USFA Headquarters,* I, 1947–49.

96. Austria, *Bundesgesetzblatt fuer die Republik Oesterreich,* Jahrgang 1952, 4. Stueck, Nr. 14, Anlage IV, "Dienstposten fuer das Jahr 1952," p. 119; *ibid.,* 1955, 7. Stueck, Nr. 27, Anlage IV, "Dienstposten fuer die Jahr 1955," p. 208.

97. *Ibid.,* Jahrgang 1956, 4. Stueck, Nr. 12, Anlage IV, p. 176.

98. On July 21, 1955, two months after the signing of the State Treaty ending the occupation, 6,500 gendarmes were transferred to the new Office of National Defense. *Die Presse,* July 22, 1955; see also Habermann for figures on the build-up.

99. Austria, *Bundesgesetzblatt fuer die Republik Oesterreich,* Jahrgang 1955, 7. Stueck, Nr. 27, p. 76.

100. *Proceedings of the Allied Commission,* ALCO/M(55)235, pp. 1–13.

CHAPTER 6

1. U.S. Senate Committee on the Judiciary, *Scope of Soviet Activity in the United States,* testimony of Seweryn Bialer, p. 1576.

2. See Spulber, pp. 172–76, for an excellent study of Sovrompetrol.

3. Best accounts of these negotiations are Heinl, pp. 299–333, and Adolf Schaerf, *Oesterreichs Erneuerung, 1945–1955,* pp. 64–67.

4. Schaerf, *Oesterreichs Erneuerung, 1945–1955,* p. 65.

5. In light of this, Schaerf felt (*ibid.,* pp. 65–66) that the former holders of the British and American properties so acquired by the Germans would submit claims against the Austrian government if the joint company was organized.

6. Schaerf, *Oesterreichs Erneuerung, 1945–1955,* p. 66.

7. Conversation with Leopold Figl on August 8, 1961. Mark Clark recounts that the Austrians were under great pressure to sign the agreement before September 10, the day before the first meeting of the Allied Council, when Four-Power control would be effective. He says that Renner was called to the

Soviet delegation on the 10th and ordered to sign it (Clark, pp. 466–68).

8. Conversation with Leopold Figl, August 8, 1961.

9. Dulles Papers, Category VIII, Council of Foreign Ministers—London—Minutes—November 25, December 17, 1947, Vol. I, USDEL(47)(1), 9th Meeting, Meeting of December 4, 1947, pp. 85–86.

10. *Proceedings of the Allied Commission,* ALCO/M(45)1, Annex 5, September 11, 1945.

11. *Proceedings of the Allied Commission,* ALCO/P(46)2, Meeting of January 10, 1946.

12. *Ibid.,* ALCO/M(46)13, p. 1.

13. *Ibid.*

14. Control of the Austrian Danube was only one link in Soviet control of the river. In addition to DDSG there was Meszhart, a Soviet-Hungarian company for navigation on the Danube, formed early in 1946, and Sovromtransport in Rumania; in Bulgaria the Danubian assets were so negligible that no agreement was necessary. In Yugoslavia is was Juspad, founded in 1947, and liquidated only in 1948 because of the break with the Soviet Union. For a good description of these joint-stock companies, see Spulber, pp. 187, 190–91, 194–95.

15. Austria, *Stenographisches Protokoll des Nationalrates,* V.G.P., 16. Sitzung, May 22, 1946, p. 217.

16. *Volksstimme,* March 22, 1946.

17. The circumstances of these negotiations were only revealed when the two Communist papers, *Volksstimme* and *Oesterreichische Zeitung,* on June 18, 1946, published both the Gruber note of April 4 and the Soviet reply of May 10 as proof of the Soviet willingness to negotiate. Prompted by this disclosure, *Wiener-Zeitung,* the official Austrian government newspaper, on June 20, 1946, published a synopsis of the original Gruber note and an extensive commentary on the entire affair.

18. *Volksstimme,* June 5, 1946.

19. The text of General Order No. 17 can be found in U.S.S.R., *Sowjetpolitik gegenueber Oesterreich, April 1945, April 1947,* pp. 8–13; see also *Wiener-Zeitung,* July 6, 1946, or *Volksstimme,* July 6, 1946.

20. *Volksstimme,* July 9, 1946.

21. *Wiener-Zeitung,* July 11, 1946. It should be noted at this point that in this letter, as well as all future statements on German assets, the United States did not contend that the Soviet Union did not have the right to take all the German assets in Eastern Austria. Potsdam had limited the position of the Western Allies on the Soviet economic enclave to demands that the order be carried out in the spirit of the Moscow Declaration.

22. Austria, *Stenographisches Protokoll des Nationalrates,* V.G.P., 27. Sitzung, July 10, 1946, p. 561. The Communist reaction to the seizure was summed up by Ernst Fischer, their best speaker in the Nationalrat, quite simply: "We are still of the opinion that it would have been incomparably better for Austria, for its economic and foreign policy development, to have accepted the offer" (*ibid.,* p. 565). If the KPO owed most of its influence in occupied Austria to the presence of the Red Army, in like manner it certainly owned much of its unpopularity to the same source.

23. For contents of the notes see *Wiener-Zeitung,* July 21, 1946.

24. See *Archiv der Gegenwart,* XVI and XVII (1946–47), p. 1049.

25. *Die Presse,* November 1, 1946.

26. Russian domestic production rose from 29.2 million metric tons in 1948 to 129.6 million tons in 1959 (*Statistical Year Book—1960,* Statistical Office of the United Nations, New York, 1961). However, in 1945 the situation was quite different. Particularly revealing is a message sent by Averell Harriman, American Ambassador in Moscow, to the Secretary of State: "Soviet output of crude oil without natural gas is estimated to have fallen from 31.1 million metric tons in 1940 to approximately 21.5 in 1945. Chief factors in drop were sharp falloff in Baku output due to almost complete lack of new drilling there during war, German devastation of Maikop Field and large part of Grozny Field, and the drop in output of largest non-Caucasus field in Bashkiria." Harriman adds that the "USSR will probably endeavor to maintain control of petroleum production in Soviet-occupied areas of Eastern Europe." *Potsdam Conference,* I, Doc. 621, p. 943.

27. U.S. Dept. of State, *State Department Bulletin,* December 9, 1945, p. 934, and March 17, 1946, p. 435.

28. *Monatsberichte des Oesterreichischen Institutes fuer Wirtschaftsforschung,* XXVIII, Heft Nr. 9, September 1955, p. 309.

29. Austria, *Oesterreichs Industrie in den Jahren 1954 und 1955* (Statistisches Zentralamt, Vienna, 1956), p. 12. This is the first, and, to my knowledge, the only official publication that gives complete and reliable statistics on the production values of the former USIA and SMV concerns. For employment figures see Austria, "Ehemalige USIA Betriebe, Beschaeftigte und Arbeitsstunden in den einzelnen Bundeslaendern im September 1955." Until September 1955 the Austrian government's only official source of information on the operations of USIA, SMV, and DDSG came from the payments made by these organizations to the social security funds on behalf of their workers.

30. *Volksstimme,* July 13, 1946. Quickly forgotten was the party's position on the oil fields in September 1945.

31. *Proceedings of the Allied Commission,* Zl.171.376-III/13 (1946) included as Annex I to ALCO/P(46)99.

32. *Ibid.,* EXCO/M(46)50, Meeting of July 23, 1946, p. 24.

33. *Ibid.,* ALCO/M(46)27, Meeting of July 26, 1946, pp. 3–4.

34. See "Die Oesterreichische Erdoelwirtschaft," Oesterreichisches Institut fuer Wirtschaftsforschung, 10. Sonderheft (Vienna, 1947), p. 21, for Soviet development of the new fields.

35. *Monatsberichte des Oesterreichischen Institutes fuer Wirtschaftsforschung,* XXIX, Nr. 11, Beilage Nr. 42, November 1956, p. 11, for production figures.

36. Great Britain, Cmd. 6958, Article 4(b), p. 23. Adolf Schaerf has called the Second Control Agreement, "after the unity of Austria achieved under Renner, probably the most important success for Austria since 1945" (*Oesterreichs Erneuerung 1945–1955,* p. 111).

37. Of the oil produced in Austria, 12,717,540 tons went to the Russians. Subtracting refinery losses that roughly amounted to 15 per cent, the Soviet export of Austrian oil from 1947 to 1955 amounted to at least 11,000,000 tons.

38. *Monatsberichte des Oesterreichischen Institutes fuer Wirtschaftsforschung,* XXVIII. Jahrgang Nr. 11, Beilage Nr. 33, November 1955, p. 6.

39. This estimate uses the 1954 figures as a base. For a more detailed breakdown of these figures, see "Oesterreichs Wirtschaftsverkehr mit der Sowjetunion," *Monatsberichte des Oesterreichischen Institutes fuer Wirtschaftsforschung*, Beilage Nr. 33, XXVIII, Nr. 11, November 1955, 8–9.

40. "Struktur und Zukunft der USIA-Betriebe," *Wirtschafts-Politische Blaetter*, III, Nr. 2 (April 1956), pp. 27–29; *Monatsberichte des Oesterreichischen Institutes fuer Wirtschaftsforschung*, XXVIII, Heft Nr. 9, September 1955, 309–10.

41. *Monatsberichte des Oesterreichischen Institutes fuer Wirtschaftsforschung*, XXVIII, Heft Nr. 9, September 1955, 309. It is interesting to note that this number fell to 44,859 in January 1956, reflecting the dependence of many of these industries on unrestrained Eastern trade and the advantages of tax-free operations ("Struktur und Zukunft der USIA-Betriebe," *Wirtschafts-Politische Blaetter*, III, Nr. 2 [April 1956], p. 28).

42. For a list of about 80 really important USIA concerns, see "Sonderdienst Staatsvertrag," *Donaueuropaeischer Informationsdienst*, XII, Nr. 10, Beilage Nr. 1 (May 1955), pp. 2–5.

43. The most reliable source on who owned what percentage of what in Austria is the *Finanz-Compass, Oesterreich*, LXXXIV (1955). In addition to giving the vital statistics on all Austrian incorporated concerns, this particular year gives accurate figures on ownership of stock in these companies for 1938 and 1945. For instance, ownership of the Wiener Lokomotivfabrik in 1938 was divided between the Credit Anstalt Bank, the Oesterreichische Eisenbahnverkehrsanstalt (a Belgian-controlled company), various members of the international Rothschild family, a Czechoslovakian firm, and even the government of Liechtenstein. After 1938, the majority of the shares were in the hands of the Lokomotivfabrik Henschel & Sohn, Kassel, Germany. The original owners were not asked at the time whether they were interested in selling, and whether just compensation was given is very questionable. Yet, in 1945 this concern was formally in German hands and was considered by the Russians to be a German asset.

44. The basic information from which these figures were compiled is an Austrian government report in manuscript, dated October 11, 1946. This report was put at my disposal by Dr. Kurt Wessely of the Oesterreichisches Institut fuer Wirtschaftforschung. In all cases where the concern involved was incorporated—that is, most of the large concerns—the information was cross-checked with the *Finanz-Compass, Oesterreich*, 1955.

45. For examples of this procedure, see the Soviet military newspaper, *Oesterreichische Zeitung*, July 12, 1946, September 1 and 26, and November 17, 1946.

46. See the *Proceedings of the Allied Commission*, EXCO/M(49)18, January 31, 1949; see also *ibid.*, EXCO/P(47), Annexes A, B, C, p. 133, for three letters from Figl on the efforts of the Russians to force the entry of the USIA concerns into the registry of landed property. This is just one of many examples of a preoccupation of the Soviets in Austria with the formalities of legality as the basis of policy. Soviet success in registering ownership of the confiscated property was limited to one small firm in Baden, the headquarters of the Russian army.

47. *Die Presse*, September 29, 1950.

48. Austria, *Stenographisches Protokoll des Nationalrates,* VI. G.P., 86. Sitzung, April 2, 1952, p. 3282; *Die Wirtschaft,* Nr. 21, May 28, 1955. An example of the prices would be cigarettes, which sold on the Austrian market for 22 cents a pack, but cost 7 cents at the USIA shop.

49. *Volksstimme,* September 17, 1950. *Oesterreichische Zeitung* (the Soviet newspaper in Austria), although carrying lists of the locations of the shops and the prices, never listed all the shops at one time. The highest number they gave (May 17, 1953) was 44, for all of Austria.

50. *Proceedings of the Allied Commission,* Annex B to EXCO/P(47)44 and Annex A to EXCO/P(46), p. 356. Annex A includes a letter from the Austrian government dated October 28, 1946, protesting the order and contending that it violated the so-called Schilling Law, which blocked many accounts in order to help stabilize the currency.

51. *Ibid.,* EXCO/P(47)44 and EXCO/M(47)73. Chancellor Figl to the Allied Council, letter of January 17, 1947, Annex A to EXCO/P(47)44.

52. Adolf Schaerf, *Oesterreichs Erneuerung, 1945–1955,* p. 115, and Heinl, p. 316. This refusal by the Soviet Union to permit nationalization in Austria is not surprising in light of what we now know of the nationalization question in other Eastern European countries. In Hungary, Rumania, and Bulgaria, reparations and joint-stock companies were pressed by the Communists; large-scale nationalization came only after the Communists had absolute power. Even in Czechoslovakia the second and greater wave of nationalization came after February 1948. See Spulber, pp. 70–83.

53. *Der Weg zum Aufstieg,* pp. 10–11.

54. *Volksstimme,* September 8, 1945. In another article (August 22, 1945) calling for nationalization, the *Volksstimme* said of German acquisition of property in Austria: "Systematically Austria was plundered, systematically everything of value was raked together and stolen." This particular point of view on the German method of acquiring the "German assets" was carefully forgotten in 1946.

55. Austria, *Stenographisches Protokoll des Nationalrates,* V.G.P., 2. Sitzung, December 21, 1945, pp. 19–27.

56. *Wiener-Zeitung,* July 18, 1946.

57. For the text see Austria, *Bundesgesetzblatt fuer die Republik Oesterreich,* "Bundesgesetz vom 26 Juli 1946 ueber die Verstaatlichung von Unternehmungen, No. 168," pp. 337–39.

58. *Stenographisches Protokoll,* V.G.P., 30. Sitzung, July 26, 1946, pp. 696–97. For text of the two notes see *Volksstimme,* July 27, 1946. Kurasov complained that the published list of firms included a large number of concerns that had, on the basis of the Berlin Conference and his orders, been "taken into custody by the Soviet Union."

59. *Stenographisches Protokoll,* V.G.P., 30. Sitzung, July 26, 1946, pp. 715–16.

60. *Ibid.,* pp. 708–11.

61. "Struktur und Zukunft der USIA-Betriebe," *Wirtschafts-Politische Blaetter,* III, Nr. 2 (April 1956), p. 27; "Sonderdienst Staatsvertrag," *Donaueuropaeischer Informationsdienst,* XII, Nr. 10, Beilage Nr. 1 (May 1955), pp. 2–3; Austria, *Bundesgesetzblatt fuer die Republik Oesterreich,* Nr. 168, 1946, pp. 338–39.

62. *Die Zukunft,* July 1948.
63. The Soviet attempt at revenge was not long in coming. On August 27 the Russians proposed to the Executive Committee measures "for the purpose of the definitive separation of Austria from Germany economically and the liquidation of industrial power created by the German Reich on Austrian Territory and not necessary to the peacetime economy of Austria." They recommended, for example, that for the next ten years production of pig iron in Austria be limited to 500,000 tons a year (this limit was exceeded by 1948 and rose to 1,738,000 tons by 1956), and crude steel to 800,000 tons a year (this was reached in 1949 and rose to 2,078,000 tons by 1956). Fortunately for Austria, the proposal was flatly refused by the other powers. See EXCO/P(46)282, and ALCO/M(46)31, pp. 2–4. For the production figures, see United Nations, Statistical Office, *Statistical Year Book—1957* (New York, 1957), pp. 269, 271, 279.
64. Austria, *Stenographisches Protokoll,* VI. G.P., 85. Sitzung, March 27, 1952, pp. 3249, 3250.
65. For example, the Erste Oesterreichische Maschinenglasindustrie in Brunn (Eastern Austria) was in 1945 the only producer of plate glass in Austria. In 1947, however, another glass factory, the Mitterberger Glashuetten, was opened in Salzburg in the American zone—theoretically a competitor. However, in 1952, the very year in which Raab was speaking of those who dealt with USIA as "traitors," the two plants agreed to divide the market and raise prices (Harry W. Johnstone, *The Restraint of Competition in the Austrian Economy* [Vienna: U.S. High Commission for Austria, 1951], pp. 51–52). This sort of arrangement also held true for the wire cable industry, graphite, and carbides. See Johnstone, p. 60, and *Neue Zuercher Zeitung,* April 25, 1954.
66. Austria, *Beiblatt zur Parlamentskorrespondenz,* 433/A.B. zu 443 J, 1. Beiblatt, May 27, 1952. Statement of Franz Thoma, Federal Minister of Agriculture and Forestry.

CHAPTER 7

1. Gulick, "Austrian Labor's Bid to Power," p. 35. He compares this figure with that of the United States, where but one-quarter of those employed are organized by labor, and of that number, the AFL-CIO has but 10 per cent.
2. For the most comprehensive and sound work on the development of the Austrian trade union movement, see Klenner, *Die Oesterreichischen Gewerkschaften.*
3. Boehm, p. 236. For the most complete description of the formation of the Austrian Trade Union Federation (OGB), see Klenner, *Die Oesterreichischen Gewerkschaften,* II, 1599f; see also the article by the Communist trade union leader Gottlieb Fiala, "Die Befreier brachten die Gewerkschaftsfreiheit," *Volksstimme,* April 13, 1951, and that of Anton Proksch, "Der Aufbau des Oesterreichischen Gewerkschaftsbundes."
4. Klenner, *Die Oesterreichischen Gewerkschaften,* II, 1601, 1602.
5. Weinberger, p. 244.
6. Klenner, *Die Oesterreichischen Gewerkschaften,* II, 1603.

7. Conversation with Fritz Klenner on February 15, 1961.

8. See the Gottlieb Fiala article in *Volksstimme,* April 13, 1951.

9. *Volksstimme,* April 13, 1951.

10. For a reproduction of the document, see Klenner, *Die Oesterreich-ischen Gewerkschaften,* II, 1604.

11. *Ibid.,* p. 1605.

12. *Neues Oesterreich,* May 8, 1945.

13. See Austrian Trade Union Federation, *Taetigkeitsbericht des oester-reichischen Gewerkschaftsbundes, 1945–1947.* Vienna, pp. 1/154–1/160.

14. *Ibid.,* 1/28.

15. Klenner, *Die Oesterreichischen Gewerkschaften,* II, 1606.

16. *Gazette of the Allied Commission for Austria,* December 1945–January 1946, pp. 28–29.

17. Boehm, p. 239.

18. Conversation with Fritz Klenner, February 15, 1961.

19. Allied Commission for Austria, *Report of the U.S. High Commissioner,* IV (February 1946), 95–96.

20. Klenner, *Die Oesterreichischen Gewerkschaften,* II, 1669–70.

21. For a comprehensive analysis of the Collective Agreements Act, see *ibid.,* pp. 1581–84.

22. Klenner, *Die Oesterreichischen Gewerkschaften,* II, 1720; Adolf Schaerf, *Oesterreichs Erneuerung, 1945–1955,* p. 388. In the 1954 elections the Communists, now running as Gewerkschaftliche Einheit (United Trade Unionists), improved their position slightly, commanding some 10 per cent of the mandates. By 1959 this figure had fallen slightly, to 6.6 per cent and 40 mandates (Oberleitner, p. 59).

23. Klenner, *Die Oesterreichischen Gewerkschaften,* II, 1718. This union included the Soviet-controlled oil fields under the SMV.

24. For a breakdown of the persons and party affiliation of the OGB leadership, see Oberleitner, pp. 53–57.

25. Klenner, *Die Oesterreichischen Gewerkschaften,* II, 1729.

26. For text see Austria, *Staatsgesetzblatt fuer den Staat Deutschoesterreich,* CI, Stueck, Nr. 283, 651–55. For an excellent analysis of the role of the Works Councils, see Kummer, pp. 110–24.

27. Klenner, *Die Oesterreichischen Gewerkschaften,* I, 480–94.

28. *Richtlinien fuer die Wahlen von Betriebsraeten und Vertrauenspersonen.*

29. *Die Gewerkschaften und Betriebsraete als Kampfinstrumente der proletarischen Revolution,* p. 5.

30. *Die Kommunistische Partei: Ihr Wesen—Ihr Aufbau—Ihre Menschen,* pp. 20–21.

31. *Das Neue Statut der Kommunistischen Partei Oesterreichs,* pp. 14–32. The work *Betrieb* defies any satisfactory translation. "Concern" or "enterprise" is perhaps the best.

32. For an explanation of the reorganization, see the *Richtlinien* distributed to party functionaries, in "Der Vertrauensmann-Ratgeber fuer die Funktionaere und Aktivisten der Landesorganisation Niederoesterreich."

33. *Ibid.,* Nr. 3 (September 1946), p. 1.

34. *Sozialpolitische Mindestforderungen,* p. 7.

35. For the text of the paragraph Honner wanted changed, see *Manzche*

Taschenausgabe der Oesterreichischen Gesetze (Vienna, 1948), par. 82, p. 138. Based on a whole series of laws going back to the time of the empire, the ordinance was very strict with those who left work without authorization or who incited others to do so.

36. *Volksstimme*, March 29, 1947. See also the speech of the Communist delegate, Viktor Elser, in the Nationalrat, March 28. Austria, *Stenographisches Protokoll des Nationalrates*, V.G.P., 50. Sitzung, March 28, 1947, pp. 1383–89.

37. The Communists demanded, in addition to co-determination for the Works Councils, influence over the hiring of workers (giving notice and firing of employees) and immunity for the members of the councils. The People's Party wanted, and received as the price of their support, exemption of agricultural workers from the law. *Ibid.*, pp. 1378–1401.

38. For text see Austria, *Bundesgesetzblatt fuer die Republik Oesterreich*, 25 Stueck, Nr. 97, pp. 587–96. An elaboration of the text may be found in Dittrich *et al.*, pp. 182–244.

39. *Proceedings of the Allied Commission*, ALCO/P(47)54, Serial I, p. 1; see also *ibid.*, ALCO/M(47)50.

40. Klenner, *Das Unbehagen in der Demokratie*, p. 33. See also pp. 26–40 for a fuller analysis of the problem of *Betriebsegoismus*. See the article by Kautsky, "Betriebsrat und Gewerkschaft."

41. "Verordnung des Bundesministeriums fuer soziale Verwaltung vom 24. Juli 1947, BGBL, Nr. 211, ueber die Wahl der Betriebsraete und Vertrauensmaenner," in Dittrich *et al.*, *Manzche Grosse Ausgabe der oesterreichischen Gesetze*, X, Part 1, pp. 244–75; see also *Betriebesrats-Wahlordnung*, Schriftenreihe des Oesterreichischen Gewerkschaftsbundes Nr. 8 (Vienna: Verlag des OGB, 1951).

42. Meisel, pp. 439–44; see also Fischer, pp. 854–71; or the article by Honner, "Die kommenden Neuwahlen der Betriebsraete."

43. *Arbeiter-Zeitung*, July 27, 1947.

44. *Ibid.*, August 31, 1947.

45. *Ibid.*, September 14, 1947.

46. *Volksstimme*, September 14, 1947.

47. Klenner, *Die Oesterreichischen Gewerkschaften*, II, 1716. Klenner gives a more detailed breakdown of the elections of 1951, including the fact that in 1951 the Communists controlled 15.4 per cent of the Works Councilors and representatives (*Vertrauensmaenner*) in the Chemical Workers Union and 13.1 per cent of both categories in all the trade unions in Lower Austria.

48. Austrian Trade Union Federation, *Taetigkeitsbericht des oesterreichischen Gewerkschaftsbundes, 1945–1947*. Vienna, pp. 1/72, 2/2, 2/3, 2/12; Klenner, *Die Oesterreichischen Gewerkschaften*, II, 1718.

49. Meisel, p. 440.

50. Austria, *Die steirischen Betriebswahlen*, 1947/48.

51. The figures for the Styrian elections, both in 1947 and 1949, came from the report of the Styrian Chamber of Labor and the more comprehensive report on the 1949/50 election. *Ibid.*, 1949/50.

52. In 1949, of the 1,319 concerns in Styria with 20 or more employees, 725 were in these three cities.

53. Austrian Trade Union Federation, *Taetigkeitsbericht des oesterreich-*

ischen Gewerkschaftsbundes, 1945–1947. Vienna, pp. 2/33. Emphasis is mine.

54. *Volksstimme,* November 15, 1947.

55. *Ibid.,* November 19, 1947.

56. *Der 14.Parteitag der Kommunistischen Partei Oesterreichs,* pp. 148–49.

57. For the new statute see *Statut der Kommunistischen Partei Oesterreichs.*

58. For a good example of the vitriolic attacks on the OGB leadership, see the article by Honner, "Der OGB auf gefaehrlichen Wegen," pp. 238–37.

59. *Arbeiter-Zeitung,* March 9, 1948; see also the *New York Times,* March 11, 1948.

60. For an interesting example of this, see Austria, *Beiblatt zur Parlamentskorrespondenz,* 206 A/B zu 236 J, September 28, 1948. Described here is the case of a Works Councilor in one of the USIA plants who was fired because of his "anti-Soviet" agitation. When the majority of the workers threatened to strike if the man—a Socialist—was fired, the Soviet authorities gave in.

61. "Die Betriebe: Kraftzentrum unserer Partei," p. 436.

62. Austria, *Die steirischen Betriebswahlen,* 1949/50, pp. 5, 15.

CHAPTER 8

1. For a detailed statistical breakdown of the results of the elections of 1945 and 1949, see Austria, "Die Nationalratswahlen vom 25. November 1945" and "Die Nationalratswahlen vom 9. Oktober 1949."

2. *Volksstimme,* January 1, 1948; see also "Bilanz der Betriebsratswahlen," pp. 1–7.

3. Austria, "Die Nationalratswahlen vom 25. November 1945," pp. 12–15, and "Die Nationalratswahlen vom 9. Oktober 1949," p. 15. See also Oberleitner, pp. 6–7.

4. An examination of the police register for the year 1949 shows that the Communists were still in control of all the police districts in the Russian sector as well as in the international district. They also controlled the administrative section of the Viennese police, with the Soviet-appointed police chief, Rudolf Hartmann, as its director. Moreover, former officers in the Honner Battalion—Max Goldberger as police commissioner in the Fourth District and Peter Hofer in the Twenty-fifth—were still in positions of great responsibility. Austria, *Provisorisches Personal-Standesverzeichnis fuer das Jahr 1949,* pp. 1–10; Austria, *Oesterreichischer Amtskalender fuer das Jahr 1950,* XVIII (Vienna, 1950), 471–73.

5. By far the best account of the general strike of September–October, 1950, is Klenner, *Putschversuch—oder nicht?* Klenner's exhaustive compilation of newspaper accounts, reports of trade union officials, and Austrian government accounts gives a thorough day-by-day account of the strike as it affected all parts of Austria. The other account is by Migsch. See also Helmer, *50 Jahre erlebte Geschichte,* pp. 287–301.

6. Nemschak, p. 11.

7. Austria, *Austria and the ERP.* Summary Report for the Period April 1948 to April 1951, pp. 6–9.

8. Austria, *Statistisches Handbuch fuer die Republik Oesterreich*, I, Neue Folge (Office for Central Statistics, Vienna, 1950), pp. 7–21.

9. Austria, *Austria and the ERP*. Fourth Quarter 1949, p. 23, and Summary Report for the Period April 1948 to April 1951, p. 9.

10. For the attitude of the ERP administration on agricultural subsidies, see *Austria and the ERP*. Second Quarter 1950, p. 4.

11. *Monatsberichte des Oesterreichischen Institutes fuer Wirtschaftsforschung*, XXIII, Heft Nr. 12 (December 1950), pp. 633–34. The best analysis of Austria's postwar currency problems is given by Rothschild, esp. pp. 33–35, 49–53.

12. Nemschak, pp. 82–88; Rothschild, pp. 46–48, 56–58.

13. Austria, *Austria and the ERP*. Ninth Quarterly Report, July–September, 1950, p. 46.

14. Austria, *Austria and the ERP*. Second Quarterly Report, 1950, pp. 7–10.

15. Klenner, *Putschversuch—oder nicht?* p. 5.

16. *Montsberichte des Oesterreichischen Institutes fuer Wirtschaftsforschung*, XXIII, Heft Nr. 10 (October 1950), 510.

17. Klenner, *Putschversuch—oder nicht?* p. 6.

18. Austria, *Stenographisches Protokoll*, VI. G.P., 31. Sitzung, October 12, 1950, p. 1094.

19. *Arbeiter-Zeitung*, September 10, 1950.

20. *Neue Wiener Tageszeitung*, September 17, 1950.

21. *Arbeiter-Zeitung*, September 19, 1950.

22. *Volksstimme*, September 14, 15, 1950.

23. *Arbeiter-Zeitung, Wiener-Zeitung, Neue Wiener Tageszeitung*, September 23, 1950.

24. *Volksstimme*, September 23, 24, 26, 1950.

25. Remarks of Oskar Helmer, Minister of the Interior, in *Stenographisches Protokoll*, October 12, 1950, p. 1098.

26. Adolf Schaerf, *Oesterreichs Erneuerung, 1945–1955*, p. 255; Helmer, *50 Jahre erlebte Geschichte*, p. 290; Klenner, *Putschversuch—oder nicht?* pp. 89–93.

27. For details see Helmer, *50 Jahre erlebte Geschichte*, pp. 293–94; Klenner, *Putschversuch—oder nicht?* pp. 16–18; and Austria, *Stenographisches Protokoll*, October 12, 1950, pp. 1098–99.

28. Conversation with Oskar Helmer, April 14, 1961.

29. Helmer, *50 Jahre erlebte Geschichte*, p 294.

30. *Proceedings of the Allied Commission*, Meeting of September 29, 1950, ALCO/M(50)131, p. 17.

31. Klenner, *Putschversuch—oder nicht?* pp. 18–19; Migsch, pp. 19–20.

32. Austria, *Stenographisches Protokoll*, October 12, 1950, pp. 1098–99; Migsch, p. 21.

33. *Proceedings of the Allied Commission*, Meeting of September 29, 1950, ALCO/M(50)131, p. 17.

34. Klenner, *Putschversuch—oder nicht?* p. 20.

35. *Ibid.;* also Migsch, pp. 14–15.

36. *Volksstimme*, September 27, 1950; Klenner, *Putschversuch—oder nicht?* p. 25.

37. *Volksstimme,* September 27, 1950.

38. Klenner, *Putschversuch—oder nicht?* p. 22.

39. Austria, *Stenographisches Protokoll,* October 12, 1950, pp. 1099–1100; Klenner, *Putschversuch—oder nicht?* pp. 27–30.

40. Migsch, p. 17; Klenner, *Putschversuch—oder nicht?* p. 34.

41. For examples of the type of propaganda distributed, see Klenner, *Putschversuch—oder nicht?* pp. 29–30, 31.

42. Conversation with Oskar Helmer, February 22, 1961; Klenner, *Putschversuch—oder nicht?* pp. 30–32.

43. *Volksstimme,* September 28, 1950.

44. *Volksstimme,* October 1, 1950; *Oesterreichische Zeitung,* October 1, 1950.

45. Klenner, *Putschversuch—oder nicht?* p. 52.

46. *Arbeiter-Zeitung,* October 3, 1950.

47. *Ibid.,* September 28, 1950.

48. For the text of the government's proclamation and a description of the circumstances surrounding its formulation, see Gruber, pp. 230–32.

49. *Proceedings of the Allied Commission,* EXCO/M(50)172, pp. 9–13.

50. Austria, *Stenographisches Protokoll,* October 12, 1950, p. 1102.

51. *New York Times,* October 4, 1950.

52. Klenner, *Putschversuch—oder nicht?* p. 78.

53. *Der Eisenbahner,* Zentralorgan der Eisenbahner im Oesterreichischen Gewerkschaftsbund, Nr. 11 (October 7, 1950), quoted in Klenner, *Putschversuch—oder nicht?* pp. 78–80.

54. The best description of these events is in Klenner's *Putschversuch—oder nicht?* pp. 61–78. See also Gruber, pp. 230–33; and Austria, *Stenographisches Protokoll,* October 12, 1950, p. 1100.

55. *Arbeiter-Zeitung,* October 4, 1950.

56. Austria, *Stenographisches Protokoll,* October 12, 1950, p. 1100; Helmer, *50 Jahre erlebte Geschichte,* pp. 300–301.

57. For the bitter Communist reaction to Olah's brutal but effective work, see *Volksstimme,* October 5, 8, 1950; *Oesterreichische Zeitung,* October 6, 1950.

58. Gruber, p. 234; Helmer, *50 Jahre erlebte Geschichte,* pp. 299–300; conversation of July 6, 1961, with Colonel Kaes, who led the gendarmerie detachment to Wiener Neustadt.

59. *Proceedings of the Allied Commission,* ALCO/M(50)132, p. 8.

60. Gruber, pp. 235–36.

61. *Volksstimme,* October 5, 1950.

62. *Wiener Kurier,* October 24, 31, 1950. For a partial list of those purged, see the issue for November 7, 1950.

63. *Beiblatt zur Parlamentskorrespondenz,* 482/A.B. to 514 J, July 28, 1952, pp. 4–5; *Wiener Kurier,* October 25, 1950; *Arbeiter-Zeitung,* August 21, 1950.

64. *Proceedings of the Allied Commission,* ALCO/M(50)133, pp. 1–2; U.S. Dept. of State, *American Foreign Policy, 1950–1955,* II, 1769–71.

65. *Wiener-Zeitung,* August 13, 1955. Where there were grounds for criminal prosecution, the Communist police official in question often disappeared at the time of the Communist withdrawal. See, for example, the

case of Albert and Egon Schlesinger, in Austria, *Beiblatt zur Parlaments-korrespondenz*, 336/A.B. to 368 J, September 24, 1955, p. 2; and *ibid.*, 378/ A.B. to 404 J, January 21, 1956, p. 1.

66. *Oesterreichische Monatshefte*, VI, Nr. 11 (November 1950), p. 675.

67. *Proceedings of the Allied Commission*, ALCO/M(52)177, p. 5.

CHAPTER 9

1. Dulles Papers, Category IX, Meeting of the Four Foreign Ministers, Berlin, FPM [Four-Power Meeting] (54)56, February 12, 1954.

2. For a description of the activities of the Austrians at Berlin and, more generally, of the genesis of Austrian neutrality, see the excellent article by Stourzh, "Austrian Neutrality—Its Establishment and Its Significance," pp. 107–32; see also Stourzh, "Zur Geschichte der oesterreichischen Neutrali-taet," pp. 269–75. An interesting account of the origins of the Austrian State Treaty is given by the former Swedish ambassador to Austria, in Allard, *Diplomat in Wien*.

3. Dulles Papers, Category IX, Meeting of the Four Foreign Ministers, Berlin, FPM(54)60, February 13, 1954.

4. Text in Supplement to *New Times* (Moscow), No. 7 of February 12, 1955, p. 23; or in *Pravda*, February 9, 1955.

5. For English text of the Soviet-Austrian Memorandum of April 15, 1955, see Supplement to *New Times*, No. 22 of May 28, 1955, pp. 5ff; for German text, see Siegler, Appendix; for an account of the Austrian mission, see Kindermann; for Figl's statement at Berlin on military alliances and foreign bases, see U.S. Dept. of State, *Foreign Ministers Meeting*, pp. 200–212.

6. Text in U.S. Dept. of State, *American Foreign Policy, 1950–1955*, I, 643–75.

7. For text of constitutional amendment, see *Dept. of State Bulletin*, December 19, 1955, p. 1011.

8. "Report of the Senate Committee on Foreign Relations, June 15, 1955," in *American Foreign Policy, 1950–1955*, I, 685.

9. *New York Times*, May 16, 1965.

10. David Dallin in *Soviet Foreign Policy after Stalin* writes that at least after the Hungarian revolution, when thousands of Hungarians fled into Eastern Austria, "the magnanimity of 1955 was clearly regretted in Moscow" (p. 261). See also the speech of Secretary of State Dean Rusk, made in Vienna on the occasion of the tenth anniversary of the signing of the Austrian State Treaty, in the *Dept. of State Bulletin*, June 7, 1965, pp. 898–99. Senator J. W. Fulbright, speaking in Vienna in May 1965, called the treaty an "example of the possibilities of East-West accord," and suggested that "the fact that Austria recovered unity and independence after years of arduous negotiations offers grounds for hope that other problems, now seemingly intractable, can ultimately be resolved."

11. U.S. Dept. of State, "An Historic Week—Report to the President," pp. 6–8.

12. Dulles Papers, Category IX, Meeting of the Four Foreign Ministers, FPM(54)74, February 16, 1954.

13. Dulles Papers, Category VIII, Council of Foreign Ministers, Moscow, vol. I, USDEL(47)(M), 15th meeting, March 27, 1947, p. 145.

14. *Ibid.,* USDEL(47)(M), 36th meeting, April 19, 1947, p. 399.

15. *Ibid.,* Council of Foreign Ministers—Moscow, Reports, March 10–April 24, 1947, vol. II, part 2, p. 403.

16. *Ibid.,* Council of Foreign Ministers—Moscow, Minutes, vol. III, USDEL(47)(M), 11th meeting, March 21; USDEL(47)(M), 16th meeting, March 28.

17. *Ibid.,* Council of Foreign Ministers, Moscow, J.F.D. [John Foster Dulles] Personal and Miscellaneous Papers, vol. I, p. 98. Letter and memorandum of Dr. Karl Gruber, marked 89—St. M/47 (Secret). Emphasis mine.

18. *Ibid.,* p. 104.

19. *Ibid.,* pp. 107–8.

20. *Ibid.,* Council of Foreign Ministers—Moscow, Minutes, vol. III. USDEL(47)(M), 34th meeting, April 18, 1947, p. 377.

21. Gruber, p. 144.

22. For details, see Gruber, pp. 164–65; see also Helmer, *Oesterreichs Kampf um die Freiheit,* pp. 19–20; *New York Times,* June 8, 10, 12, 1947.

23. Dulles Papers, Category VIII, Council of Foreign Ministers—London, Minutes, November 25–December 17, 1947, vol. I, USDEL(47)(L), 1st meeting (revised), pp. 2–15; and USDEL(47)(L), 9th meeting, December 4, 1947, p. 90.

24. *Ibid.,* USDEL(47)(L), 17th meeting, December 15, 1947, p. 186; and Annex to same, pp. 196–97.

25. *Dept. of State Bulletin,* February 15, 1948, p. 213.

26. *Ibid.,* June 6, 1948, pp. 746–47.

27. *Ibid.,* p. 747.

28. The bulk of the material used in this section is drawn from the Dulles Papers on the Paris meeting of the foreign ministers in May and June of 1949. In the various background and position papers of the United States' delegation at Paris, there is considerable material on the 1948 deputies' conferences in London. Unfortunately, the original minutes of deputies' meetings are as yet unavailable. For a revealing firsthand account of the negotiations as seen from the Austrian side, see Gruber, pp. 183–201.

29. For the text of the French plan as first proposed by General Cherrière, the French representative on the Deputies for Austria Commission, see Dulles Papers, Category VIII, Council of Foreign Ministers—London, Proposals, Statements, J.F.D. Misc., vol. II, CFM/47/L/8, November 27, 1947; for the Soviet counterproposal, see *ibid.,* Official Papers, vol. II, CFM/D/L/48/A/1 (Con.), January 24, 1948, pp. 139–40.

30. Text of the April 6, 1948, agreement can be found in Dulles Papers, Category VIII, Council of Foreign Ministers—Paris, Official Papers, vol. II, "Report of U.K., U.S., and French deputies on Article 35," CFM/P/49/8, June 1, 1949, pp. 52–53.

31. Gruber, p. 191.

32. *Ibid.,* pp. 192–94.

33. See Djilas, pp. 87ff.; Dedijer, pp. 249ff.

34. Dulles Papers, Category VIII, Council of Foreign Ministers, Minutes, May 23–June 16, 1949, vol. IV, p. 250. Letter dated June 13, 1949. Italics in the original.

35. Shulman, pp. 1, 259.

36. Dulles Papers, Category VIII, Council of Foreign Ministers—Paris, Minutes, May 23–June 16, 1949, vol. I, pp. 152–57. Carbon of minutes of restricted meeting held June 12, 1949, at 8:00 P.M. at the Palais de Marbe Rose.

37. *Ibid.*, USDEL(49)(P), 20th meeting (first session), p. 159.

38. From "Report of the Senate Committee on Foreign Relations, June 15, 1955," in U.S. Dept. of State, *American Foreign Policy, 1950–1955*, I, 685; see also the report of John Foster Dulles to President Eisenhower on the treaty, *ibid.*, pp. 676–82.

39. Austria, *Austrian Information*, VI, No. 5 (March 7, 1953).

40. U.S. Dept. of State, *American Foreign Policy, 1950–1955*, I, 679.

41. For an admirable rendition of the Soviet Union's economic troubles in 1954, see Schwartz, esp. pp. 55–73.

42. Dulles Papers, Catalogue IX, Conference Dossiers, "Verbatim Report of the Fifteenth Meeting of the [North Atlantic] Council," C-VR(54)50, p. 21.

43. "Statement of the Soviet Government on the German Question, January 15, 1955," *New Times* (Moscow), No. 4, January 22, 1955, Supplement, pp. 3–4.

44. For details on the Austrian controversy, see Boffa, pp. 29–30, Dallin, pp. 254–55, 227–33; U.S. Senate Committee on the Judiciary, *Scope of Soviet Activity in the United States*, testimony of Seweryn Bialer (Polish Communist Party defector), pp. 1573–74.

45. Eisenhower, pp. 504–6.

46. Dulles Papers, Category IX, Conference Dossiers, Special Subjects, December 1954–55. Big Four Meeting. Memorandum dated July 6, 1955. Italics mine.

47. *Ibid.*, "Estimate of the Prospect of the Soviet Union Achieving its Goals," undated.

48. Statement of N. A. Bulganin on May 11, 1955, at the Warsaw Conference, *New Times*, No. 21, May 21, 1955, Supplement, p. 9. Italics mine.

49. E. Ambartsumov, "The Political Situation in Italy," in *New Times*, No. 23, June 4, 1955, p. 13; see also *New Times*, No. 22, May 28, 1955, p. 30.

50. *Pravda*, April 16, 1956, translated in *Current Digest of the Soviet Press*, VIII, No. 16, pp. 17–18. Talk in the West German press of a similar solution forced the Bonn government to publicly rule out neutralization. See *Frankfurter Allgemeine Zeitung*, May 21, 1955.

51. Dulles Papers, Category IX, Conference Dossiers, Special Subjects, December 1954–55. From a memorandum proposed by Dulles for the President and then sent to United States chiefs of missions for background information. Dated August 15, 1955.

52. *International Affairs* (Moscow), No. 9, September 1958, p. 85.

53. *Ibid.*, September 1964, p. 60.

54. Kissinger, pp. 220–23.

Bibliography

Akt zu 1603/57; Akt zu 1159/59; Akt zu HV 1573/47–VglVr 4492/47, *see under* Austria.

Allard, Sven. Diplomat in Wien. Cologne: Verlag fuer Wissenschaft und Politik, 1965.

Allied Commission for Austria. Gazette of the Allied Commission for Austria. Vienna, 1945–55.

———. Letters from the Federal Chancellery to the Allied Council. Vienna, 1946–55.

———. Proceedings of the Allied Commission. Official minutes of the meetings of the Allied Council (ALCO) and the Executive Committee (EXCO), and verbatim accounts as recorded by the U.S. element, as well as other papers and annexes. Vienna.

———. Protocol of the First Meeting of the Four (Allied) Commanders in Chief in Austria, August 23, 1945. Vienna.

———. Record of the Quadripartite Meeting Prior to the Establishment of the Allied Commission. Minutes of the Allied Chiefs of Staff Conferences. Vienna, July 16, 24–25, 1945.

———. Report of the United States High Commissioner. Vienna, Nos. 1–53, 1945–51.

Aus der Vergangenheit der KPO; Aufzeichnungen und Erinnerungen zur Geschichte der Partei. Herausgegeben und Verlegt von der Historischen Kommission beim ZK der KPO. Vienna: Globus Verlag, 1961.

Austria. 80 Jahre Wiener Sicherheitswache. Bundespolizeidirektion Wien. Vienna: Verlag fuer Jugend und Volk, 1949.

———. Akt zu 1603/57; Akt zu 1159/59. Landesgericht fuer Strafsachen Wien II.

———. Akt zu HV 1573/47–VglVr 4492/47. Landesgericht fuer Strafsachen Wien I.

———. Amtsblatt der Polizeidirektion Wien. Bundespolizeidirektion Wien, 1945–50.

———. Austria and the ERP. Federal Chancellery, 1948–51.

———. Austrian Information. Austrian Consulate General, New York.

———. Beiblatt zur Parlamentskorrespondenz. Vienna, 1945–55.

————. Bundesgesetzblatt fuer die Republik Oesterreich. Vienna, 1945–55.

————. Denkschrift der Provisorischen Staatsregierung der Republik Oesterreich ueber die Organisation der Zusammenarbeit der militaerischen und zivilen Behoerden. Vienna: Austrian State Printing Office, 1945.

————. "Ehemalige USIA Betriebe, Beschaeftigte und Arbeitsstunden in den einzelnen Bundeslaendern im September 1955." Bundeskammer der Gewerblichen Wirtschaft-Sektion Industrie.

————. HV 1573/47–VglVr 4492/47. Landesgericht fuer Strafsachen, Wien I.

————. "Die Nationalratswahlen vom 25. November 1945," Beitraege zur Oesterreichischen Statistik, Nr. 2. Statistiches Zentralamt, Vienna, 1946.

————. "Die Nationalratswahlen vom 9. Oktober 1949," Beitraege zur Oesterreichischen Statistik, Nr. 4. Statistisches Zentralamt, Vienna, 1950.

————. Oesterreichisches Jahrbuch. Vienna: Austrian State Printing Office.

————. Provisorisches Personal-Standesverzeichnis fuer das Jahr 1949. Bundespolizeidirektion Wien, 1949.

————. Red-White-Red Book. Descriptions, Documents and Proofs to the Antecedents and History of the Occupation of Austria. Vienna: Austrian State Printing Office, 1946.

————. Die steirischen Betriebswahlen. Kammer fuer Arbeiter und Angestellte in Steiermark. Abteilung Statistik, Graz, 1947/48 and 1949/50.

————. Stenographisches Protokoll des Nationalrates der Republik Oesterreich, 1945–55.

————. Tages Befehl. Bundespolizeidirektion Wien, 1945–50.

Bader, William B. "Oesterreich in Potsdam," *Oesterreichische Zeitschrift fuer Aussenpolitik,* II, Nr. 4 (June 1962).

Balfour, Michael, and John Mair. Four Power Control in Germany and Austria, 1945–1946. London: Royal Institute of International Affairs, Oxford University Press, 1956.

Bauer, Otto. Bolschevismus oder Socialdemokratie. Vienna: Verlag der Wiener Volksbuchhandlung, 1920.

————. Die Illegale Partei (Aus dem unveroeffentlichen Nachlass). Paris, 1939.

Black, Cyril E., and Thomas P. Thornton, eds. Communism and Revolution: The Strategic Uses of Political Violence. Princeton, N. J.: Princeton University Press, 1964.

Becker, Hans. Oesterreichs Freiheitskampf. Vienna: Freie Union der Oesterreichischen Volkspartei, 1946.

Benedikt, Heinrich, ed. Geschichte der Republik Oesterreich. Munich: Oldenbourg Verlag, 1954.

"Die Betriebe: Kraftzentrum unserer Partei," *Weg und Ziel,* VI, Nr. 6 (June 1948).

"Bilanz der Betriebsratswahlen," *Weg und Ziel,* VI, Nr. 1 (January 1948).

Birke, Ernst, and Rudolf Neumann, eds. Die Sowjetisierung Ost-Mitteleuropas. Berlin: Alfred Metzner Verlag, 1959.

Boehm, Johann. Erinnerungen aus meinen Leben. Vienna: Verlag des Oesterreichischen Gewerkschaftsbundes, 1953.

Boffa, Giuseppe. Inside the Khrushchev Era. New York: Marzani & Munsell, 1959.

Buttinger, Joseph. In the Twilight of Socialism. New York: Praeger, 1953.

Byrnes, James F. Speaking Frankly. New York: Harper, 1947.

Churchill, Winston S. Triumph and Tragedy. Vol. VI of The Second World War. Boston: Houghton Mifflin, 1953.

Clark, Mark. Calculated Risk. New York: Harper, 1950.

Clay, Lucius D. Decision in Germany. New York: Doubleday, 1950.

Dallin, David. Soviet Foreign Policy After Stalin. New York: Lippincott, 1961.

Dedijer, Vladimer. Tito Speaks. London: Weidenfield & Nicolson, 1953.

Deutsch, Julius. Ein weiter Weg. Zurich: Amalthea-Verlag, 1960.

Dittrich, Robert, Karl Wahle, and Rolf Veit, eds. Manzche Grosse Ausgabe der oesterreichischen Gesetze, X, I Teil. Vienna: Manz Verlag, 1953.

Djilas, Milovan. Conversations with Stalin. New York: Harcourt, Brace & World, 1962.

Dulles Papers. John Foster Dulles Library, Princeton University, Princeton, N.J.

Eden, Anthony. Full Circle. The Memoirs of Anthony Eden. Boston: Houghton Mifflin, 1960.

Eisenhower, Dwight D. Mandate for Change: 1953–1956. New York: Doubleday, 1963.

Engelmann, Frederick C. "Haggling for the Equilibrium: The Renegotiation of the Austrian Coalition, 1959," American Political Science Review, LXI, No. 3 (September 1962).

Erickson, Edgar L. "The Zoning of Austria," The Annals of the American Academy of Political and Social Science, CCLXVII (January 1950).

Feis, Herbert. Between War and Peace—the Potsdam Conference. Princeton, N.J.: Princeton University Press, 1960.

————. Churchill—Roosevelt—Stalin: The War They Waged and the Peace They Sought. Princeton, N.J.: Princeton University Press, 1957.

Fellner, Fritz. "Oesterreich in der Nachkriegsplanung der Alliierten 1943–1945," in Oesterreich und Europa. Festgabe fuer Hugo Hantsch. Vienna, 1965.

Fischer, Walter. "Die kommunistische Betriebsorganisation," Weg und Ziel, V, Nr. 12 (December 1947).

Fodor, M. W. "Finis Austriae," Foreign Affairs, XVI (July 1938).

Fuernberg, Friedl. "Der Weg Oesterreichs zum Sozialismus," in Der 17. Parteitag der Kommunistischen Partei. Vienna: Zentralkomitee der KPO, Stern Verlag, 1957.

Die Gewerkschaften und Betriebsraete als Kampfinstrumente der proletarischen Revolution. Vienna: Auftraege des Gewerkschaftsrates der KPO, 1921.

Goldinger, Walter. Geschichte der Republik Oesterreich. Munich: Oldenbourg Verlag, 1962.

Grayson, Cary Travers, Jr. Austria's International Position, 1938–1953. Geneva: Droz, 1953.

Great Britain. Foreign Office. Agreements Between the ... United Kingdom, the United States of America, the Union of Soviet Socialist Republics, and the ... French Republic concerning Control Machinery and Zones of Occupation in Austria and the Administration of the City of Vienna. London, 4th July, 9th July, Vienna, 28th June 1946. Cmd. 6958.

Gregory, John Duncan. Dollfuss and His Times. London: Hutchinson, 1935.

Grew, Joseph C. Turbulent Era: A Diplomatic Record of Forty Years, 1904–1945. 2 vols. Boston: Houghton Mifflin, 1952.

Gruber, Karl. Zwischen Befreiung und Freiheit: der Sonderfall Oesterreich. Vienna: Ullstein Verlag, 1953.

Gulick, Charles A. Austria from Habsburg to Hitler. 2 vols. Berkeley: University of California Press, 1948.

————. "Austrian Labor's Bid to Power: The Role of the Trade Union Federation," *Industrial and Labor Relations Review*, XII, No. 1 (October 1958).

Gunther, John. "Dollfuss and the Future of Austria," *Foreign Affairs*, XII (January 1934).

Habermann, Gustav. "Der Neuaufbau des oesterreichischen Bundesheeres," in Unser Heer. 300 Jahre oesterreichisches Soldatentum in Krieg und Frieden. Vienna: Forum Verlag, 1963.

Heinl, Eduard. Ueber ein Halbes Jahrhundert. Vienna: 1948.

Helmer, Oskar. 50 Jahre erlebte Geschichte. Vienna: Verlag der Wiener Volksbuchhandlung, 1957.

————. Oesterreichs Kampf um die Freiheit. Vienna: Verlag der Wiener Volksbuchhandlung, 1949.

Hiscocks, Richard. The Rebirth of Austria. London: Oxford University Press, 1953.

Holaubek, Josef. "Der Schwierige Personalaufbau in der Wiener Polizei," *Oeffentliche Sicherheit*, XIX, Nr. 4 (April 1954).

Honner, Franz. "Die kommenden Neuwahlen der Betriebsraete," *Der Vertrauensmann*, Sondernummer (August 1947).

————. "Die Kommunisten in der Provisorischen Regierung," Aus der Vergangenheit der KPO.

————. "Der OeGB auf gefaehrlichen Wegen," *Weg und Ziel*, VI, Nr. 5 (May 1949).

Hull, Cordell. The Memoirs of Cordell Hull. 2 vols. New York: Macmillan, 1948.

Hurdes, Felix. "Wie die oesterreichische Volkspartei entstand," *Oesterreichische Monatshefte*, October 1945.

Jedlicka, Ludwig. "Heer und Demokratie," in Jacques Hannak, ed., Bestandaufnahme Oesterreich, 1945–1963. Vienna: Forum Verlag, 1963.

Johnstone, Harry W. The Restraint of Competition in the Austrian Economy. Vienna: U.S. High Commission for Austria, 1951.

Kautsky, Benedikt. "Betriebsrat und Gewerkschaft," *Die Zukunft*, January 1954.

Kelsen, Hans, ed. Die Verfassungsgesetze der Republik Deutschoesterreich. Parts I–III. Vienna: Franz Deuticke, 1919.

Kindermann, Walter. Flug nach Moskau. Vienna: Ullstein Verlag, 1955.

Kirchheimer, Otto. "The Waning of the Opposition in Parliamentary Regimes," *Social Research*, XXIV, No. 2 (1957).

Kissinger, Henry A. The Troubled Partnership: A Reappraisal of the Atlantic Alliance. New York: McGraw-Hill, 1965.

Klenner, Fritz. Die Oesterreichischen Gewerkschaften. 2 vols. Vienna: Verlag des Oesterreichischen Gewerkschaftsbundes, 1951, 1953.

———. Putschversuch—oder nicht? Vienna: Pressereferat des Oesterreichischen Gewerkschaftsbundes, 1950.

———. Das Unbehagen in der Demokratie. Vienna: Verlag der Wiener
Volksbuchhandlung, 1956.

Die Kommunisten im Kampf fuer die Unabhaengigkeit Oesterreichs. Vienna: Stern Verlag, 1955.

Die Kommunisten Partei: Ihre Wesen—Ihr Aufbau—Ihre Menschen. Vienna: Stern Verlag, 1945.

Kummer, Karl. "Works Councils in Austria," *International Labour Review,* LXXXI (January–June, 1960).

Kunschak, Leopold. Oesterreich 1918–1934. Vienna: Typographische Anstalt, 1934.

Leonhard, Wolfgang. Die Revolution entlaesst ihre Kinder. Berlin: Kiepen-
heuer & Witsch, 1955.

Macartney, C. A. The Social Revolution in Austria. Cambridge: Cambridge
University Press, 1926.

MacCormac, John. "The Improbable Coalition that Governs Austria," *The
Reporter,* January 23, 1958.

Marsalek, Hans. Mauthausen mahnt! Vienna: Mauthausen-Komitee des
Bundesverbands der oesterreichischen KZler, 1950.

Matejka, Viktor. Katholik und Kommunist. Vienna: Verlag der "Berichte
zur Kultur und Zeitgeschichte," 1945.

Meisel, Josef. "Die Betriebsorganisation, die wichigste Einheit der Partei,"
Weg und Ziel, V, Nr. 6 (June 1947).

Migsch, Alfred. Anschlag auf Oesterreich. Zentralsekretariat der SPO. Vienna, 1950.

Molden, Otto. Der Ruf des Gewissens; der oesterreichische Freiheitskampf,
1938–1945. Vienna: Herold, 1958.

Mosely, Philip E. "The Treaty with Austria," *International Organization,*
IV, No. 2 (May 1950).

Nemschak, Franz. Ten Years of Austrian Economic Development, 1945–
1955. Vienna: Austrian Institute for Economic Research, 1955.

Das Neue Statut der Kommunistischen Partei Oesterreichs. Zentralkomitee
der KPO. Vienna: Globus Verlag, 1946.

Oberleitner, Wolfgang. Politisches Handbuch der Republik Oesterreich,
1945–1960. Guarda-Information Nr. 4. Vienna: Guardaval, 1960.

Die Oesterreichische Erdoelwirtschaft. Vienna: Oesterreichisches Institut
fuer Wirtschaftsforschung, 10 Sonderheft, 1947.

"Oesterreichs Wirtschaftsverkehr mit der Sowjetunion," *Monatsberichte des
Oesterreichischen Institutes fuer Wirtschaftsforschung,* XXVIII, Nr. 11,
Beilage Nr. 33 (November 1955).

Pollak, Oskar. "The Rebirth of Austria," *The Contemporary Review,* No.
951, March 1945.

Potsdam Conference, see under U.S. Dept. of State.

Proceedings of the Allied Commission, *see under* Allied Commission for
Austria.

Proksch, Anton. "Der Aufbau des Oesterreichischen Gewerkschaftbundes,"
Der Oesterreichische Arbeiter und Angestellte, July 28, 1945.

Renner, Karl. "Austria: Key for War and Peace," *Foreign Affairs,* XXVI
(July 1948).

————. Denkschrift ueber die Geschichte der Unabhaengigkeitserklaerung Oesterreichs. Zurich: Europa Verlag, 1946.

————. Oesterreich von der Ersten zur Zweiten Republik. Vienna: Verlag der Wiener Volksbuchhandlung, 1960.

Richtlinien fuer die Wahlen von Betriebsraeten und Vertrauenspersonen. Vienna: Verlag des Oesterreichischen Gewerkschaftsbundes, 1945.

Rothschild, Kurt W. The Austrian Economy since 1945. London: Royal Institute of International Affairs, 1950.

Schaerf, Adolf. Oesterreichs Wiederaufrichtung im Jahre 1945. Vienna: Verlag der Wiener Volksbuchhandlung, 1960.

————. Oesterreichs Erneuerung, 1945–1955. 2d ed. Vienna: Verlag der Wiener Volksbuchhandlung, 1955.

Scharf, Erwin. Ich darf nicht Schweigen—Drei Jahre Politik des Parteivorstands der SPOe—von Innen Gesehen. Vienna: Herausgegeben von Nationalrat Edwin Scharf in Selbstverlag, 1948.

Schuschnigg, Kurt. My Austria. New York: Knopf, 1938.

Schwartz, Harry. The Soviet Economy since Stalin. New York: Lippincott, 1965.

Secher, Herbert P. "Coalition Government: The Case of the Second Austrian Republic," *American Political Science Review*, LII, No. 3 (September 1958).

Shell, Kurt L. The Transformation of Austrian Socialism. Albany: State University of New York, 1962.

Shepherd, Gordon Brook. The Austrian Odyssey. London: Macmillan, 1957.

————. Prelude to Infamy: The Story of Chancellor Dollfuss of Austria. New York: Ivan Obolensky, 1961.

Shulman, Marshall D. Stalin's Foreign Policy Reappraised. Cambridge: Harvard University Press, 1963.

Siegler, Heinrich V., ed. Oesterreichs Weg zur Souveraenitaet, Neutralitaet, Prosperitaet, 1945–1959. Bonn: Verlag fuer Zeitarchive, 1959.

Simon, Walter B. "The Political Parties of Austria." New York: Ph.D. dissertation, Columbia University, 1957.

Sobek, Franz. KZ-ler der Staatspolizei," *Mahnruf fuer Freiheit und Menschenrecht (Der Mahnruf)*, Nr. 3, March 1947.

"Sonderdienst Staatsvertrag," *Donaueuropaeischer-Informationdienst*, XII, Nr. 10, Beilage Nr. 1 (May 1955).

Sozialpolitische Mindestforderungen. Zentralkomitee der KPOe. Vienna: Globus Verlag, 1946.

Spulber, Nicolas. The Economics of Communist Eastern Europe. New York: The Technology Press of the Massachusetts Institute of Technology, 1957.

Statut der Kommunistischen Partei Oesterreichs. Zentralkomitee der KPOe. Vienna: Stern Verlag, 1949.

Stearman, William L. The Soviet Union and the Occupation of Austria. Bonn: Verlag fuer Zeitarchive, 1961.

Stourzh, Gerald. "Austrian Neutrality—Its Establishment and Its Significance," *Internationale Spectator*, No. 5 Jaargang XIV (March 1960).

————. "Zur Geschichte der oesterreichischen Neutralitaet," *Oesterreich in Geschichte und Literatur*, V (1961).

Strong, David F. Austria (October 1918–March 1919), Transition from Empire to Republic. New York: Columbia University Press, 1939.

"Struktur und Zukunft der USIA-Betriebe," *Wirtschafts-Politische Blaetter*, III (Nr. 2, April 1956).

Thayer, Charles. Diplomat. New York: Harper, 1959.

Truman, Harry S. Year of Decisions. Vol. I of Memoirs. Garden City, N.Y.: Doubleday, 1955.

U.S. Dept. of State. American Foreign Policy 1950–1955. No. 6446, 2 vols., 1957.

————. The Austrian State Treaty. An Account of the Postwar Negotiations, Together with the Text of the Treaty and Related Documents. No. 6437, 1957.

————. Correspondence between the Austrian Chancellor and the USFA [U.S. Forces in Austria] Headquarters, 1947–1955.

————. Correspondence between the British Element and USFA Headquarters, 1947–50.

————. Correspondence between Various Ministries and the USFA Headquarters, 1947–49; 1950–52.

————. Foreign Ministers Meeting: Berlin Discussions, January 25–February 18, 1954. No. 5399.

————. Foreign Relations of the United States, the Conference of Berlin (The Potsdam Conference) 1945. 2 vols. Nos. 7015 and 1763, 1960.

————. "An Historic Week—Report to the President," May 17, 1955. Public Services Div., Series S—No. 34.

U.S. Senate Committee on the Judiciary. Scope of Soviet Activity in the United States. Hearings of June 8, 11, and 29, 1956. Washington, D.C.: U.S. Government Printing Office, 1957.

U.S. Senate Foreign Relations Committee. A Decade of American Foreign Policy: Basic Documents, 1941–1949. Senate Doc. No. 123, 81st Cong., 1st Sess., 1950.

U.S.S.R. Sowjet-Politik gegenueber Oesterreich (April 1945–April 1947). Vienna: Oesterreichische Zeitung, 1947.

"Der Vertrauensmann-Ratgeber fuer die Funktionaere und Aktivisten der Landesorganisation Niederoesterreich." Herausgegeben von der Landesleitung Niederoesterreich der KPOe, Sondernummer, I (August 1946).

Der 14. Parteitag der Kommunistischen Partei Oesterreichs. Vienna: Zentralkomitee der KPO, Stern Verlag, 1949.

Vodopivec, Alexander. Wer regiert in Oesterreich—Ein politisches Panorama. Vienna: Verlag fuer Geschichte und Politik, 1960.

Der Weg zum Aufstieg. Bericht ueber die Wienerparteiarbeiterkonferenz der Kommunistischen Partei Oesterreichs am 6. August 1945 im Wiener Konzerthaussaal, 1945.

Weinberger, Lois. Tatsachen, Begegnungen und Gespraeche. Vienna: Oesterreichischer Verlag, 1948.

Wiener Polizei oder Polizei gegen die Wiener? Herausgeber Kommunistische Partei Oesterreichs. Vienna: Stern Verlag, 1945.

INTERVIEWS

Heinrich Duermayer, former chief of the Austrian State Police, April 1961.

Leopold Figl, former Chancellor of Austria, August 1961.

Oskar Helmer, former Austrian Minister of the Interior, February–April 1961.

Obstlt. Ferdinand Kaes, Commandant, Gendarmerie Schule des Bundesministeriums fuer Inneres, July 1961.

Fritz Klenner, Austrian Trade Union Federation, February 1961.

Samuel Reber, chief American negotiator during most of the Austrian State Treaty negotiations, summer, 1965.

Index